The

Breakup

BIBLE

The
Breakup
BIBLE

The Smart Woman's
Guide to Healing
from a Breakup
or Divorce

Rachel A. Sussman

Three Rivers Press | New York

Cataloging-in-Publication Data is available from the
Library of Congress

ISBN 978-0-307-88509-8
eISBN 978-0-307-88510-4

PRINTED IN THE UNITED STATES OF AMERICA

Book design by Donna Sinisgalli
Illustrations by randomway/Veer
Cover design by Alison Forner

3 5 7 9 10 8 6 4

First Edition

For Gary

and Isabelle

with love and gratitude

Contents

The
Breakup
BIBLE

Introduction

*I*f you have experienced the ending of a romantic relationship, you are not alone. Every day women all over the world suffer from debilitating breakups or divorces. In a split second the life you know evaporates. The pain can feel agonizing, all-encompassing, and eternal. Many describe that the actual breakup and ensuing weeks feel like an out-of-body experience. I often hear women exclaim, "This can't be happening to me!" Along with the suffering comes a roller coaster of complex feelings: embedded grief, abandonment and fear, guilt, monstrous rage. I've witnessed completely healthy people behave insanely when they have been rejected.

Right now you may be thinking that your life will never get better and that you can't live without your ex. I'm here to tell you that life *does* get better, and not only *can* you live without him, but in time you'll see that *it is even possible to thrive*. Thriving can entail creating an entirely new and healthier life for yourself, including regaining trust, self-confidence, and love. This book gives you the evidence to believe that and the tools to make it happen. So please keep an open mind and allow me to lead you out of your sorrow and into a much improved state.

Through the process of loving and losing we have the capacity to learn tremendous life lessons. When viewed wisely and with insight we learn who we are as individuals and as partners. We gain knowledge about what we did correctly, and when we're astute, we learn where we erred. We come away from the experience fuller and wiser. Although breakups can feel unbearable, we don't die from them. The old adage "If it doesn't kill you it will make you stronger" is definitely true in this circumstance. The most interesting humans are multifaceted, having experienced pleasure *and* pain. They have survived, and so can you.

Many factors inspired me to write this book. Breakups and divorces are one of the biggest reasons that people come to me for therapy. Over the past several years I have witnessed the demise of lengthy relationships affecting close friends, relatives, and clients. I was moved by their suffering, and incredibly inspired by their strength as they slowly regained their lives and eventually recovered. I too am quite familiar with the unbearable sadness that comes when a relationship ends. Regrettably, I spent too many years nursing a continually broken heart after several failed long-term relationships. I made decisions that weren't always in my best interest, that chipped away at my self-esteem, and that kept me in a state of suspended melancholy. Never once did I stop to evaluate my behavior or see that there were other ways to live my life.

One day a close male friend sat me down and said, "Rachel, you are such a great girl and have so much to offer. I scratch my head wondering why you are constantly dating toxic men when so many nice guys ask you out. I really hope you can figure this out, because I am worried about you." I trusted this friend—he was kind and mature (the type of guy I *never* would have dated back then) and we really understood each other. After our talk, I suspected that I had some issues that needed tending when it came to romance. That conversation was the catalyst for what eventually would become my change and growth.

I strongly believe that anyone can alter undesirable feelings and behaviors and completely turn his or her life around. You simply need two components: the wish for change and the motivation to do something about it. Sometimes it takes a crisis to get us to contemplate the opportunity for resurrection, and that's how it happened for me. I committed to figuring out what was interfering with my ability to have a successful love connection. I immediately stopped dating and spent a solid year in counseling, meticulously examining my entire life to search for answers. As difficult as this work was (and believe me, it was tough), I trusted that it was a huge chance for me to come to a place of great understanding, strength, and growth. My work eventually paid off and I was finally able to connect the dots and see what had transpired in my earlier life that was driving my less-than-stellar dating track record. From that moment on, I fully committed to an entirely new way of dating—and living. I would not be here today as a happily married woman—and an expert on breakups and divorces—if I didn't put in my time to take a revealing look at myself and pledge to learning new and healthier behaviors. I am now going to take you on a journey to teach you everything that I learned plus so much more. I can't wait to watch your sorrow turn into spectacular growth, as did mine.

Once I began my initial research for this book, I discovered a few common themes shared by the women I spoke to:

- They were ready to begin a journey of personal recovery, and requested the advice, tools, and support needed to make it happen.
- They wanted an intelligent and realistic resource—such as a book—for women that deals with both the emotional havoc caused by the ending of a relationship *and* how to recover and move on.
- All were eager to hear tales about other women who had been through similar situations and recovered.

I seriously pondered these valuable comments. *Women were telling me exactly what they were lacking and what resources they needed to recover.*

I started meeting with women who had been through difficult breakups or divorces and had survived their ordeals in impressive ways. I then started sharing *their* stories with others in earlier stages of recovery. Upon hearing these narratives, women reported feeling comforted, validated, and vindicated. One declared, "This is the first day I've felt better in months" after I read her a tale with similarities to her own.

I had identified the power of shared experience. Just as with addiction, sexual abuse, or physical illness, when a person who is suffering hears from someone who has gone through what she's going through *and* has come out the other side, she feels understood and encouraged. She feels compassion and validation from a healing community.

Additionally, I discovered that the healing went full circle—women were healed by both listening to stories *and* telling their stories. This is what you are about to experience with *The Breakup Bible*. Using the ancient art of storytelling, I created a community for you to listen to others who have gone through experiences similar to your own. This will allow you to feel validated, which will expedite your healing. Please allow yourself time to grieve, be comforted, and be educated. You're welcome to become part of this kinship for as long as you require it.

Our Community

It was of great importance to me to introduce you to a cast of exemplary women who have made their share of mistakes, done their work, learned their lessons, and fully recovered. All of their stories are genuine, yet some of their identities and personal facts have been changed at their request. Although all special in their own ways, just like you, every woman who appears in this book has something profound to offer. I have learned so much from their stories, their hardships, and their bravery—and I hope you will too. They will tell you their tales and leave you with anecdotes. I think that you'll see a bit of yourself in each one, which will help to validate your own personal experience. Each woman is at a different stage in the recovery process—but all of their suffering has ended and they have moved on. Many proclaim to be leading their best life ever. And one day, so will you. Please understand that these women are your sisters—they are neither more nor less extraordinary than you. Some may be a bit further along in their recovery, but please use that knowledge to motivate and try not to get frustrated. Remember that every woman's recovery runs along a spectrum, and your healing is unique to you.

I have tried to make my community as inclusive as possible. I spoke with women from varied age groups, ethnicities, socioeconomic backgrounds, and sexual preferences. Some have children, and others are childless. I have discussed breakups with women who were left by their significant others, and those who did the breaking up themselves. There is a myth floating around that those who are left experience more pain than those who leave. This is a complete untruth. Please keep in mind that endings affect us all in profoundly different ways.

Some of you have lived through the catastrophe of infidelity, while others have gone outside of your relationship as a remedy for the alienation you have endured from being with the wrong partner. If you discovered your partner's infidelity, that reality is agonizing. If you desperately wanted to save your relationship and your ex had no interest in that plan, that rejection is awful. But it is equally horrid to live day by day in a relationship where you feel misunderstood, controlled, abused, or lonely, and you are petrified of letting go out of fear or the thought of causing irrevocable harm to your ex or your innocent children. Whether you have been abandoned by your lover or were the one who ended your relationship—we are all in this together. No woman's suffering is worse than the next one's, it is just different. It is not for any one of us to judge who has it harder or easier, because it is all messy and difficult. We are a sisterhood here—everyone is invited to read, learn, share, and participate.

All that matters is that you are doing the work and giving yourself hugs and accolades along that way. Just the fact that you are reading this book proves so much. If you are determined to recover, rest assured, you will.

How to Read This Book

The Breakup Bible is divided into three sections: healing, understanding, and transformation—my unique and proven method for recovery. In the *healing* phase I will explain that proper healing is a marathon, not a sprint. I'll encourage you to be patient with yourself, to care for your body and soul, to build a cohesive support system, and to navigate your emotions. *Understanding* is a crucial phase that is typically omitted or minimized in books on this topic. In this phase we will explore and eventually uncover the psychological ramifications of your relationship choices, patterns, and ultimately, your breakup. Doing this work and "owning" the implications of what you discover is the only closure you will ever need! *Understanding* also introduces you to many new concepts including the creation of a "Personal Love Map." Your Personal Love Map was formed the moment you were born. Deciphering your map reveals why you chose your lover, how you behaved in the relationship, and how you mourned your loss. With your emotions in check, and a full understanding of your breakup under your belt, you are ready to be launched into your new life. This is the premise behind the *transformation* phase.

In each chapter, I will give you important information and useful tools that will allow you to experience your breakup and the more challenging aspects of your recovery in healthy and productive ways. Each chapter builds upon the preceding one. At the end of each chapter, I offer a review list that can easily be called upon whenever you need a refresher course. Feel free to read each chapter or favorite sections over and over again. It may also be helpful for you to read with some sticky notes, markers, or a notebook/journal next to you. This book is designed to be a focused and interactive solution—I want you to dig deep, question yourself, and take notes.

If you take your time, keep an open mind, do the reading and exercises, and follow the plan, you will recover. You will also emerge armed with new insight and confidence, which will enable you to make better and healthier choices in the future. This book is about hope. You will heal. You will survive. You will thrive and move on to live your best life yet.

PART I

Healing

There is no remedy for love but to love more.

—Thoreau

1

A Room of One's Own

Finding Comfort in the Early Stages of Grief

"The first months after our breakup are still a blur to me. I was in terrible shape. I could barely get out of bed. I missed work. I was in shock at first. I kept thinking that it was a huge mistake, and he would come to his senses and come back to me. When he didn't, I was completely devastated. I didn't know if I was coming or going. I was an absolute wreck. It was an awful moment in time, but it's way behind me now." —*Gia*

A Window into Your Soul—
Assessing the Damage

The breaking apart of a romantic relationship is an extraordinarily painful event, whether you've been dating for a year or married for thirty. Even if you initiated your split, you are going to be overcome with interminable sorrow. You are not only mourning the loss of someone significant in your life, but saying farewell to your dreams of an eternity together.

The first weeks and months tend to be the most treacherous in the road to recovery. Pervasive grief invades your existence. You question everything, including your self-worth, your choices, your career, your friendships—everything. Numerous thoughts, feelings, and emotions run through your brain. The majority of the women I interviewed had at least half of the following experiences:

• You're in shock—unable to comprehend why your relationship ended, or feeling as if it can't be happening to you. You feel devoid of feelings, numb and detached.

• You wonder if you can ever trust again, if the pain will ever subside, and if you will ever feel joy or happiness again.

• Depression and despondency permeate your body and soul. You feel hopeless, helpless, unable to cope. Your self-esteem is shot. You have lost your ability to concentrate and feel ill equipped to make decisions.

• You have anxiety and anxiety attacks as early stage symptoms. You feel paralyzed with fear and dread, unable to sit still. You tremble and shake, have heart palpitations and trouble breathing.

• You understand intellectually that your relationship is over, but you cannot accept it emotionally. Some days you are convinced you can salvage it, or that in time your partner will return.

• You are unable to control your emotions. You can't contain yourself. You cry or rant constantly and call friends obsessively.

• You feel embarrassed that your relationship ended. You're ashamed to tell anyone and you feel humiliated.

• You contact your ex repetitively via phone, e-mails, texts, or Facebook. Or you may find yourself glued to your telephone, waiting for it to ring.

• If you are ending a marriage, you have the lengthy process of divorce to consider. You feel incredibly overwhelmed thinking about what you'll do and how to divide the life you and your ex have accrued.

• You are obsessed about your breakup. These thoughts intrude most of your day, and you dream about your ex at night. You re-create and dissect the last moments, weeks, and months, again and again. The final conversation loops through your brain repetitively.

• If you have children, you worry about how they will handle the separation and feel guilt ridden that you have imposed psychological damage on them. You feel too inundated to deal with parenting.

• You are filled with self-blame, self-loathing, doubt, and regret.

You're convinced that you blew it. You think, "If I were only a better partner. If I were more loving, giving, attentive. If I only did this better. If only . . ."

• You are filled with rage. You have huge, uncontrollable outbursts of anger.

• If your ex supported you, or carried part of your financial load, you are frightened about finances.

• If your relationship ended over your partner's affair, your healing is even more complicated. You feel completely betrayed, blindsided, shaken, and shocked. Your sense of justice, order, and good in the world has evaporated.

• You think that your final ship has sailed. Time is running out. You wonder if you'll ever meet someone again, if you'll be able to bear children.

• You have trouble eating and sleeping. Weight loss and insomnia are quite common after a breakup. Or you eat too much and sleep excessively.

• You feel unlucky, victimized, as if nothing ever works out quite right for you. You're steeped in self-pity.

• You feel completely overwhelmed and "out of sorts." Food shopping, caring for your home, and washing your clothes seem like insurmountable tasks. Or, perhaps you have unending, manic energy. You've refolded every item in your closet and can't stop cleaning.

• You may be filling up every single waking moment with plans, or sitting at home, completely isolated.

The Importance of Validating Your Feelings

Perhaps you recognize yourself in some of these statements. Or possibly you have experienced them all. Every single declaration represents the normal range of emotions that we experience after a separation. The first step that you must do on the road to recovery is to validate each emotion you are feeling as natural.

Let me take this opportunity to offer you my sincerest condolences over the sorrow that has befallen you. Breaking up is so incredibly difficult. What could possibly prepare you for this monumental heartache? I know it can feel all encompassing and very scary. I've been there, and so have millions of others.

You are now officially submerged in the early stages of breakup grief. Life has become a daily barrage of emotionally charged thoughts and feelings—uncharted territory for most. Many discuss feeling absolutely insane as they observe their moods swinging wildly back and forth like an out-of-whack pendulum. You are entering a whole new and frightening world. You are feeling and thinking things that are quite foreign to you.

It's very important to take the time to validate your feelings. It will allow you to see that you are right where you should be, which will help to ease the anguish you are experiencing.

Unfortunately, the validation you crave rarely comes from your ex, which can be extremely upsetting. We go through all sorts of machinations to try to get our partners to take responsibility, yet only a few do. And often friends and family members, although well meaning, cannot fully understand the gravity of your situation, which can be equally frustrating. The absence of having your experience acknowledged can make you feel even more alone. If you haven't found a way to validate yourself, it's important that you do so right now using this book and my words to enhance your healing. Please remember, *you are allowed to feel what you feel.* This is your essential right. It is OK that you feel miserable and it is absolutely necessary that you accept your grief. Validating yourself and feeling your feelings is a vital part of the healing process.

Taking Time to Grieve:
Making Peace with Your Discomfort

"The first few months after my marriage ended were just horrific. I was extremely devastated yet kind of numb. After that, the tears came. Rivers upon rivers of tears. Sadness of such depth, like I'd never experienced before. I hated the way I felt and went through all sorts of motions to try to escape. I finally realized that I needed to stop running and find a safe place to work with my emotions. Finding that place helped me survive." —*Helene*

"Immediately after my breakup I scheduled myself 24/7. I ran myself ragged trying to avoid my pain. That was a mistake and made me feel pretty depleted. Finally I slowed down, and that's when I started feeling better. I realized I needed time to grieve, time to clarify my situation. You must leave time for reflection—it's extremely important and very worthwhile." —*Abby*

In order to survive the early stages after a breakup, you have to make peace with your sorrow, and accept the realization that it's going to stick around for a while. I understand that the idea of patience and gradual healing is counterintuitive to most. Unless you are a naturally patient person (and most of us, including me, are not), practicing the art of tolerance is no easy feat. Our natural inclination toward suffering is to press the fast-forward button and get out of the experience as quickly as possible. But bucking up against how you are feeling right now will accomplish little. In fact it can backfire and make you feel even worse than you already do. It is important to try to master patience, and to realize that there are many valuable lessons for you to learn at this juncture. Your journey will be much more comfortable if you reconcile the fact that healing takes time and there are no shortcuts.

Often women in the early stages after a breakup or divorce say, "When will I feel better?" "Why aren't I feeling better?" "I hate feeling this way!"

These statements are *completely* valid. Does anyone ever enjoy suffering? Of course not. It's extremely uncomfortable. It is a good thing to eliminate unnecessary suffering, but breakup suffering *is* necessary—it's an important step on the road toward healing, understanding, and transformation.

Consider a spiritual response to suffering. According to the ancient Buddhist teachings, the way to end suffering is to follow a gradual path of self-improvement and enlightenment. Suffering will disappear when progress is made on the path. I think this philosophical approach makes a great deal of sense, and in time, you will too.

Although the heartache can feel insurmountable, I promise you that if you do the work to process the ending of your relationship correctly, over time, you will recover fully. Together we will navigate this rocky terrain and find healthy outlets for your pain. We will clarify your emotions, figure out why your relationship ended, gather useful tools, and crawl out of the hole. Although it may sound inconceivable today, it is highly probable that you will become your best possible self, healthier and happier than you could ever imagine.

Taking Care of Yourself

Most of us are not comfortable with the notion of taking care of ourselves. Women are hardwired to care for others before thinking of ourselves. Recently I attended a dear friend's milestone birthday celebration, which was for women only. During dinner the conversation turned to summer plans, and one woman announced that she was visiting a spa with her family. I commented that I thought it was a lovely idea and perhaps I would visit a spa in the future—on my own. A woman sitting next to me, whom I barely knew, replied, "Oh, you'll never go!" Her comment intrigued me. She didn't know me, yet she was predicting that I wouldn't do what I just said I would. "Why would you say that?" I inquired. "Because you're a woman. You put your family first, you put your job first, you put everything ahead of taking care of yourself. This is what I do too. This is what we all do!"

Her words startled me, yet they were true. We are caregivers as opposed to caretakers, and there is a greater percentage of women than men in our country caring for children, spouses, and parents. We are programmed to go, go, go—putting the needs of our family, friends, and lovers way ahead of our own. In fact, many of us measure our self-worth by this selfless behavior.

I'm asking you to break the mold and find a way to put yourself first. To take care of yourself. To take your own nurturing seriously, even though it may initially feel very strange. Mark it off on your calendar and pick a time for a daily meeting with yourself—a daily comfort session. This is a gift to yourself that you deserve.

Creating a Comfort Zone

"After my divorce when I was very down, a friend suggested I find a photograph of myself at the happiest moment of my life, frame it, and put it someplace where I'd see it every day. My husband had just moved out and I decided to fix up my bedroom to be a sort of shrine to myself. I looked at this photo daily and remembered who I was when I was a happy person. Remind yourself that you can be that person again—you will be that person again. This worked for me and it can work for you." —*Roberta*

"The concept of taking care of myself was very new to me. I had to remind myself each day that it was my mission to allow myself to grieve. I turned my bedroom into a sanctuary. I immediately bought new bedding as a symbolic act—out with the old, in with the new. I didn't want any reminders of my ex. I used that room to relax, stay calm, sort through my feelings, and journal. I created a comfortable place where I could feel secure." —*Sabrina*

What I'd like you to do now is create "a room of your own." This room will be a safety zone while you pass through this complicated yet necessary stage in the healing process. Trust me, it will be incredibly beneficial to you: a secure place, complete with your imprint, where you can go to grieve on your own terms. Perhaps there is a place in your home—even a quiet corner of a room will do—that you can designate as your *special place* to experience comfort while mourning your loss. It doesn't matter which room you choose, but it must be someplace where you can create a sense of peace, harmony, and security.

I suggest using your bedroom, as I do when I need a serene place to escape to. Here are some ideas on how to create a calming atmosphere:

- Burn aromatic candles or incense.
- Use good mood lighting.
- Get some stunning accent pillows.
- Purchase some new bedding (especially if your ex slept in your bed). Many women I spoke with describe this as a must-do!
- Play soft and soothing music.
- Buy a white noise machine to mask unwanted sounds.
- Add some beautiful flowers or plants.
- Give the room a mini makeover—relocate furniture, repaint the walls, and consider new window treatments, paintings, photographs, or posters.

The Healing Power of Nature

Basking in nature's glory can be a soothing and majestic experience. When I'm feeling down, a walk in a park always helps me put things in perspective and perks me back up. Why don't you try taking a long walk or hike, or even having a picnic in a park or a forest? If you live near the water, a beach stroll is a great way to unwind. I'm sure you too will have that special feeling that comes from being surrounded by nature.

Once you have this room set up, find some time each day to spend there, basking in this newly created comfort. Many women report that while in their special place they take time to journal, read spiritual or motivational books, meditate, or watch movies. You can also do any hobbies you enjoy in this sanctuary.

Journaling

Journaling is a useful tool following a breakup or divorce and I strongly recommend it. It allows you to track yourself and your relationship in a very meaningful way. It will help create clarity and accelerate your personal development. It will improve your self-awareness and self-knowledge. It will also reduce stress and obsessive thinking; the simple act of writing something down clears your head and reduces the tendency to fixate.

I found journaling cathartic after a terrible breakup, so I suggest you buy a notebook or journal and write in it daily. You can write absolutely anything you feel like. Let your thoughts spill onto the blank page. After each writing session rate your mood on a scale from one to ten (one being extremely depressed and ten being your personal best). This way you have a clear history of your progress. Often we feel stuck in our gloom and frustrated that our lives are not getting any better. When we note our moods and progression through journaling, we can track our evolution more objectively. As the months pass you can literally see where you have been and where you are going.

> "I started journaling two months after my husband and I separated. I just needed to write down some thoughts. Through this process I realized that the demise of my marriage was not entirely my fault. It was a huge aha moment. After that I bought several journals and made a commitment to keep writing at the same time each day. It was a conversation with myself. You have to have these conversations because you are the only one who truly has the history of your relationship. The questions

and answers are yours to discover. Also, this was a very useful way to contain my obsession with my situation. I didn't want my obsessional thinking bleeding into my career, friendships, or mothering.

During the first few months when I was trying so hard to contain myself and be in control, my writing was orderly and neat. As I got in touch with my anger, my writing was tense and scribbly. Then one night, months into the process, I noticed my handwriting was incredibly big and curly. Totally free form. I realized that night I was starting to feel very free. I was being released from the months of pain I had carried inside of me. Ten months later I had a huge revelation. I became angry that he was taking up so much of my emotional time. I said, 'Screw him, this should be about me. Not how he messed with me.' That's the day I bought a new journal and called it 'The Book About Me.' Everything started changing after that. That's when I started writing about myself. My joys, my fears, my needs, my future. Today if I have any thoughts about my ex, it goes into the old journal, because I'm working so hard to keep that toxicity out of my life."   —Sara

Although it may be difficult for you to comprehend today, in time you will certainly heal, and life will go on. Eventually the hurt and the pain will dissipate and clarity will arrive. But until then, it's important to accept the inevitable and find a safe space to experience your feelings and some comfort in the process.

Deep-Breathing Exercise

Deep breathing is unequivocally one of the best ways to quiet your mind and create a deep state of relaxation. Deep diaphragmatic breathing (a mainstay of yoga and meditation) can be done every morning and evening to soothe, calm, and provide restoration. Follow these simple steps:

Find a quiet spot. Sit silently and comfortably. Take several deep breaths in and out through your nostrils. Breathe deeply and slowly.

Start for five minutes and increase your time by a minute or more each day. Try to work up to at least fifteen minutes and please try to do this daily.

If you truly focus and concentrate on your breathing, it is difficult to think of anything else at all. This is a wonderful respite from the stressful thoughts that may be causing you sadness and anxiety.

Grounding Exercises

Grounding exercises will help bring you back into your senses when you are slipping into unpleasant thoughts or feeling out of control. These easy and effective exercises will be very helpful when you are attempting to process that your relationship has just ended and are feeling shocked or panicky. Here's how it goes:

• Take several deep cleansing breaths. Breathe in deeply until your lungs are full. Slowly, breathe out. Relax.

• Look around at your surroundings and name out loud five things that you can see. "I see a book on my night table, I see my plant on my windowsill, I see my couch," and so on.

• Name five things you can hear. "I hear the television, the birds chirping, a car passing by," and so on.

• Name five things you can physically feel. "I feel my sweater on my skin, my shoes on my feet, the breeze on my face," and so on.

Repeat this exercise five times at first, then four times, and so on down to one time. Try to pick new examples each time. This will both calm and distract you. It will also allow you to get refamiliarized with your surroundings, which will help you feel safe and in control. These exercises can be done anywhere, not just at home. If you are at work, or out with your friends, and feel overwhelmed, just excuse yourself and find a place to go where you can spend five minutes grounding yourself.

~~~~~~~~~~~~~~~~~~~~~~~~~~~~~~~~~~~~~

A Room of One's Own
Tips and Tools

1. Validate yourself. Consider writing a list of everything you feel and then write a comforting thought next to it. For example:
   Feeling: I feel so ashamed of my breakup. I can't tell anyone.
   Comfort: There is no reason to feel embarrassed. Millions of women are suffering just as I am today. I am not alone. I have a right to ask for help.
2. Accept that healing will take time. You are on a long marathon, not a sprint, and there is a finish line up ahead.
3. Create a comfortable and peaceful area to grieve. Turn your bedroom or another room into a place of tranquillity.
4. Practice your deep-breathing exercises several times a day.
5. Journal your thoughts daily. Let your emotions flow onto each page and don't hold back. This is a place where you can totally be yourself and write anything that you desire.
6. Use grounding exercises as needed—they are very helpful.

~~~~~~~~~~~~~~~~~~~~~~~~~~~~~~~~~~~~~

2

Creating a Support System

"I tended to my relationship above everything else. I put my boyfriend first in every way—ahead of my social life, family, and friends. When it ended, my life was shattered. I was isolated, and sometimes went entire weekends without seeing or talking to anyone. One day at work I broke down in front of a colleague. He was so kind and sympathetic. He listened and valued what I was saying. He offered very good advice. After that experience I realized that in order to rebuild my life, I had to start talking. It took a lot of courage on my part, but slowly I began reaching out to a variety of people—friends, family, coworkers. Reaching out made me feel supported, validated, and valued." —*Iris*

We all tend to feel lonely and isolated after a relationship ends. The emptiness we feel can seem utterly unbearable. Being part of a couple often consumes your life; it can even mimic a secret society. Couples have their personal routines and habits, shared inferences and jokes, and friendship and intimacy. Many describe their partner as their best friend, or someone they spend the majority of their time with. Filling that void can feel daunting. You are probably wondering how you will fill your days, nights, and especially frightening, weekends and holidays. The emptiness can feel enormous, as if it can never be filled, even by well-meaning friends and loved ones.

It's possible that along with your breakup you've lost not only your mate but some friends and family as well. It's unfortunate, but people do tend to take sides, which can cause you to feel even more isolated and abandoned. I often hear women cry out, "I'm all alone. No one cares about me any longer. I have no one to turn to." Although these statements can feel very real, in actuality, they are rarely true.

The loss of companionship is a theme that came up repeatedly in my interviews, along with all-consuming loneliness—feeling as if no one exists in the world but you; thinking that you'll never be part of a couple again and that all of life's challenges must now be tackled single-handedly. Facing loneliness can seem insurmountable, but it must be done. It's one of the most important steps of healing. Please resist the urge to give in to your isolation. While I have touted the importance of self-reliance and reflection, this is not to be confused with seclusion. Too much time alone can be extremely dangerous—it will fuel your sorrow and may lead to a deeper and more profound depression. Too much time in your own head is not helpful. You will obsess about your breakup and put an inordinate amount of blame on yourself. Support from many different sources will help you in a variety of ways. It will combat isolation and put you firmly on the path toward recovery. It will validate your experience, as it affords you an audience to talk through your narrative. There are scores of people out there, both lay and professional, who really do want to help. Many are already in your life, and others are waiting to be discovered. You simply have to be open to the process and willing to do the work.

Many of you report that even with loneliness as a motivator, creating a support system feels too difficult. Reasons may include:

- Inertia from depression
- Uncertainty regarding where and whom to turn to
- Fear of further rejection
- Embarrassment over the circumstances surrounding your breakup
- A limited number of friends
- Worries about being judged
- Fears that you have either alienated or burned out family and

friends during the course of your relationship and ensuing breakup, and you don't know how to ameliorate this problem.

• Discomfort reaching out for fear of burdening others, or perhaps you are unfamiliar with asking for help. You may be more comfortable being the helper as opposed to being the one seeking assistance.

Although all of these reasons may seem valid to you, I am urging you to reach beyond the paralysis and move ahead, as challenging as it may feel.

Friendships

"My friends are my estate."
—Emily Dickinson

"On the day my husband left, I immediately reached out to my closest friends. They flew to my rescue. Someone was either physically or on the telephone with me for the first twenty-four hours. I don't know how I would have made it through that day without this safety net. Today I have an unbelievable social life and amazing girlfriends. We support each other when the going gets rough. It's so important to have that validation and to realize that you're not the only single girl out there." —*Hailey*

It is nearly impossible to survive the aftermath of a separation without the support of friends. Time after time women reported to me that friendships literally saved their lives. You are going to need to talk about your breakup, and good friends will supply you with this crucial outlet. Human beings, especially women, need to feel connected. The absence of close friendships will increase your sense of isolation and loneliness. A ten-year Australian study concluded that friendships can actually increase our life span, and I've read that friendships actually have a greater impact on our psychological health than familial relationships—or even a spouse! Friendships will help to reduce stress, provide recreation, improve your overall sense of well-being, and much more. And did you know that when you spend time with positive and upbeat people you will actually feel better? This is because the mirror neurons in our brains pick up the mood of the folks we're with, making their state of mind literally contagious.

Two years ago a dear friend was left unexpectedly by her husband, and her brave journey was one of the factors that inspired me to write this book. Andrea struggled greatly to make sense of the breakup of her twenty-five-year relationship and relied on me for both support and guidance. We were always good friends, but our connection deepened substantially as I became a vital part of her support system. I tried my best to be available and compassionate. I used humor with her, because I've found that laughter is a marvelous tonic. When it was called for, I served as a reality check, I redirected her as needed, and I was always honest and at times frank. Using our relationship as a model, she came to further understand the benefits of both friendships and talking, and she turned to more friends for comfort and companionship. Eventually she amassed a wonderful group of female friends, both old and new, whom she calls "my amazing group of girls."

Intellectually, I'm sure most of you agree with what I'm saying regarding the necessity of friendship, but there are many factors that may inhibit you from reaching out to touch someone. You could be confused about whom to turn to, or who is the "right" friend to call. Here are the most common statements I hear that hinder us from connecting with friends, and tips to coach you along. Breaking through will help you build, nurture, and keep friendships alive and well while you are recovering.

• **I have some good friends, but I'm not sure whom I can count on.** This is a very important issue to consider before you reach out. Connecting with the proper friend will help you greatly, while reaching out to the wrong person can be a setback. If you contact a friend who is unable to provide the comfort or validation you are craving, it can feel very hurtful and alienating. Don't limit yourself to only "best friends" when deciding whom to contact. I heard really great stories of "good friends" and even acquaintances coming through in a variety of ways.

• **My best friend totally let me down. Now I really have no one.** It's very upsetting when we feel disappointed by someone we really treasure. Try to remember that not all people are naturally empathetic and understanding. Friends can have their own issues and agendas; plus, hearing about another's misfortune can sometimes trigger them into recalling one of their own. Although it may sting to be disappointed by a friend, this is also a good opportunity for you to assess your relationships and work on having healthier ones in the future. This doesn't mean you have to totally remove these people from your life. They may be better for laughter or for recreation—and eventually you're going to need that too.

• **I'm too embarrassed/afraid/ashamed to ask for help. I'm afraid that people will judge me.** Approximately one million couples divorced in 2009 in the United States alone. That does not even include the millions of dating and cohabiting couples that broke up. Nearly everyone at some point in his or her life has gone through a debilitating split. Even so, when people discuss breakups, feelings such as judgment, embarrassment, guilt, and humiliation come up repeatedly. Please try to understand that you are not alone.

I remember a new friend who dragged me to lunch during a particularly painful breakup of my own. Diana was the recent girlfriend of an old friend, and I'd only met her a handful of times. I was nervous when she reached out to me—I was ashamed about my situation, disappointed and angry with myself, and didn't know if I felt comfortable enough to share with someone I wasn't fully acquainted with. As I recall, I almost canceled our date. But luckily, I did go, and it was a remarkable experience for me. Diana boldly shared her own breakup stories (some of which were quite colorful!), which helped comfort and validate me in innumerable ways. She was so sweet and completely nonjudgmental. After that day Diana became an integral part of my support system and we remained close friends for many years. Remember, asking for help is a strength, not a weakness.

• **I'm afraid I've burned out my friends with my story.** While asking for help and relying on friends is crucial, leaning solely on anyone can be somewhat problematic. Burning through friendships during a breakup is something many do, so it's good to be aware of this now so it won't happen to you. Friendships, even in times of need, are two-way streets. Do be careful not to depend too heavily on one person, as it may be too difficult for him or her to handle. Be sure to always thank friends for taking the time, and try to remember, even when you're not feeling your best, to ask them about their lives too.

• **All of my friends are married and I'm sure they don't have time for me. It's hard to make new friends as I get older.** Although this statement may ring true for you, I promise you we can prove otherwise. Believe it or not, even married or committed people make good friends, and even married people want single friends. I suggest that you create a friendship list and look at it with a finely tuned eye. I'm sure you will be able to come up with several people to call. Regarding making new friends, this is an excellent time to expand your network. Potential friends can be found at your gym or on a team, at your job, through volunteering, taking a class, at a restaurant, on Facebook, through travel, hobbies, by getting a dog, and so much more. You simply have to find the time and desire to build up your network. You'll be way ahead of the game if you start this process today.

• **I'm a very private person and don't feel comfortable talking about personal things.** Not everyone is an extrovert and many people do feel uncomfortable sharing private information. Perhaps you are naturally shy and reticent, and may have large boundaries when it comes to defining friendships. Talking equals healing. It's through the process of communicating that you will be able to put the pieces together, create a cohesive narrative, and open yourself up to the recovery process. It is nearly impossible to make sense of your relationship patterns and understand the full impact of your separation, including your role in it, without discussing it. Breaking through these discomforts and letting people in will be valuable in many ways. The right friend will be kind, open to meeting with you, supportive, willing to listen without giving unsolicited advice, and nonjudgmental. I know it can feel unnerving to push through these fears, but I promise you the rewards will be there.

Friendship Formula

Ask yourself these questions when deciding whom to reach out to:

Who is a caring and sympathetic person?

Who is not a "tough-love" person?

Who is a good listener? (Be cautious with friends who give *too much* advice, or expect you to always listen to them. Ultimately you want to be able to figure out your own truth.)

Who is not judgmental?

Who is more selfless than selfish?

Who may best relate to my experience?

Who has the time for me?

Whom have I been a good friend to?

Who is a positive and upbeat person (avoid negative and/or bitter people)?

Do I have a friend who handled herself with class and finesse after her breakup? Someone whom I admire?

Contemplate these questions while looking through your address book. This is a great exercise and the answers may surprise you. However, if you do not have many close friends at the time of your separation, fear not. There are many other places where you can get great support.

Family

"My father flew in to visit me unexpectedly the weekend my boyfriend and I broke up. We were close, but had never spent too much time together alone. It was such a pleasant surprise. He was both comforting and wise." —*Patricia*

"My brother and his wife were incredibly supportive to me. They called constantly, visited me (although we lived in different cities), and insisted that I visit them. They went above and beyond. After I recovered I sent them a gift certificate for a weekend at a spa. I felt so proud to be able to pay them back for their care."   —*Charla*

If you are fortunate to come from a close and loving family, navigating the world's myriad problems can feel a lot easier. Families can provide unconditional love, abounding wisdom, tradition, community, willingness to help, confidence, friendship, and fun. Scores of women I interviewed described how the love and support of their family, or certain family members, helped them heal in a variety of ways.

If you are close to your family, including them in your support system is a very good choice. They innately know and understand your personality and your behavior patterns, and chances are they have known your ex from the start. These factors can give them an important role in both discussing and dissecting your story. I've regularly heard stories of parents and/or siblings who are ready, willing, and able to sign on for the long haul. When families work, when they are close and devoted, healing and growth are accelerated. I've also heard many stories about women being let down by one member, while being pleasantly surprised by another.

Even if you come from a close family and the love is there, many are not equipped to provide the kind of support you may need during this difficult time. I've heard umpteen stories about women being gravely hurt by expecting support from family and not receiving it. It is always disappointing when family lets you down, but it can be especially sorrowful at the end of a relationship. There is a good chance if there has been a history of complex or dysfunctional family relationships, even now, when you're in crisis, this scenario may play out.

As painful as these encounters can be (and I understand, they hurt so deeply), paradoxically there is rich material here that can serve you in your healing. Once you brush yourself off, this is actually a golden opportunity to take a look at your family relationships. Trying to piece together and understand why they reacted to your breakup as they did will provide crucial clues for you to dissect and study. Knowing your role in your family, plus how family relationships have tinted your view of the world and impacted your relationships, will be a huge component in your understanding phase.

As previously discussed in the friendships section, I suggest you take some time to consider who may be the most sympathetic and helpful to you during this complicated time.

Here are some further tips to reflect on when reaching out to family.

• **Parents.** For many women, especially younger ones, reaching out to Mom and Dad is generally the first choice. When parents are able to assist, the outpouring of love can feel like a warm and cozy blanket. I've heard touching stories of parents (and even grandparents) stopping their lives to help out in any way that's needed. But remember, as we've discussed, some parents may be more equipped to help than others.

Most mothers really do want to help, and when it works it's wonderful. Other moms get too involved, and this can feel overwhelming and controlling. Fathers can provide both love and practical guidance. Some dads may be uncomfortable with the outpouring of emotion or may just not know how to be helpful. Put them to work. Let them fix things around the house, help with the kids, garden, shop, and so on.

Often parents need to be instructed on how they can best be useful, so try to communicate exactly what you need from them. Can they help emotionally? Financially? Can they chip in with chores and children?

• **Siblings.** Overall I heard very positive stories about love and support from siblings. Sisters, and even brothers, stepped up to help in a whole host of ways. There is no generation gap with siblings, and generally they can better relate to what you're going through than parents or children. They understand you and your situation. If you have siblings you can count on, this is a very good choice.

If you are an only child or not close to your siblings, try to expand your family network in other ways. Think of cousins or other relatives.

• **Children.** If you have children, you are probably very concerned about how your split will affect them. Chances are your kids are conflicted and confused. Most vacillate between feeling sad, confused, and angry about the circumstance that has befallen them and you. Relying on children for support is tricky. I have heard wonderful stories about children providing love, validation, and comfort—especially if they are teenage or young adults. However I've also known of women making the common mistake of over-involving their children in their pain and healing.

Truly the best thing you can do for your children is to take care of yourself and stay healthy. Your kids will absolutely reap the benefits of your taking time to heal and taking care of yourself. There are many wonderful resources readily available to help you assess how your children are faring, and what role, if any, they can play in your recovery.

Colleagues

"People at work knew my marriage was ending and they totally rallied to help me. Every day someone checked in on me. Many of us keep in touch today. They're all proud of my progress."   —*Gretchen*

"At first people tried to respect my privacy, but one day my boss came in and asked if everything was OK. I broke down in front of her and was very embarrassed. I started talking nonstop and explaining that my personal problems weren't going to affect my performance. She looked at me like I had three heads and said, 'I'm only here because I'm concerned about you—this is not about the job.' That was such a relief for me."   —*Pritti*

Getting along with your coworkers and superiors does make for a happier and healthier life. Colleagues can become a makeshift family celebrating life's successes and mourning tragedies. I have many fond memories of colleagues brightening my day with friendship, camaraderie, gossip, and humor. In fact, a boss introduced me to my husband. So consider reaching out for support at the place where many of us spend the majority of our time: on the job.

Some of you may feel that there should be very strict boundaries between your personal life and work life. One woman described to me how she felt it was imperative to keep her divorce private from her colleagues, stating, "I have an executive position in a mostly male company. There is plenty of sexism there. There was no way I was going to share anything about my private life on the job. I was afraid it could be used against me." She did go on to explain that the decision cost her in other ways. "It made things a lot more difficult for me because I felt so isolated while at work. I work at least ten hours a day. Acting like nothing was wrong for that amount of time took its toll. I spent a great deal of time crying in the rest room."

If you have friends at work, adding them to your support system is a smart choice. Do, however, use some prudence when deciding with whom to share, and how much to discuss. Please always be mindful not to let your personal life overly affect your performance or behavior.

Consider the following when deciding whom to reach out to:

• What is the culture of your company? Does it encourage fraternization? If not, are you taking too much of a risk by bringing your personal life into work?

• Who may be the best choice to lean on for support? (See the friendship formula on p. 21)

• How can I strike a proper balance between getting support at work, yet not allowing my situation to interfere too much with my job performance?

Therapy

"My therapist became a trusted friend. She was actually the most helpful component of my support system. She had no agenda, and was simply there to listen and help in any way that I needed. She really cared and was concerned for me. Truly, I couldn't have healed without her love and support."   —*Maura*

"You may need that objective observer to help you put your story together. You must gain insight and take responsibility before you can really move forward." —*Laura*

Therapy offers abundant emotional benefits to someone recovering from a breakup or divorce, and support is definitely one of them. For many of us in the psychotherapy field, what we do is a calling as opposed to a job. We are available to help individuals be the best they can be using a combination of psychology, education, research, and devotion. Therapy is many things, including a caring relationship between two people. The right therapist has lots of experience to help you understand and overcome the numerous stages and implications of your breakup.

We know that talking things through, particularly for women, helps process our thoughts and feelings. Through this progression, information will come out that you have never been able to articulate or even understand before. Many truths flow in this way. The therapeutic relationship is completely confidential. It is unequivocally a safe haven where you can open up and say anything that is on your mind. There is no need to be ashamed—your therapist will never judge you.

Many excellent and highly skilled therapists are ready, willing, and available to help you through this trying time. Making the right match is very important. Feel free to contact several therapists and be sure to spend time on the telephone asking questions. You

Animals to Soothe

Perhaps you'd consider making a pet part of your support system. Animals can provide emotional connection and love, and physical comfort too. Having a pet to climb onto your lap, lick your face, or curl up next to you in bed may help fill the void of physical touch that you are missing. If your pet needs to be walked, it will catapult you into the world. Dog parks are excellent places to meet people and feel connected. There are many ways to make a pet part of your healing regimen. You can purchase, adopt, borrow, pet-sit, or foster. Volunteering for your local rescue organization is also a wonderful choice for someone who loves animals but may not wish to parent full time—and this is something to consider during this time of upheaval. Volunteering will provide you with an opportunity to do good deeds, be around animals needing your love, and meet others in the process.

can also make appointments with different therapists and interview them to find the right fit. I recommend they have experience in understanding relational dynamics, are actively involved in the session, and believe in giving feedback and suggestions. If you have insurance during your breakup you can go directly to your plan to locate a therapist. If you don't have insurance and cost is an issue, most cities have low-cost counseling centers available to help during difficult times.

Groups

"Joining a support group really helped me cope. I realized I was not alone and that most women do really suffer after a breakup. My pain was finally validated. I was able to express my feelings, be consoled—plus help others. That's the power of a group." —*Olive*

Groups can be a wonderful addition to your support system. As a group therapist I can fully attest to the power of being part of a healing community. Discovering that you are not alone in your suffering, and that others are having similar thoughts and experiences, can work miracles. I've witnessed people from all different walks of life come together and deeply bond over the one issue they have in common. Groups will help you to feel less isolated, address the challenges you are experiencing, foster communication and connection, and validate your circumstances. Through both the group leader, who can be a therapist or a layperson, and other participants, you will learn facts about both the psychological and logistical aspects of your breakup or divorce. Psychological issues can include a better understanding of your feelings, how family patterns may have influenced and impacted your relationship, and a clearer narrative about the details of your relationship and its ending.

If groups interest you, there are plenty out there. Some are topic specific and others are more therapeutic in nature. Here's a list of the type of groups that you may encounter in your search:

• **Breakup or Divorce Support Groups.** I highly recommend that you consider attending one of these. They offer abundant comfort and validation because you will be meeting with others who are in your shoes. You will meet folks at all different stages in their healing who will offer support and education. Topics will be discussed such as how to deal with your ex, career decisions, how and when to relocate (if necessary), and financial matters. If you are going through a divorce, discussion may include knowledge of laws and rights, and parenting issues. Support groups encourage fraternization, so this is also a great opportunity to expand your support system.

• **Group Therapy.** This is a form of psychotherapy where several people come together to form a therapeutic community. These groups are run by licensed and experienced group psychotherapists. The group is used as a vehicle for change as you explore your thoughts and feelings while receiving feedback from both group members and the counselor. Ultimately the process serves as a "mirror," which helps to enlighten you about how your personal style and behavioral patterns are viewed by and affect others. People enroll in these groups for a variety of reasons; however, relationship issues are a common motivator. Through the process of the group you become aware of who "pushes your buttons" (i.e., who in the group reminds you of your ex, your mother, father, etc.), understand the dynamics causing those feelings, and work toward making the changes that will enable you to have healthier relationships.

• **Twelve-Step Groups.** If alcohol, drugs, or any other addiction (including spending, sex, pornography, or gambling) affected your relationship and contributed to its termination, you may be very well served by attending a twelve-step meeting. These meetings, which are widely available, help addicts or those affected by addiction by offering camaraderie, support, education, and guidance.

Faith

"My faith has grown since my divorce. My relationship with God definitely helped me through. I knew I wasn't alone, and that others go through tragedies much worse than mine. Prayer helped me a lot. My faith also allowed me to forgive my ex." —*Bonnie*

"As an atheist, I never expected to have religion play any role in my life. After my breakup, when I was in the dumps, a friend invited me to mass at a small neighborhood church. I enjoyed the experience and the feeling of community that it afforded. They had a soup kitchen and many worthwhile projects. Slowly I made my way into their volunteer program and it helped me in many ways. I made some friends and felt I was doing some good in the world, which helped me to feel better about myself and my situation." —*Susan*

A relationship with a higher power or being affiliated with a religious community can be comforting in difficult times. After a breakup there can often be a reevaluation of your entire life. Faith can help you to find your way while allowing you to feel less conflicted and alone. Even if you have no belief system or a tenuous relationship with a higher power, it could be helpful to you to think of God, or a higher being, as someone who can simply listen without judgment, who can hear and accept your pain.

There are definite benefits to getting involved in a religious or spiritual community. Most clergy are well trained to assist people going through challenges in their lives, and many offer guidance through individual meetings. Organized religion offers you an opportunity to get involved in a community, which will help to ease your loneliness and allow you to get out of yourself and get involved. Most churches, temples, and other places of worship offer a variety of activities such as charity or volunteer work, becoming part of a committee, lectures and workshops, and activities for new members.

Eastern religion interests me, and I assure you, Buddhism has much to offer in your time of need. The Buddha was an awakened being who taught people how to end their suffering by understanding what caused it, and more important, by accepting it. Buddhism teaches that life includes both joy and pain, and learning about this concept may ease your suffering as it did mine in times of difficulty.

Consider adding religion or spirituality to your support system. Prayer and belief can help to comfort you, which will undoubtedly speed your healing.

Now is the time to create a caring and sympathetic group of people who are willing to help you through this period of difficulty. Adding support to your life will ease your journey, provide abundant comfort, and greatly expedite the healing process. In today's age of electronic effortlessness, reaching out is easier than ever before. Call, text, e-mail, or Facebook someone right now. The more people and resources you contact, the more comfortable your journey will become. You will benefit greatly by filling your schedule with upbeat experiences, taking a needed break from your thoughts, and re-creating many of the positive benefits that your prior relationship afforded you.

Creating a Support System
Tips and Tools

1. Continue your journaling practice in a comfortable and peaceful space. Let your thoughts and feelings flow on each page. Take time to think. Take time to write. Take time to feel.
2. Work hard to create an outstanding support system that may include both lay- and professional persons. Try not to be too deflated if someone lets you down. Take a deep breath, give yourself a much-deserved hug, and move on to the next person.
3. Make a list of all the individuals you can reach out to. Make a commitment to contact each person by a certain date. Check this list weekly to monitor your progress.
4. Review the friendship formula. Continue to be mindful regarding the type of friendships you currently have and the type you may wish to create.
5. Consider adding therapy or group therapy to your support system.
6. Consider adding religion or spirituality to your life. It can really help to find belief in something greater than ourselves.

3

Nourishing Your Body and Soul

"Caring for myself was the last thing I would think about. I didn't eat healthy, didn't exercise, and I stopped attending church. That took quite a toll on me. My depression just became worse and worse. Finally I came to the realization that I couldn't go on like this. I just felt mentally and physically depleted. Once I started to put the steps in place to eat right, exercise, and reconnect to my spirituality, I started feeling better—more like myself. Those small changes really helped me feel much more hopeful. I was proud that I was pushing through my pain and accomplishing even small things. I realized that it was worth taking care of myself and it was worth living." —*Carolyn*

The dissolution of a relationship causes both physical and emotional distress. Many of the emotions you are experiencing take a huge toll, interfering with your ability to function minimally let alone optimally. Caring for yourself, even in simple ways, can seem like an insurmountable task. This is an unfortunate but normal cycle—and one we must break to speed your recovery. If you are not eating properly, exercising, and taking care of your spiritual and emotional needs, your progress will be greatly slowed. Taking care of yourself will help you get out of bed each day and enable you to present your best self to the world—even when you feel terrible. It will also help you achieve peace and harmony and better prepare you for the road ahead.

Following my suggestions for health and healing will place and keep you firmly on the path to recovery. You will start to feel less depressed, calmer, and more energized, and you will be extremely proud of yourself. Breaking the cycle of lethargy is a major leap forward. I believe in you, and I know you can do it!

Nutrition

"I gained over ten pounds on this ridiculous diet of junk food. This further injured my self-esteem. Losing the weight was hard, but I eventually knew that I had to do it. Today I eat very well and I've seen and felt the positive results." —*Amelia*

It's commonly understood that if you eat well you will reap many wonderful benefits, and that poor nutrition can cause a myriad of health issues. When you're going through the ordeal of a breakup, healthy eating is one of the first good habits to disappear.

There are a variety of reasons that food takes on a new significance after a painful experience. Many of us initially use food to cope with our distress. If you are imploding with worry or anxiety, your appetite may be severely restricted. This response can make eating unpleasant and at times physically difficult. Even your favorite foods can seem extremely unappetizing and unappealing. Under-eaters may also believe that they are able to get some control in their disorderly lives by constraining food intake. Some may have an obsession with losing weight or staying thin, which they believe may better prepare them for future dating.

On the other hand, some use food to numb, distract, or comfort after a breakup. This pattern may lead to binge eating and extensive weight gain. It's normal to change eating patterns after a stressful experience—nearly everyone does. Modified eating habits over a few days or a week is normal and acceptable, but unfortunately for many, this pattern can often continue much longer than is healthy.

Both under- and overeating will restrict your ability to function optimally and heal properly.

• It will impede your cognitive functioning, which can worsen your mood and cause you to feel irritable.

• If you are starving or gorging on the wrong foods, you will have volatile swings in your blood sugar, which will make you feel imbalanced.

• If you allow yourself to become disabled by poor nutrition, gain or lose excessive weight, and become dissatisfied with your appearance, it will damage your esteem, and you will not be as free to present your best self to the world.

Food for Thought

Several women I spoke with described the act of cooking and eating comfort foods as caring for both their body *and* their soul. Cooking is about nutrition, but it's also about creativity, fun, and love. It is a great hobby, especially if you are looking for new ways to fill your time. You can experiment with different recipes and styles of food. You can thank those who have supported you by inviting them to break bread or baking them a treat.

I'm urging you to get your nutrition under control before it becomes harmful and hinders your recovery. I know you have the power to do this and I will help you by suggesting a healthier approach toward food.

• Nutritionist and *Today* show correspondent Joy Bauer says that breakfast is the most important meal of the day and should not be skipped if possible. Even if you can only eat a yogurt or a piece of toast in the morning, just be sure to eat.

• Many find that comfort foods are the easiest to get down. Try taking a healthier approach to your favorite foods by substituting whole grains, less white sugar, and lower fat and carbs wherever possible.

• Try eating several healthy "mini" meals during the day to keep yourself nourished and satiated.

• Consider visiting a nutritionist, who will help you by creating an individualized plan and monitoring your progress.

One of my favorite books on nutrition is *Joy Bauer's Food Cures*, which covers everything from how to achieve radiant skin and hair, to foods that actually cure aches and pains! I also like her cookbook *Slim and Scrumptious*.

Exercise

"No one wants to exercise when they're feeling shitty. That's perfectly normal. But it's the very best medicine that you can take. You have to force yourself to get out there and work up a sweat. It will make you feel good about yourself. There are tons of options for exercise no matter where you live—it can be done solitary, like running or riding a bike, or in a group setting."   —*Allegra*

"I gained nearly twenty-five pounds after my divorce. All I did was sit on the couch, cry, and eat. One day I walked up a flight of stairs and I had trouble breathing. That's when I knew I was in trouble. The next day I committed to losing the weight through diet and exercise. I started slowly—walking thirty minutes a few times a week. Then I got back to the gym and started doing yoga. It wasn't easy, but slowly the pounds started to shed. That's when I really felt I was back in the driver's seat."   —*Maria*

Never underestimate the physical and mental benefits of exercise. If you want to feel better, have more energy, and live longer, exercise is the way to go. Exercise has been positively linked to *decreased* anxiety, stress, and depression, and *increased* self-esteem and mental focus. And several studies, including one from Duke University

Beware of Alcohol and Other Addictives

"After my relationship ended I found myself drinking more than I usually did. The more depressed I became, the more I would drink. And, with drinking and depression came isolation. Getting treatment and stopping drinking saved my life. I was finally able to process the end of my relationship and get to work rebuilding my shattered life. About a year after I stopped drinking, I met a wonderful man, who is my husband today. It never would have happened if I was still drinking." —Taylor

The use of alcohol is woven into the fabric of our society. We often drink to be social and celebrate, yet many turn to alcohol to drown their sorrows in times of distress. What you probably don't realize is that increased use of these substances actually causes the exact opposite effect that you may be looking for. For example, alcohol and sedatives are mood depressants, thus they will *increase* depression, anxiety, and insomnia. This book is loaded with suggestions to promote relaxation, so please try those instead.

Medical Center, discovered that a regular exercise routine can be as effective as taking an antidepressant medication, due to the endorphins (chemicals released in your brain that cause you to feel calmer and happier) that are emitted. Many of you described how your involvement in sports or movement allowed you to feel better about your bodies and increase your energy. Others reported that it helped them feel both physically and emotionally stronger, improved feelings of angst and hopelessness, increased confidence, and created a huge sense of achievement.

After a breakup or divorce, exercising is the last thing you may feel like doing. If you're suffering from depression, insomnia, and lethargy, barely getting out of the house each day is a monumental accomplishment. And if you're not an exerciser to begin with, you're probably thinking, "She wants me to start going to the gym *now?*" I understand that pushing through your resistance is not going to be easy, but it's a battle that I am strongly urging you to fight.

I am an avid exerciser and can fully attest to its benefits, yet many mornings I find myself struggling to find motivation, especially if I'm unusually tired, or if it's cold or gloomy outdoors. On those days I remind myself about how great I'm going to feel when I'm running my last mile, or doing my final push-up. I feel as if I've achieved a goal, and that's something I can hang my hat on all day long.

Here are some suggestions to help you get into an exercise routine:

• Make a commitment to yourself to begin a fitness regimen. Make a chart and fill it in with your goals and your progress. Start slow—even if you can commit to only ten or fifteen minutes a day, that is fabulous! You'll be surprised how a small promise to yourself can easily turn into a larger one.

• Exercising first thing in the morning is a great way to begin the day. Depression and anxiety are generally worse in the morning, so this is a natural way to push through.

• Working out with a friend can be a lot of fun and help to motivate you. Ask a friend to exercise with you.

• Work out to great music. When I'm jogging with a favorite tune on my iPod it's just as fun as dancing.

• Another strong motivator—if you are lonely or isolated, joining a gym or sports team will get you out of your house and foster socializing.

• Consider hiring a trainer, even for a few sessions. A trainer will ease you into the gym, show you the ropes, and create a personalized routine for you.

• Join an adult recreation league, where you can play everything from soccer to softball. Found in many cities, they accept all levels, offer great exercise, and are a wonderful way to meet people.

• Start an exercise program at home by purchasing an instructional DVD of any activity that interests or intrigues you.

• Taking a yoga, Pilates, or stretch class in the evening is an excellent way to end your day, fill your time, and promote relaxation.

• Once you've started your exercise routine, reward yourself by downloading a new song on your iPod or purchasing a cute exercise top or outfit.

I strongly recommend that you add some form of exercise to your life to help speed up your recovery. It will improve both your mental and physical health, allow you to have some needed fun, and enable you to take crucial steps to regain your sense of self. Start today and feel your power. Just do it!

Sleep

"Sleeping literally became a nightmare for me. I couldn't fall asleep—I'd toss and turn for hours. When I fell asleep I was plagued with dreams about my husband. The dreams made me not want to sleep and I'd become very anxious around bedtime. It became paradoxical because I knew I needed to sleep but I was afraid to. I knew I needed a better bedtime routine to kick this. I started journaling and taking hot showers to promote relaxation. I told myself not to be afraid, that sleep was a good thing. After awhile it got much better." —*Sonia*

"I couldn't stop sleeping. It's all I wanted to do. Sometimes I stayed in bed or in my pajamas for days. After a while I knew I needed to face the world, and I pushed myself to get into a better routine by setting my alarm and asking friends to call me in the morning to help me get up. I felt much better when I rejoined the human race!" —*Elisa*

Sleep is a necessity—it's something we simply cannot live without. Nobody likes the effects of sleep deprivation, yet insomnia is a common by-product of a breakup. If you are suffering from insomnia, you are not alone. Women report having problems getting to sleep and staying asleep, and many complain of waking up much earlier than they are used to. Others describe that they *are* sleeping, but still feel exhausted upon awakening, which could indicate a disruption in REM sleep (the normal stage of restful sleep). Sleep deprivation will prevent you from feeling and performing well, which are extremely important features in your healing. Symptoms of insomnia can include exhaustion, moodiness, headaches, increased depression and anxiety, and an inability to focus or concentrate.

Some women report that their primary break-up response is to sleep—hours upon hours, days upon days. They are hiding from problems, responsibilities—from the world. This bad habit will cause you to feel constantly lethargic and unmotivated. It will also make it harder for you to keep up with your errands and tasks, which may cause you to feel overwhelmed.

These new patterns can feel very frustrating and add to the despair you are already experiencing. Promoting good sleep hygiene is a crucial element in your recovery. There are many important things you can do to improve your sleep patterns. Here are a few suggestions:

- Try to stick to a regular sleep routine; retire and rise at the same time daily.
- Proper nutrition, exercise, and limiting alcohol are key ingredients for healthy sleep.
- Beware of using stimulants such as caffeine in excess. Try switching to decaffeinated beverages after noon.
- Make sure your bedroom is set up for maximum relaxation. This includes having comfortable bedding and the right mattress, proper temperature control and lighting, and good noise control.
- Don't forget old-fashioned remedies such as a glass of warm milk, a hot shower, or a bath.
- Deep breathing, meditation, yoga, reading, and guided imagery can also be helpful and relaxing.
- Journaling before bed is a wonderful way to get all your

thoughts out of your head and down on paper before you retire. This will help to eliminate the rumination, which can tend to keep you awake.

Try to begin your unwinding routine at least one hour, if not more, before your bedtime. Once you start sleeping regularly you *will* start to feel better.

Soul Food

"My spirituality has helped me to keep a positive outlook through difficult times. One of the beliefs of Hinduism is that everything unfolds the way it is supposed to and it's important not to become too attached to any one particular idea or egotistical view of self. It also preaches the concept of loving others, forgiveness, and letting go of anger, which is disruptive not only to oneself but to the fulfillment of one's potential. These can be difficult concepts to live by, especially when you want to blame or find an immediate explanation for something. Over-all I have found it gives me the peace to open myself up to the next person or opportunity." —*Victoria*

In times of turmoil, providing nourishment to your soul will bestow enormous benefits to your emotional being. When your soul is well cared for, life's complexities become easier to handle. When you take the time to keep in touch with your soul, it will help you stay bonded to your true essence now and for many years to come.

There are numerous ways to create a soul connection that are easy, enjoyable, and effective. Caring for your soul means finding time, even on hectic and stressful days, to relax, unwind, and sit quietly with your emotions. This will enable you to contemplate how to bring harmony and joy to your life, even while it's in flux. This could be accomplished in a fifteen-minute meditation session where you clear your mind of negative thoughts and allow yourself to develop feelings of loving-kindness and compassion toward yourself. In a few scheduled moments you can temporarily make peace with your suffering and remind yourself that in time, and with devotion to your care, you will heal. The simple act of sitting quietly with your thoughts and feelings without running from them will prove that you are strong, and that you can survive your ordeal. It will also increase your capacity for introspection, which is a key component to understanding and, eventually, recovery.

Many described to me that dabbling in a spiritual practice both calmed and centered their turbulent souls. I was regularly told that yoga, meditation, prayer, and other activities that were good for your spirit helped lessen the pain of bleak moments. Several women I interviewed explained that focusing on their spirituality and reading about Buddhism, the law of attraction, positive visualization, learned optimism, or other sources of inspiration helped them get to a much-improved place.

Yoga offers a lot to women after a breakup, and it's a great way to nourish your soul. It is a form of exercise and meditation, and as an added attraction, it also offers the ability to become part of a community. Many studios offer a variety of classes, lectures, and workshops, which encourage students to get acquainted and involved. During a particularly difficult time in my life I turned to yoga and found it incredibly healing. I located a beginner class and started attending. Mastering some of the more challenging postures gave me a real sense of power and accomplishment, and listening to the instructor's wisdom both consoled me and helped keep my thoughts in perspective.

So please find time to add some soul food to your life. It will provide comfort and clarity, warm your heart, and lighten (or "enlighten") your load.

Nourishing Your Body and Soul
Tips and Tools

1. Caring for your body and soul are crucial after a breakup. It is very important that you take care of yourself and stay healthy, which will give you strength for the road ahead.

2. Remember to eat, and to eat nutritiously. Losing or gaining weight will impede your ability to stay clearheaded and look your best.

3. Make exercise your new best friend. There are many ways for you to participate in an exercise routine, and you will feel so proud of yourself when you get up, get out, and move.

4. Congratulate yourself every single day when you eat healthfully and get some movement in your life.

5. Nourish your soul by adding yoga, meditation, or some sort of spirituality to your life. It will help to provide comfort and clarity.

4

Navigating the Emotional Roller Coaster

> "You've got to feel every single emotion. Give yourself
> time to heal. It simply cannot and should not be rushed.
> Do not try cutting corners—it will bite you later on. Try
> to be patient and give yourself time. I am not the same
> person that I was a year ago." —*Jennifer*

> "When I'd feel hopeless or sad, I'd constantly remind
> myself, 'This is how I feel now, and it's not going to be
> this way forever.'" —*Iris*

The variety of feelings experienced after a breakup or divorce can
only be described as an emotional roller coaster. Remember the
amusement park? The roller coaster goes up, it goes down, it sus-
pends you in midair, and then it comes crashing down. You scream,
cry, panic, and hold on for dear life. For many this jumbling of emotions is an entirely new experience. There will be many times when
you are going to feel completely lost.

Emotions play an important part in all of our lives. As humans
we have the capacity to identify, process, and use our feelings in
healthy and productive ways. The ability to comprehend what we
are feeling creates emotional intelligence and self-awareness, which
is something worth striving for. Emotional intelligence will allow
you to fully know yourself and your behavior, have a better understanding of others, and have improved relationships throughout
your life. Developing a keener emotional intelligence will be an

additional benefit for you when we begin to explore the full ramifications of your breakup in phase 2, "Understanding."

As distasteful as it can be, feeling, discussing, and understanding your varied emotions is extremely useful and important. It is through your personal exploration that answers will materialize. They will help to normalize your experience and move you into a deeper and richer state of personal growth.

Let me take a moment to remind you that you are still in the earliest stages of healing and this new endeavor should not begin unless you have put into place many of the suggestions we have discussed in previous chapters. If you are doing the work we've already discussed, it's time to read on. But if you are reading and not putting the suggested tools into action, I urge you to go back and put some more time and effort into the earlier chapters. It's through the combination of reading, acting, and truly challenging yourself, that progress will be made and outstanding growth will occur. You will get through the journey in due course with the combination of a curious and open mind, a diligent work ethic, and the passage of time. If you rush into dissecting your emotions, it can be disruptive to your healing. You have to take time to take care of yourself. You have to settle in. So buckle up, work hard, and breathe. You can do this!

Resilience

I have interviewed more than one hundred women for this book in all stages of recovery, and I have come to a wondrous conclusion: The bereaved and wounded are far more resilient than anyone would have imagined. If you work hard you will emerge triumphant from your breakup experience. I believe there is always an opportunity hidden within a crisis. Surviving your breakup is indeed an opportunity. It will make you stronger, smarter, and more resilient. There are many valuable lessons to be learned, and you will in time fully recover.

Processing Your Emotions

I'm going to take you step by step through the emotional roller coaster that has temporarily become your life and offer ample explanations and suggestions to expedite your healing. Through this process you'll have an opportunity to identify and explore your predominant moods. You may see yourself in a few categories, or you may identify with all of them. A huge component of recovery is acquiring an honest inventory of yourself. Knowing intuitively what makes you tick is going to be of great value to you now and for many years to come. It may be useful for you to take notes during this next section. After I discuss each emotion, take a few moments to ask yourself these evocative questions:

- How do I see or experience this emotion in my life?
- Am I satisfied with how I am dealing with it, or do I think there is more that I can do?
- What would be one positive phrase (or mantra) I can repeat to myself when grappling with a particularly challenging emotion?

I think you will find the answers to these questions particularly meaningful, and I assure you it will help in the exploration of your feelings.

Stages of the Roller Coaster

Shock and Denial

My friend was having a romantic dinner with her husband one evening when he suddenly burst into tears. He explained he didn't feel "in love" with her any longer and needed to move out and begin the process of "finding himself"—after twenty years of marriage. "It was as if the rug had been pulled out from under me," my friend told me. "In a million years I never, ever would have expected this. For many months afterward I refused to believe it was true. I felt as if it was happening to someone else, not me. I expected he'd walk through the door any moment and say he had made a mistake. I think it may have taken me six months or even more to realize my marriage really was over and he wasn't coming home."

No matter what the circumstances are surrounding a breakup, most women describe a feeling of full-blown disbelief when their relationship ends. If your relationship finished suddenly or unexpectedly, or you surprisingly discovered your partner was in a clandestine affair, you may be in a state of shock, which can actually feel like or mimic the symptoms of a trauma.

You may feel paralyzed and unable to plan any sort of strategy, unable to decide what to do next or whom to call. If you have children, you wonder how to tell them, and if you're married, you wonder how to protect your assets and legal rights. You may feel frozen in your tracks, unable to make the simplest of decisions.

Common feelings and reactions associated with shock may include numbness, denial, and dissociation—as if it can't be happening to you. You may be re-creating over and over in your head the last weeks, days, and hours leading up to the actual breakup. Alternatively, you may be walking around in a foggy daze, going through the motions yet pinching yourself to see whether this is real or not. Waiting for your life to return to normalcy. Or you may be completely subjugating every feeling—pretending that nothing has changed and everything is fine. Others try to keep up their same "coupling" routines, thinking that the breakup is a temporary situation and that life will return to usual in a matter of time.

Denial is a perfectly normal and necessary reaction to your breakup. Temporary denial is a needed function because it gives you time to adjust to the shock and reality of your loss. It will keep you from getting overwhelmed, and protect you from spiraling too rapidly into your feelings. It will allow you time to adapt to your new circumstances.

"The initial period following my separation was surreal. I'd wake up in the morning or in the middle of the night and say, 'No this isn't happening—this can't be happening.' You feel sideswiped. No idea what to do. I walked around for months in total shock. Eventually that feeling subsides, and you start to accept what's transpiring. I think that phase is nature's way of preparing you for what's ahead. I mean, you wouldn't be human if you didn't feel that kind of disbelief in the first few weeks and months." —*Audrey*

In time your shock and denial will pass, and reality will seep in. An important step toward getting out of this stage is recognition. Ultimately you will learn to recognize when you are in denial and take steps to give yourself a gentle reality check. Often close friends and family will nudge you when they feel you are falling back into denial, and that can be very helpful. Be sure to listen when that occurs and redirect yourself.

Bargaining

If you are thinking that your relationship is not really over, that it can be saved, that you can change the course of events and your partner will come back—you are in the bargaining stage. This is the stage where you convince yourself that you can get your ex back, and you make it your mission in life to do so. You may find yourself insisting, begging, groveling, and taking full blame for your breakup, even if you bear little fault. You refute his reasons for the breakup point by point, convinced, as if your life depended on it, that you can get him to see he is wrong and you are right.

Because of the bargaining routine we hear stories of breakups taking months, and, at times, years. Kristen described to me how she repeatedly called her boyfriend, begging him to reconsider.

"I would call Avery constantly and lure him into meeting me. I was sure I could convince him to come back, and I set out on a plan to do exactly that. When I went out at night and looked particularly attractive, I'd stop by his house so he could see how sexy I was and what he was missing. I would repeatedly reiterate how I would change and promised to be the best girlfriend ever to him should he reconsider. This pattern went on for months, and in hindsight, it was extremely damaging to my recovery and kept me stuck in dysfunction. I eventually understood that it was over and he wasn't coming back, and then I started working toward my own self-repair."

Prolonging the bargaining stage is troublesome. As long as you are continually engaged with your ex, you are reopening your wounds, which will cause you repeated despair. Eventually you will have the courage to admit that your attempts at negotiation have been futile and you will let go. Bargaining may continue to crop up from time to time as you move through your recuperation. Try to be firm with yourself and understand that it is ultimately harmful and will hinder your recovery.

Hero Worship

Even when we're in a fabulous relationship, we have a laundry list of issues with our partner. The mind is a funny thing. Regularly after a breakup we forget about the bad times and focus solely on the good ones. This is a primary reason why you may be having a hard time letting go. I repeatedly see this in my practice. A relationship with many flaws is nearing completion, yet when it ends, it's as if the problems never existed. Suddenly the ex-partner takes on a halo and the relationship, deemed perfect, must be saved.

Putting your ex on a pedestal will not serve you. When you put someone up high and only look at him through rose-colored glasses you are incapable of viewing the situation with objectivity and rationality. This will distort facts and cause you to long for something that is unrealistic and potentially injurious. Hero worship will keep you stuck because you will inordinately concentrate on your ex, which causes you to think less about your own recovery. Moreover, if you are focusing unrealistically on what you've lost, it will magnify negative thinking about yourself.

"I always put my boyfriend on a pedestal. I think I made him into something he just wasn't for many, many years.

Of course after the breakup I continued to idolize and deify him, thinking nonstop about how perfect he was and how I lost the best thing ever. And of course if he was so great, and he ditched me, then I must be pretty awful. You've got to get them off the pedestal. Keeping them there will taint your thinking and stunt your growth." —*Rebecca*

When hero worship creeps in, I strongly suggest to my clients that they make a list of everything that was wrong with their relationship and their ex. I advise them to write as much as they possibly can, and if they get stuck, that they query friends and family members for some assistance. I recently heard from a former client who reminded me that I gave her this assignment years ago during a trying breakup. She reported that it was a huge turning point in her recovery.

"Rachel made me write a list of everything that was wrong with the relationship and look at it whenever I felt like reconnecting with him. When I got to page four, and I wasn't even done, and it was all there right in front of me, I finally realized that it wasn't ideal, and in fact really needed to end. Whenever I get melancholy or doubt the breakup, I return to the list!" —*Stephanie*

Be persistent, even if it feels uncomfortable, and write this list. Once it is written, I urge you carry it with you and study it several times a day. It will also be helpful to read it to a friend so you can practice saying it out loud.

Sorrow and Grief

As the shock and denial fade away they are often replaced with a very deep and intense feeling of melancholy. Whenever we experience an important loss in our lives we grieve. Your life is taxing right now and you are being called upon to adapt in completely new ways. As we discussed in chapter 1, it's OK to be distressed and it's necessary to grieve. Aristotle wrote that crying cleanses the mind. You are not going to be able to truly make sense of your breakup if you don't take the time to feel and experience your pain. One woman I met expressed this point well.

> "My predominant emotion was anger. I was so angry. I needed to get my say. I wanted to get revenge. Over time I realized that I didn't like my angry self. And then I discovered that it was a cover-up for my sad self. Finally I decided that I needed to allow myself to feel sad and grieve. It was hard. It was scary. But once I did, I was able to let go of the anger, and that's when I started to move on." —*Mila*

Even if you initiated your split, you too may feel sorrow. It is extremely painful to say good-bye to someone you once loved and cherished, and to mourn for the life you had. Many discussed that even with life's inevitable ups and downs, their separation caused them to feel an impenetrable sadness, like nothing they'd lived through before. Some reported that it felt as if a fatality had occurred and they were literally experiencing a process that mirrored bereavement. Others concurred with that sentiment, including a friend who called her divorce "a death without a corpse." However, along with a real death comes support and a mourning process. This unfortunately is not always the case when a relationship ends. You may feel that you are left with excruciating distress without any ritual to help you through.

The progression out of the mourning stage is a slow and steady one. The more you put into your recovery the better you will feel. And no matter how hard it gets, you must maintain a degree of hope. Repeat this phrase every single day: I am a survivor, and this too shall pass.

Depression

Some women report that after a while their mourning turns into a depression. Depression is a catch-22. You need to work hard to get out of one, but the nature of depression often stifles the ability to do so. Even when you're feeling down, please try very hard to do this work. Find the strength to soldier on.

Exercises for Depression

• Make peace with your sorrow and create space for it to be there. A new study in the *Archives of General Psychiatry* found that if you can accept and not judge your thoughts, it is just as good at fighting depression as an antidepressant. Other studies have shown that mindfulness (deep breathing, yoga, meditation) is also effective.

• Exercise is one of the best depression busters available. Even if you can get to the gym or yoga studio, or take a run or a walk, for just fifteen minutes a day, it will be extremely helpful.

• The very nature of depression causes us to have countless negative thoughts circling through our brains. And those negative thoughts exacerbate the depression. Both *identifying* and then *talking back* to those thoughts is crucial. Try very hard to counter each negative thought with a positive one. For example:

Negative Thought: My life is over. No one will love me again.
Positive Thought: I acknowledge that this is a time of great upheaval. I am strong. I will get through this. I will find love again.

Mastering this skill takes time and practice, but you'll be doing yourself a huge favor when you commit to this change.

• Write a gratitude list. I know what you're thinking—but please try this. Write down *every little thing* that you are grateful for, and read this list several times a day. It really does help.

• Do not isolate. Even when you are feeling sad and lonely, get out of the house. Call someone upbeat from your support system (remember those mirror neurons!). Catapult yourself back into the world.

• Get a makeover. Have your hair blown out. Go to a cosmetics store and have your makeup redone.

• Force yourself to try something new, even if it means going solo, like visiting an exhibit or attending a lecture. See a movie. Take a class. Travel. Tackle a new hobby. You'll feel proud of yourself when you do these things, and that feeling of accomplishment will help alleviate the depression. Also, according to Temple University's School of Medicine, trying new activities stimulates your brain's septal zone, the "feel-good" area, which actually makes you happier!

Fear, Anxiety, and Paralysis

> "I thought I would be fine, but I wasn't at all. I thought, Oh my God, this is really happening. I'm single. I'm alone. I'm lonely. I was afraid about everything. Afraid my life was over. That I'd never meet anyone. Your mind plays these tricks on you and you really believe these scary thoughts. They are not really true, but at the time you think they are." —*Allie*

Any life change that is challenging will induce stress, and stress can often manifest itself as anxiety. It's very probable that you are having difficulty relaxing, concentrating, sleeping, or eating. You may feel a heightened sense of alert, heart pounding, and thoughts racing. Although unsettling, experiencing fear, panic, and anxiety are commonly reported after a breakup or separation. Many women who were unusually calm and strong before their ordeal describe being flooded with paralysis and fear, stuck and afraid to make the simplest moves. I completely empathize with how disturbing these feelings are. When fear and anxiety are pervasive, you can feel like life is closing in on you. The best way to calm your anxiety is through stress-management tools. These include exercise, meditation, yoga, and guided visualization. Here are some other tips that can be quite helpful:

• Make peace with your anxiety and create space for it to be there. Acknowledging its presence will help you better tolerate it.
• Write down the thoughts that are making you anxious. This

will help you clear your head. Then ask yourself, "Is this really true? Does this really make sense?" Then talk back to your thoughts. Practice having a strong and optimistic internal dialogue:

Anxious Thought: I'm going to be alone forever.

Response: I am not alone even now. There are many people in my life who love me and want to help.

• Don't put too much pressure on yourself, especially if you are in the earlier stages of healing.

• Avoid if possible making too many sudden decisions or changes. Take time to think through your new circumstances.

• Take comfort in routines.

• Force yourself to schedule relaxing time. Take a hot bath, play soothing music, read. Drink soothing herbal teas and light aromatic candles.

• Try shifting focus when enveloped in anxious thoughts. Changing activities may be helpful.

• Practice deep breathing regularly. It really helps to relax you.

• Be careful with stimulants such as coffee or soft drinks with caffeine and sugar. Also be mindful with alcohol usage. These substances, which are not healthy, will make you more anxious.

• Review the grounding exercises I suggested in chapter 1. They are quite useful when dealing with anxiety. Do give them a try.

Loneliness

Breakups leave an emptiness that can feel hard to fill. Being part of a couple is about companionship, and the absence of that can feel very barren. If you've been in a long-term relationship, it's habitual to assume you will always be together, and many plan their daily and extended life with this in mind. When you've lived a part of your life thinking in terms of "two," changing that mind-set is definitely an adjustment. Even simple tasks such as preparing a meal for one can be a constant reminder of what you've lost. If you were living with your partner at the time of your ending, learning how to live alone will take time. Nearly everyone I spoke with described daily remembrances of their loss, such as not having someone at home to discuss their day. They missed simple activities such as watching a TV show together and laughing at the same scenes. Others worry about who will help them change a bulb on a high chandelier, fix a dripping sink, or open a stuck jar. Many people complain about the deafening silence of an empty home.

If you deplore being alone, you are going to have to work hard to make some modifications. Numerous women described initial overpowering and overwhelming isolation. This feeling can be unpleasant for those who crave to be surrounded by warm, loving relationships. There is, however, a big difference between being alone and being lonely—and I urge you to consider this. I encourage you to reach out to your support system. I also challenge you to do a variety of activities on your own. Take some interesting advice from a woman I interviewed:

"Getting used to being alone is completely different than being lonely. I have always enjoyed my time alone. I have many hobbies. I'm a voracious reader and have a very curious mind. I love learning things, traveling, exploring. I kept up these traditions after my divorce. There was no way I was going to let my ex take these things away from me. My independence is very important—it defines me. I see many women get hysterical about not having plans for Saturday night, and it's a mistake. It's OK to stay home with a great book or a DVD. Cook yourself a delicious meal, have a glass of wine, and learn to enjoy your alone time. This is the very best gift you can give yourself—and it will last a lifetime." —*Hannah*

The Healing Power of Volunteering

One of the projects I often recommend if you are battling loneliness is to become involved with volunteerism. I recall one particularly hurtful breakup when I was feeling rather alone and isolated. It seemed as if everyone I knew was in a relationship, including both of my roommates. One day I read an article about an Ivy League–educated corporate lawyer who gave up her successful law practice to become a minister after the untimely death of her brother. She was pastoring at a church in an impoverished neighborhood and desperately needed volunteers for a children's program she had developed. Her story moved me. I picked up the phone to contact her, and she actually answered and invited me to visit her the next day. Getting up the gumption to do this caused me to push past my comfort zone, plus it helped put my life (and breakup) in perspective, and I met some of the most wonderful people along the way. Think about a population or project that may interest you. You can take on an endeavor in your community or someplace far away. Let your breakup be a catalyst for you to do something you'll be proud of.

Obsession and Rumination

"I would obsess for hours. Obsess about missed opportunities and fantasize about different outcomes. When I retold stories in my head and to my friends it made me feel I was still in the relationship. It was exhausting. Eventually it does get better—and then one day you go through an entire day without thinking of your ex. That's a great day!"   —*Elisa*

Even when you intuitively comprehend that your relationship is over, you may have a hard time mentally disengaging. For most of us, worries come and go, but after a breakup your mind may be fully consumed with obsessive thoughts. You may feel distracted, miss parts of conversations, and forget appointments. In the time it takes for our brains to extricate from our powerful mating chemicals, obsession and rumination can be very prevalent. Even if you are a mellow soul—someone who generally is happy to let it roll—you too may be overthinking your breakup. It's common, and it's very upsetting. So many of the women I spoke with reported a barrage of intrusive thoughts occupying every waking moment of their lives. It's hard to focus and get things accomplished when an endless loop of commentary about your relationship occupies the majority of space in your brain.

It's normal to obsess, and everyone does it. Obsession will be at its peak during the first month or two, and then, with effort on your part, should gradually subside. Unfortunately, attempts to simply dismiss these thoughts are generally unsuccessful and can actually make the obsessing worse. A better alternative is to accept that you are going to ruminate and make peace with it. Once you've accepted that it's going to stick around, these exercises will help reduce and eventually eliminate obsessing:

• Acknowledge that you are obsessing and tell yourself that it's a normal stage of healing.

• Instead of trying to *stop* obsessing, make an agreement with yourself that you are going to postpone the obsessing for a while.

• Make a specific date in the future to return to your obsessing. For example, "I'm going to postpone thinking about my ex while I'm at work, and pick it up tonight at seven p.m. when I'm home."

• When seven p.m. rolls around, see if you can postpone again, let's say until nine p.m. Keep distracted until nine p.m. by using some of the tools I've suggested in this and previous chapters.

• At nine p.m. allow yourself a specific time (for example, fifteen minutes) to obsess. You can write your obsessions, discuss them with a friend, or sit quietly and focus on your thoughts.

• After you are finished, change activities again. You are done obsessing for the day.

Eventually try to stall your obsessing time for *as long as possible*. The longer you use these stalling tactics, the less powerful your obsessions will be. Although I encourage you to reach out for support, please be aware that obsessing breeds more obsessing. If you are going to discuss your breakup all day with friends, colleagues, and anyone who is willing to listen, you are going to keep perpetuating your obsessing and your agony.

Abandonment and Rejection

> "I felt very abandoned. Childlike. Like I couldn't survive without him."   —*Maryanne*

If your ex initiated your split, feeling abandoned is a very normal part of the grieving process. For many, this stage is agonizing because it can trigger memories of every abandonment and breakup you've carried your entire life. And if you have suffered from childhood abandonment, it will be even harder for you to cope.

I was recently spending the day with my friend Pam, whose husband had left the marriage more than a year ago. She was on the mend, but some of her statements led me to believe that she may not be progressing as well as I had thought. Our conversation turned to something that had recently transpired at her job, and she commented, "Well I was more successful then—it was the year before Mark dumped me. I'm off my game now." The word "dumped" set off an alarm. That word was clearly making her feel like a victim. If you allow yourself to feel victimized, you are putting your healing in jeopardy.

Upon further digging I discovered that Pam was still feeling extremely rejected because of her divorce. She was taking too much responsibility, which was causing her to feel down about herself. These unexamined feelings were arresting her healing. I rolled up my sleeves and we got to work.

• I asked Pam to spend some additional time exploring her abandonment feelings to see if they went deeper than her breakup with her husband.

• We reviewed the circumstances surrounding her divorce. I reminded her that she was a very good and loving wife, that her husband had made some bad choices, and that she was minimally responsible for his decision to leave the marriage.

• I explained that using phrases like "dumped" and "off my game" were examples of negative thinking, which was putting her in an inferior position and causing her to feel victimized. I requested she create a new and healthier vocabulary to describe her feelings, and to be aware when negative words snuck up so she could talk back to them.

• Pam enjoyed her job and her colleagues, loved spending time with supportive friends, had a great relationship with her children, and took pleasure in biking and reading. I praised her for using her tools from her "bag of tricks" and working toward her recovery.

• I asked her to think about some new goals for herself. She suggested speaking to her boss and requesting some new projects, and taking some updated classes and workshops to facilitate career growth. Pam also had an amazing relationship with her grandparents, who had both passed away during the last few years. She missed them very much, and said for some time she had wanted to volunteer to help the elderly. We added that to her list of goals.

I checked in with Pam a month later and she reported feeling much better. Until our conversation she didn't even realize how abandoned and victimized she was feeling.

I hope you have gained some knowledge and tools from my "mini workshop" with Pam. Please use this as a model to work hard through your own feelings of abandonment. It is so important to remind yourself, even when feeling very low, that you are a worthwhile person. Even though you momentarily *feel* rejected does not mean that you are not valuable and lovable. Put together your own personal bag of tricks, and add to it habitually.

Anger

> "You have to get to the anger, process it, and release it in a positive way. I tried exercise, karate, and using voodoo! It all helped. Someone told me she went to a skeet-shooting range and it helped her a lot." —*Jody*

For many years women have been given messages that it isn't OK to feel or express anger. We should be caring, loving, and nurturing—but not angry. History abounds with stories of women being scorned, punished, or considered unstable for expressing displeasure, let alone rage. It is not supposed to be "in our nature" to have or display feelings that are explosive or eruptive. Thus most women are extremely

One of My Favorite Healing Tools—Humor

Laughter is said to boost your immune system and increase the production of serotonin, a neurotransmitter known as the "happiness hormone." And a Vanderbilt University study claims that a hearty chuckle actually burns calories. It's also one of the best coping mechanisms that I know of. I come from long line of funny people and I regularly use humor to get through dire times. When appropriate, I also try to use it with my clients—I've found that when we can laugh at ourselves it makes things easier. In fact, several women remarked to me, "If I couldn't laugh at my situation, I just don't know how I would have survived." Also, when you start to create and increase your support system through socializing, humor is a great icebreaker. So do have a laugh on me—it really does help.

"The best depression killer ever is comedy and laughter. Read David Sedaris. I watched every rerun of Seinfeld *and* Curb Your Enthusiasm. *You have to surround yourself with laughter and positive people. And you have to try to laugh at yourself and your situation."* —Jaci

uncomfortable expressing anger. But in reality, anger is a legitimate feeling and getting in touch with it is very important. Even if your parting was amicable, there will be times when you will feel angry at your ex and your circumstances. And if your split was malevolent, or if lying or infidelity was involved, you may be feeling enraged.

It is important and useful to get in touch with your anger for many reasons. It can help release you from some of the other emotional stages you may be reclining in. It will take your ex off the pedestal. It's a great motivator. It can boost you out of a depression and it will help you feel less like a victim. However, there are healthy and unhealthy ways to deal with anger. Anger can be a deflector for other feelings that you are going to need to come to terms with, including abandonment, guilt, and sorrow. At times we hide behind it for fear of our deeper feelings. If anger becomes disruptive, if it infuses into other relationships, that's a definite warning sign for you to pull back and reevaluate. Be cautious with these types of anger:

• Many women describe a type of anger I call righteous anger, meaning, "How could *he* do this to *me*?" This is a common default response that many fall into. It's a way of protecting our bruised egos and dealing with humiliation and rejection. Please be careful to avoid this type of anger. Getting overly involved with your ego will keep you from accepting any accountability and stifle your ability to learn from your breakup.

• Revenge tends to appear from time to time. While it's common to fantasize about it—fantasize is the operative word—we never, ever want to act on revenge. As one woman humorously put it, "Revenge is like drinking the cyanide and watching your ex die!" Inordinately focusing on revenge will keep you from rebuilding your life, and *acting on revenge can ruin your life*. A better way to use vengeful feelings is to put all of your resources into pulling your life together and moving on. Get busy, be healthy, look terrific.

Here are some healthy ways to express anger, which is especially important if children are involved, and that will ultimately help your recovery:

- Accept your struggle with anger, even if it feels uncomfortable.
- Don't be too angry at yourself. While I certainly encourage taking responsibility for your part, be careful not to carry the full burden.
- If your relationship ended over infidelity, keep your anger directed at your ex and not at the other person. I've seen too many breakups get incredibly overcomplicated because of this. Blaming the other person will keep you from focusing on what you need to focus on: figuring out why your relationship ended and healing yourself.
- Anger is good as a *protector* but can be dangerous if used too much as a *projector*. You need to feel it, but be mindful that it's not seeping into other relationships or responsibilities.
- Journal about your anger. It's a very safe place to express yourself.
- Exercise is a major anger release. Try a kickboxing class.
- Buy a voodoo doll. Punch a pillow. Go into the woods (or a park, or your shower) and scream.

Over time, letting go of your anger will definitely help you move on. But to do so you need to feel it, experience it, and express it.

Guilt and Regret

> "I knew I had to call off my engagement. The relationship was bad and I had to leave. Even so, I doubted myself for a long time. I felt very guilty for what I had done, for hurting someone else—even though I had to do it and we had to end."   —*Tamara*

We all feel guilt and remorse at times in our lives—it's part of the human condition. And even the most assured tend to question themselves, especially over significant decisions. Many women I spoke with described having a bad case of "woulda, coulda, shoulda" after the ending of their relationship. For some people, leaving is just as hard as being left. If you initiated your breakup, even if you had solid grounds for ending it, there is a chance you will question your decision and worry about causing harm to your partner or others. I've sat with many women who carry enormous weight on their backs while they come to terms with the fact they ended their relationship and caused suffering to someone they once loved.

Getting past the guilt is an important step toward getting healthy. If your guilt is primarily regarding your children, I can certainly understand your concerns. Please remember that marvelous resources are out there to help you with parenting through a divorce. If you are feeling too culpable or being too hard on yourself, you are not going to be able to put your healthiest self forward—and that is exactly what your children really need to feel safe.

If you ended your relationship, I'm sure you had some very good reasons for making that tough choice. Write down those reasons and study them every day. Stop worrying about your ex, or obsessing about different outcomes, and please attempt to make peace with your decision and with yourself.

In actuality, no one is faultless in his or her relationship, and you probably made some mistakes—just as the rest of us. You will have ample time to discern your truth and take responsibility. So please consider forgiving yourself. It is very important that you take yourself off the hot seat and get back on the road to recovery. Tell yourself that you did the best job that you could *with the resources that you had at the time.*

Feeling guilt and regret will accomplish little. Guilt is one of those emotions that we all grapple with but doesn't serve much purpose. You won't be able to honor or validate yourself, or look at your relationship with objectivity, if you submerge yourself in regret and guilt.

Failure and Self-Blame

"It was my second divorce, and I was under forty. I felt like such a failure. I was so accomplished in so many ways, and I felt like a complete failure in romance. It's an awful feeling, but you must forgive yourself. Enduring a second divorce or breakup is very very hard." —*Tina*

When a relationship ends you can feel like a failure and have a diminished sense of self-worth. Our society tends to cherish winners, and we hear many messages that the ending of a relationship equals failure. These messages can make us feel even worse about our circumstances than we already do. Although breakups and divorces are commonplace within our society, the burden of shame and blame does tend to fall on the shoulders of many women. We hold ourselves up to a very high standard and are too quick to take full responsibility if we feel as if we failed at something or disappointed someone.

If you were in a relationship that included emotional abuse, you may have an overabundance of these feelings. If your partner inordinately blamed you, took limited responsibility, or outright told you that you ruined the relationship, you are going to have to work very hard to revise those thoughts and see your behavior in a more lucid way.

Getting too caught up in these feelings is perilous. Depression is often associated with feelings of self-loathing and blame. If you take too much accountability you are in danger of losing your truth and foundation, which can catapult you back into a place of darkness. Here's a wonderful motivational quote from a woman who fully blamed herself until she finally saw the light.

"I felt like it was all my fault. I had made mistakes, I wasn't perfect—but he fully blamed me for the breakup. I ate it up and fell into a terrible depression. But then I realized that he was not blameless. He had made a lot of mistakes too. Then I got angry—and that was such a release! Taking too much responsibility is really dangerous. It makes you feel ashamed, sad, unlovable. I really believe that it is important to take responsibility and know why your relationship ended, and how you contributed to it—but it does take two to mess it up. You've got to work hard to find the reality, the truth." —*Lydia*

Blaming yourself doesn't accomplish anything positive—it will only make your situation worse. Just because your relationship didn't work out doesn't mean that you have failed. So stop listening to what your ex said, or to the negative loop in your brain, and focus on yourself. Use your tricks and tools to redirect negative thoughts. Replace them with positive ones by reminding yourself of all you have accomplished in your life and how successful you actually are.

Embarrassment and Humiliation

"There is a certain amount of shame about the whole situation and I felt ashamed that my husband had an affair. When I first found out, I didn't want to tell *anybody*! I felt like it must have been my fault . . . like I did something wrong."   —*Anne*

"I remember the first time I went to a company function alone. People knew I just got divorced. It was uncomfortable. I didn't know how to act, what to do. I felt like a deer in the headlights. I felt ashamed, like I wasn't good enough. Over time you do get used to flying solo, and it eventually becomes the new norm. Time passes. It's actually not nearly as bad as you anticipate, and you do realize that you have nothing to be embarrassed about."   —*Sabrina*

I recall a meeting with a client who tearfully described how her relationship had just ended. Teri and Jeff were quite devoted to each other and had hoped to eventually marry, but the relationship was not without complications. Jeff was somewhat enmeshed with Marissa, his former girlfriend of a decade, and all three worked in the same industry, one that was small and incestuous. Jeff's ex never accepted that their relationship had ended, and regularly interfered with his courtship of Teri, often trying to lure him back. Jeff didn't set great boundaries, and Teri, kind and patient, never put pressure on him to do so. Eventually Jeff caved under pressure and returned to his former relationship, which crushed Teri.

Q&A

It's been six months since my breakup. I'm still feeling very bad, but my friends are encouraging me to start dating. What do you think?

I am a strong believer that dating should not occur until you've fully worked through healing, understanding, and transformation, and your recovery is firmly in place. Dating for distraction, or before you are ready, can be a mistake. If you haven't taken the time to fully understand your breakup, and your role in it, you may be destined to repeat the same mistakes in the future. I have heard too many tales of women putting themselves out there before they're ready, only to get hurt again. And, if you are not healed from your breakup, you are not going to be putting your best foot forward, and you are not going to attract the right sort of match. There is a reason I have included a detailed dating guide as the last chapter of this book. So please be patient—there is ample reason to wait.

"I dated too quickly after my breakup because I didn't want to think about it. That was a big mistake. I was making bad decisions regarding whom to date. I decided to swear off men for a full year. I stopped concentrating on dating and focused on myself instead. I spoke to a therapist, I started planning dinner parties, read books, worked hard at my job. I really turned my life around. Then I went back out there. I'm dating an amazing guy at the moment. Today I really know what I want." —Melanie

When Teri and I discussed the situation she repeatedly spoke of her humiliation. "Everyone is going to know what happened! Jeff and Marissa are going to look like the golden couple. She got him back. She won! I'm going to look like the fool. The fallen woman. The loser. It's so embarrassing. How am I going to go to work and face my peers?"

Teri truly believed that she had suffered a terrible defeat. She was steeped in shame and humiliation. She was isolating, avoiding colleagues, and had stopped going to work events, fearing that people would be gossiping about her or feeling sorry for her. I had to run some interference. I explained that *she had it all wrong*. Marissa was obstructive and manipulative, Jeff was a spineless coward, and Teri was the victorious one. She had worked hard to be a supportive, understanding, and caring girlfriend, and the breakup was actually going to be a huge opportunity for her. It would free her to be with someone much less complicated, who was truly able to be a mature partner to a wonderful woman such as herself.

Teri fully recovered and is now involved with a great guy who is crazy about her, completely ready to have a healthy adult relationship—*and* is worthy of her love.

If you were left by your partner, or if infidelity was involved, your ending can definitely feel like a fall from grace. Please remember, you have absolutely nothing to feel embarrassed about. Hold your head up high. Your breakup is a badge of courage—wear it with pride.

Hope

> "People said to me around New Years, 'I bet you're happy to see this year vanish!' It made me think. 'Yes, it was the most difficult year of my life, but it was also the year I accomplished the most personal growth ever.' I reviewed my journal. I hadn't kept a traditional journal like people suggested, but I did write notes and passages and I'd put interesting quotes down. Then I started writing. For every difficult word I had written prior, I wrote a new, positive word. Pain became growth. Suffering turned into strength. Blindness, insight. Confusion, clarity. It's been a long haul, but I'm starting to feel hopeful. I've learned so much and I'm finally seeing that I will be able to make a good life for myself." —*Lyla*

Various women told me about having a moment or two, seemingly out of the blue, where suddenly and unexpectedly they felt hopeful. It could be subtle (an hour without obsessing about him) or more obvious (a girls' night out where you actually have fun). It can creep up on you (your first full night of sleep) or arrive with a bang (feeling successful about something *you* created). Once you start to string together small accomplishments, you are most definitely entering a new stage.

It may be hard to conceive at times, but you will venture to a new land. One that is bright, fresh, and hopeful. You have suffered, worked hard, and acquired valuable knowledge and growth. You are on a path that is practical, insightful, and ultimately meaningful. You are making new connections and discoveries about yourself every day. These discoveries will enable you to make important decisions about where you've been, and what you want from your life in the future. Try to remember that you had a life before your relationship ended, and in time, you will undoubtedly have one again. And there is a very good chance that it will be an excellent life—better than you can even imagine. I've witnessed hundreds of women emerge triumphant from their break-up experience—stronger, healthier, and more vibrant. They are making better relationship choices and living life on their own terms. You too will enter your stage of hope.

Navigating the Emotional Roller Coaster Tips and Tools

This chapter is loaded with tips and tools. Many of the exercises I've suggested have a proven track record and can help you now, through the duration of your recovery, and for many years to come. Dig in and get to work! Here are a few more tidbits:

1. Get a "sponsor." See if you can get a friend to read through this chapter with you. Go through the roller coaster with someone who can offer both support and guidance. Take time to read each emotion out loud and discuss how each category has affected you. For example: how do you feel when you are sad, mad, or afraid? What comes to mind?

2. Practice talking back to depressing, negative, or scary thoughts. Make your own worksheet with negative statements and contrasting positive statements. The more you do this, the quicker you will *permanently* change your brain. This exercise can be your companion for life.

3. I mentioned the phrase "bag of tricks" earlier in the chapter. I'd like you to literally pack a bag full of tricks. Put anything inside it that is helping you through your recovery. It can be filled with books, tapes, lotions, potions, a bit of candy. It can have a magic wand and a crystal. It can have a motivational tape, a letter from a friend, or a letter to yourself. Pack that bag and keep filling it and pulling out items as needed. This bag will literally be your security blanket. Keep it close by and use it repeatedly!

4. Dare to dream. What might your "hopeful" stage look like? Ask yourself what I call the "miracle question." If a miracle happened in your sleep, and you woke up having the life you've always dreamed of, what would that life be? (Hint: your ex cannot appear in the miracle!)

5. Journal daily about your feelings, and be mindful about which are the predominant ones and what they represent.

6. Remember how I suggested that you take notes about each stage of the emotional roller coaster, and assess how each is affecting you? What emotion did you most relate to? What exercise did you find most helpful? Be sure to spend some time reviewing your answers. Understanding how each stage is affecting you will be quite helpful to your recovery.

5

The Rules of Engagement

"It took me a while to realize that every time we spoke or met it definitely set me back. At first I thought it was good, that it was closure, but we kept it going for too long. Eventually I had to give up all contact with him. Once I had the distance, although it was hard, I was finally able to get the clarity and objectivity I needed to move on." —*Maura*

"During the breakup I missed him so much, and I just wanted him to help me through it, to comfort me. But every time I reached out he was so withdrawn, so mean. And that hurt me even more. I understand now that the more I reached out the more he withdrew. I wish I had realized that back then. It would have saved me from a lot of misery." —*Megan*

With her exotic looks and girl-next-door personality, Linda is finally recapturing her life. Today she is in graduate school and making plans to open her own business, and there is a light in her eyes that had dimmed six months earlier when we started working together. Linda sought me out to help her cut ties with her ex-boyfriend. She had dated Scott for five years and was currently entangled in a vicious cycle of negative and destructive interactions that had been ongoing for three years past their breakup. One conversation was so upsetting that she spent the night on the bathroom floor retching.

What do Linda and thousands of other women have in common?

They share the inability to separate from their exes and move on following a breakup or divorce. This familiar problem, which produces abundant anguish, is experienced by many of us during the disentanglement of a romantic relationship.

As you know by now, there are numerous reasons why some splits and recoveries are more challenging than others. Staying embroiled in a dysfunctional post-break-up pattern is on top of that list. Scores of women I interviewed described a deep-rooted desire to engage. Others compared it to an obsession or even an addiction, claiming that although they wanted to cut ties, they simply couldn't cease contacting, engaging, prying, or spying. As one woman aptly put it, "Whenever I was feeling bad, angry, or lonely, I'd reach out to him, only to get socked in the jaw. And, knowing it was wrong and I'd get hurt, I still did it again and again and again. It was the gift that kept on giving!"

Although there is plenty of evidence to support the theory that zero contact is the only way to go, that option is not always available to all. If your ex is intertwined in your social circle, if you work at the same company or in the same industry, if you live in the same neighborhood or participate in similar activities, there is a possibility that until you make some modifications, your ex will continue to be in your life. And if you share custody of children, your ex will always be a part of your life.

As much as I empathize with the despair that your breakup has caused you, continuing on a path of negative or harmful engagement is treacherous. You will remain stuck in the past and lose your ability to move forward in a productive way. You will be constantly opening old emotional wounds, which will limit your capacity to feel good about yourself and create a proper recovery program. A definition of full recovery means either total detachment or learning how to coexist within properly defined boundaries. In this chapter, together we will analyze this tricky dilemma and spend some time exploring, formulating, and committing to brand-new rules of engagement and disengagement.

Why We Engage

What might be your fantasy of the perfect breakup? An emotionally mature couple slowly grows apart, and after much healthy discussion jointly decides to terminate the union. Both take responsibility, feel validated and respected, and promise to stay in touch and be friends. Although some breakups do transpire in this fashion, it is unfortunately not the norm. If you are reading this book there is a strong probability that your separation was involuntary and that it ended with unanswered questions and much emotional upheaval. Most likely, you've been unable to receive any form of validation or closure.

There are several reasons why we feel compelled to stay entangled with an ex. The most common ones are:

• Thinking you can save the relationship and convince him to return (the bargaining stage).

• Fearing of abandonment and/or fearing of an unknown future.

• Being unable to accept that it's over.

• Worrying that if you fully detach you will literally be out of sight and out of mind—and then the relationship is truly over.

• Feeling as if you have failed. Or feeling guilty or overly responsible about your part in the split.

• Needing to be heard.

• Attempting to get your ex to take responsibility for his faults, flaws, and mistakes, which may have contributed to the breakup.

• Craving an apology for hurtful actions, which may include dishonesty, infidelity, or unkind or inappropriate behavior or statements.

• And, most prominently, seeking validation, vindication, and closure.

It is extremely exasperating when the above conditions are not met, and most times, they are not. We need to talk and be heard in order to work things through, and during a breakup healthy communication generally starts to collapse. And if your ex wasn't a good communicator to begin with, or if he wasn't capable of engaging in honest open dialogue during the relationship, chances are he is going to be even worse now.

Certain men, especially if they have erred or are doing the breaking up, tend to shut down emotionally, lose their ability to communicate, or even physically disappear. A woman I knew hired a private investigator to find her boyfriend of seven years who literally vanished.

Other men become cold, withdrawn, defensive, or intellectualized. Some take the offensive, refuse to listen to logic, play the blame game, and come out swinging. They bring up past problems (many exposed for the first time), rewrite the history of the relationship, and become provocative, aggressive, and even cruel.

These dynamics make us feel and act hurt, angered, perplexed, and excessively emotional, which may cause our exes to disengage even further or fight back even harder.

This detrimental pattern accomplishes little and can feel absolutely maddening. It is precisely this cycle that devastates, frustrates, and infuriates us all, which regrettably keeps us begging, digging, and engaging for way too long. This is the primary reason why women feel crazy after a breakup.

The Myth of Validation and Closure

One of the biggest mistakes I continually see women making is going back to their exes seeking validation and closure. Validation is an enormous component of healthy healing, and we have discussed its importance in earlier chapters. If you are seeking validation from your ex, you are hoping (fantasizing) that he will apologize and take responsibility. That he will tell you he made a huge mistake. That you didn't do anything wrong—and it was all about *his* crisis, which had absolutely nothing to do with you. That he acknowledges he has destroyed the life you shared together, and in turn, ruined *your* life. That he takes responsibility for hurting the children and shat-tering their stability. That his affair/addiction/dishonesty/identity crisis (fill in the blank) was a huge blunder and never should have happened.

I understand your need for validation from your ex. You desper-ately crave for him to accept some accountability, and healing is in-deed a bit easier when this occurs. But, fair warning, it is the craving for validation that makes us do silly and at times risky things, and keeps us enmeshed for way too long. I repeatedly see women calling, e-mailing, writing, texting, and stalking their exes. This destructive cycle can last for months and even years.

Seeking closure from your ex is equally as destructive. I know it's hard to just walk away—and for many breaking up is indeed a lengthy process. It's perfectly normal to want to try to get closure from your ex. When we can engage in constructive closure it does lighten our load. But the fact is that most of us are unable to achieve this sort of closure, and I've seen really bright women do really unwise things in the name of getting it. If you're trying to reach out to your ex, and he won't give you the respect of returning your call, this says a great deal about *him*. Unfortunately, and problematically, we wrongly internalize this message to mean, "You're not worth five minutes of my time," and this produces an overwhelming feeling of abandonment and devastation. Continuing on this path is ex-tremely injurious to your state of mind and self-worth.

There are messages out there that unless validation and closure are achieved it is not possible to move on. I'm here to tell you that this is not the case. It is extremely important and necessary to get validation and closure—but chances are you will never get it from him. Let me share a valuable secret with you, one that will save you ample grief, embarrassment, and heartache:

> You do not need validation or closure from your ex. At-tempting to get it is a huge waste of your time and energy. It will make you feel drained and deranged, and will derail your healing. It is completely unnecessary and even dangerous.

There are many valuable and even better sources where you can get resolution. You will get it from this book, you can get it from friends and family, you can get it from a therapist, and eventually, you will get it from yourself. The sooner you accept this fact, the better off you will be. Although I know you understand and agree with what I'm saying, many of you are nodding your head yes and texting your ex while reading this. And if your ex is on his way to pick up the children, you may be rehearsing yet another speech or planning to take him aside to make one last point. Please stop right now and continue reading so you can acquire all the tools you will ever need to disengage.

Inquiring and Spying

With the advent of electronic communications and social networking, inquiring and spying has never been easier. As wonderful as technology is, it definitely makes breaking up in the modern world more challenging. When I was dating the only way you could contact your ex was through a landline telephone. And if your boyfriend lived at home or with roommates, the notion of speaking to his parents or leaving a message that anyone could hear was extremely unappealing. Today you can reach your ex within a matter of seconds and get an instantaneous reply. Even if the reply is not the one you had hoped for, that level of engagement really hooks you in. In our society of immediate gratification, the back and forth of texting and e-mailing feeds your obsession, which at times can mimic an addiction.

Spying on your ex via Facebook (or Internet dating sites) is a really bad idea. Although everyone does it from time to time, it is another form of addiction. You are subjected to a constant stream of status updates, messages, and photos. And watching your ex's status change from "single" to "in a relationship" is the ultimate dagger in the heart. Also, men heal and move on in vastly different ways than we do. Through Facebook spying you may be subjected to seeing photos of him at parties laughing it up or with other women. He may *appear* to be having too much fun for someone newly single.

And of course this isn't always the case, but it certainly does hurt, plays into the fixation, and keeps you going back for more.

Another common yet bad habit I see is asking mutual friends (or his friends) about your ex's whereabouts. When we do this it's obvious that we're looking for someone to tell us that he's sad, hurt, lonely, and so on. Unfortunately, we don't always get this info, and it puts others in an uncomfortable position. A young woman I met on an airplane explained to me that her best friend was repeatedly coming to her to either discuss her breakup or inquire about her ex—one year after the breakup. It was profoundly affecting their friendship and she didn't know how to handle it. Although I'm a huge proponent of turning to friends for support, I have warned that overdiscussing your breakup may endanger you. The more you discuss and ask about him, the more you perpetuate your depression, anxiety, and rumination—*and* you risk losing friends. This additional "abandonment" will be extremely distressing. Continuing

Do Women Suffer Disproportionately to Men?

Many women I spoke with complained that their exes appeared to be moving on more rapidly than they were. This common belief generally adds to one's distress. Believing that your ex has moved on can feel very real, yet often it simply isn't valid. It's important to remember that men and women heal and cope in fundamentally different ways. In terms of survival, women are designed to be in stable relationships, and when that is disrupted, our brain chemicals and emotions require time to disengage. So next time you think, "How did he get over me so quickly? He must never have really cared," try to remember that we are wired differently, and that our natural tendency is to feel our feelings and to mourn our losses. Try not to compare your recovery to your ex's. It is wiser to compare yourself to other women who have gone through similar experiences—you will feel more validated this way.

with any of this behavior is extremely disruptive to your healing. You will keep chipping away at your esteem, losing your focus, and delaying the act of becoming better acquainted with yourself. This will undoubtedly affect your ability to recover.

The Negative Engagement Dance

At some point during a breakup or subsequently, a couple will fall into a style of communication that I call "the engagement dance." If you are having a heated discussion and becoming upset, aggravated, or angry, or if you are desperately attempting to achieve some measure of validation or closure, you are participating in "the negative engagement dance." While communicating in this style, arguments escalate, conversations become circular, emotions flare, and there is a limited chance of reaching any sort of conclusion or détente. Furthermore, this absence of resolution will keep you going back for more. This is precisely the pattern that keeps you hooked in and ultimately stuck. Occasionally these negative engagement styles pop up throughout the course of our relationships when we are discussing tricky subjects. If you had these sorts of problematic patterns during your relationship, rest assured they will be amplified during the breakup and after.

A visual learner myself, I've created these charts so I can further educate you about what exactly transpires during these interactions. Although I'm leading with your ex's communication style, please also pay close attention to your part in this dance. And while I've chosen to make this particular dialogue about your breakup, the topic could be any number of things that couples quarrel about, such as scheduling, children, sex, or finances. Identifying your partner's style *and* your own is a crucial first step toward learning how to break bad patterns, which will expedite your healing.

Your Ex's Style: The Avoider

- Poor emotional communicator
- Has little understanding of what is transpiring and is incapable of articulating his feelings
- Fears confrontation and will attempt to avoid it at all costs

The break-up model on the next page ends with many unanswered questions, which causes you ample confusion and frustration. The main dynamic at play here is that the more you push, the more your ex will pull back and continue to be noncommunicative and avoidant. These men often refuse to respond to any form of communication because they are afraid of confrontation *and* can't articulate how they are feeling. This pattern makes you even more hurt, frustrated, angered, and rejected. This model causes women to engage in "pestering" behavior such as repetitive attempts at communication. If your ex has completely cut you off, your fury and abandonment may be so immense that you consider showing up at his work, home, gym, and so on, to get answers, validation, and closure. This is always a bad idea.

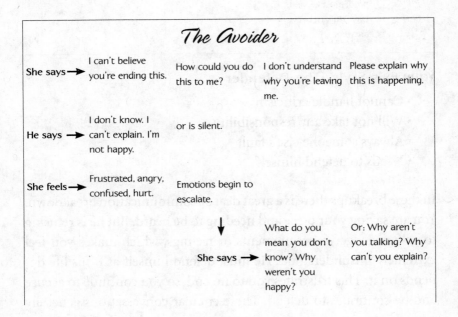

The Avoider

She says → I can't believe you're ending this.   How could you do this to me?   I don't understand why you're leaving me.   Please explain why this is happening.

He says → I don't know. I can't explain. I'm not happy.   or is silent.

She feels → Frustrated, angry, confused, hurt.   Emotions begin to escalate.

↓

She says → What do you mean you don't know? Why weren't you happy?   Or: Why aren't you talking? Why can't you explain?

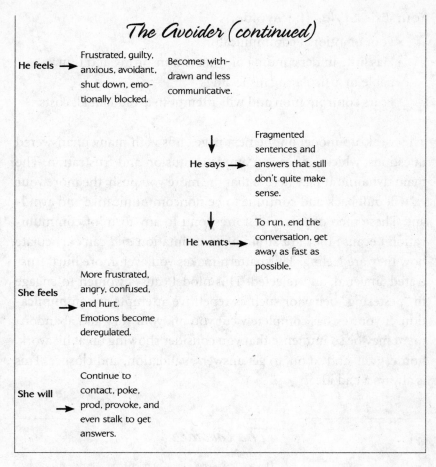

The Avoider (continued)

He feels → Frustrated, guilty, anxious, avoidant, shut down, emotionally blocked.

Becomes withdrawn and less communicative.

He says → Fragmented sentences and answers that still don't quite make sense.

He wants → To run, end the conversation, get away as fast as possible.

She feels → More frustrated, angry, confused, and hurt. Emotions become deregulated.

She will → Continue to contact, poke, prod, provoke, and even stalk to get answers.

Your Ex's Style: The Defender

- Cannot handle criticism
- Will not take any responsibility
- Always someone else's fault
- Needs to defend himself

In these breakups there is a great deal of communication breakdown. You are saying your piece and needing to be heard. But he is refusing to acknowledge your statements or feelings, which makes you feel extremely misunderstood. He must defend himself as if his life depends on it. This frustrates you to no end, so you continue to accuse and he continues to defend. These circular conversations generally escalate, causing anger, tears, aggravation, and a lot of problems.

The Defender

She says →	I can't believe you're ending this.	How could you do this to me?	I don't understand why you're leaving me.	Please explain why this is happening.
He says →	(Rolling his eyes, sighing)	I already explained myself; there is nothing more to say.	This isn't my fault.	I've been unhappy for a long time. I have a right to end this and be happy.
She feels →	Frustrated, angry, hurt, not heard.	Emotions begin to escalate. ↓	I can't believe you won't take any responsibility. You ruined my life.	
She says →			You destroyed everything we had together! How can you do this to your children?	
He feels →	Frustrated, attacked, anxious.			
He says →		↓	(Needing to defend himself *even harder*) Stop blaming everything on me! It's over. This isn't my fault. You expect too much from me.	I didn't ruin your life. I was a good boyfriend/husband. The kids will be fine. Everyone is divorced these days.
She feels →	More frustrated, more angry, deregulated.			
She will →	Continue to push him to stop defending himself until he takes responsibility.			

Your Ex's Style: The Prosecutor

- Aggressive
- Offensive
- Angry
- Provocative
- Has to be right
- Creates his own reality, which gives him *permission* to break up

These are really painful breakups. Your ex refuses to take any responsibility, and worse, he's determined to walk away clean and pin the blame on you. He will fight till the death. Maybe there were signs before of his aggressive and confrontational communication style, but you never expected him to turn on you like this. These types of breakups cause women to become hysterical, scream, cry, pull their hair out, and feel absolutely crazy. Yet they continue to engage, frantically trying to get their exes to take back their words, tell the truth, and apologize.

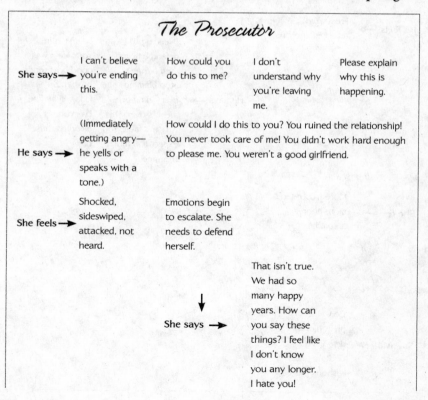

The Prosecutor

She says →	I can't believe you're ending this.	How could you do this to me?	I don't understand why you're leaving me.	Please explain why this is happening.
He says →	(Immediately getting angry— he yells or speaks with a tone.)	How could I do this to you? You ruined the relationship! You never took care of me! You didn't work hard enough to please me. You weren't a good girlfriend.		
She feels →	Shocked, sideswiped, attacked, not heard.	Emotions begin to escalate. She needs to defend herself.		
She says →		That isn't true. We had so many happy years. How can you say these things? I feel like I don't know you any longer. I hate you!		

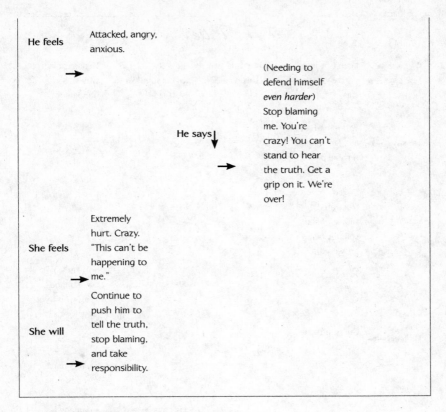

He feels   Attacked, angry, anxious.

→

He says ↓

(Needing to defend himself *even harder*) Stop blaming me. You're crazy! You can't stand to hear the truth. Get a grip on it. We're over!

→

She feels   Extremely hurt. Crazy. "This can't be happening to me."

→

She will   Continue to push him to tell the truth, stop blaming, and take responsibility.

→

Your Ex's Style: The Pitier

- Steeped in self-blame, but mostly self-pity (feels sorry for *himself*)
- Says he can't control his behavior (a passive-aggressive way to not take any responsibility)

These are frustrating breakups. These types of men, who are steeped in self-pity, aren't addressing what caused the breakup or answering your questions. Their behavior is actually passive-aggressive and even manipulative. This style allows them to deflect taking any responsibility, and it's also a way for them to avoid discussing the breakup. Unfortunately, this engagement style regularly make us feel guilty and sorry for our exes, which causes us to lose our focus and have lax boundaries. That is exactly what your ex is looking for.

The Pitier

She says ➤	I can't believe you're ending this.	How could you do this to me?	I don't understand why you're leaving me.	Please explain why this is happening.

He says ➤ You must hate me. I'm such a terrible person.

She feels ➤ Guilty, frustrated, (questions are still not being answered).

She says ➤ So why won't you change? Why won't you fight for us?

He feels ➤ Guilty, attacked, anxious.

↓

He says ➤ It's too hard. You deserve better. I'm a damaged person. I don't even know what I want anymore.

She feels ➤ Angry, frustrated, sad, guilty.

She will ➤ Continue to push him until he starts answering questions.

Your Ex's Style: The Intellectualizer

- Blocks all emotion
- Proficient at intellectualizing and rationalizing during all conversations
- Must stay in control—refuses to lose his cool

This is another frustrating yet common break-up pattern. These men block their feelings out of guilt, fear, and lack of self-awareness. They are afraid to show any emotion so they get very comfortable using their defense mechanisms. Women can feel crazy in these breakups. They wonder what happened to the "nice" guy he used to be, and work very hard to try to uncover the "real him" under this cold facade.

The Intellectualizer

She says → I can't believe you're ending this.   How could you do this to me?   I don't understand why you're leaving me.   Please explain why this is happening.

He says → I don't understand why you can't stay calm. Many relationships end, and now so has ours.

She feels → Frustrated, angry, not heard.

She says → What are you even talking about? This isn't about "many relationships." It's about us. What's wrong with you?

He feels → Attacked, anxious, detached.

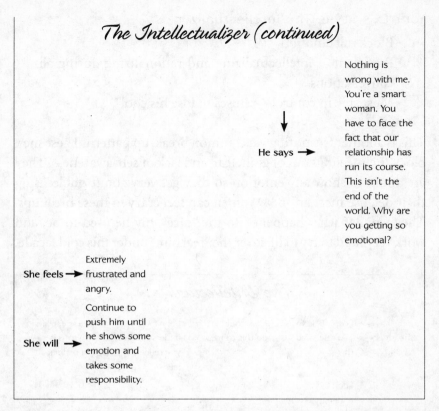

The Intellectualizer (continued)

He says → Nothing is wrong with me. You're a smart woman. You have to face the fact that our relationship has run its course. This isn't the end of the world. Why are you getting so emotional?

She feels → Extremely frustrated and angry.

She will → Continue to push him until he shows some emotion and takes some responsibility.

Now that you've identified which style of communication best depicts your scenario, and seen how you play into it, it is my job to help you break this cycle. One definition of insanity is doing the same thing over and over and expecting different results. If you are still entwined with these dynamics you are trying, either consciously or unconsciously, to get something from your ex. Perhaps you're still attempting reconciliation, waiting for that apology, or wanting to get a taste of revenge. Women regularly say to me, "It's not fair. My life is so awful right now—why shouldn't he suffer too?"

You need to understand that this push-pull pattern will always stop you from achieving whatever result you want. The more you push, become emotional, blame, act like a victim, or use sarcasm or anger, the more your ex will disappear, defend, or destroy. If you are approaching your ex in a heightened emotional state; if you are making demands, begging; if you are furious—he is going to do everything he can to avoid you at all costs, stick up for himself, or fight back. This behavior doesn't accomplish anything constructive, and truly, there is absolutely nothing in it for you.

Pulling back and stopping the madness is the very best thing you can do for yourself right now. I know dozens of stories of women taking back their lives once they realized this and changed directions. Stopping equals regaining your strength and power. Stopping means getting healthy. Stopping means being able to deal with your ex in a mature and responsible fashion. And in some cases, stopping means that your ex will actually apologize and take responsibility. Some men will reach out for their own closure once they've had time to process the breakup on their own terms. And of course we've all heard stories of exes coming to their senses once they see how well you're doing and that you've finally moved on. I'm not saying that should be a motivation to stop engaging, but it sure feels nice to have that little victory. And by the way, when this does occur, although flattering, most women report that they come full circle, realize that the relationship was flawed, and have absolutely no interest in going backward. So let's get to work and break this cycle right now!

Step one:	Identify your negative engagement dance.
Step two:	Become familiar with your ex's style. Know exactly what sets him off.
Step three:	It takes two to tango. Please take responsibility for *your* part in perpetuating the cycle. What is it that *you* do or say that incites him to avoid, defend, prosecute, pity, or intellectualize?
Step four:	Make a pledge to stop.
Step five:	Commit to learning how to either fully disengage *or* engage in healthy communication with defined boundaries.

Once you stop (and I will give you tools to enable you to do so), miracles will occur. Your healing will accelerate and everything offered in this book will make even more sense.

When you stop you can:
• Take time to breathe, care for yourself, and become more familiar with yourself.

• Remove this toxicity from your life, which will make you feel less anxious and depressed.

• Create distance from the relationship, the breakup, and your ex. This space will enable you to receive full clarity, which you are going to need during your understanding phase.

• Feel better about yourself. You will recover your strength and be so proud for accomplishing this difficult feat.

• If children are involved, it will give you more energy to be a better mom. You'll be in an improved space to think through new ways of engagement, which will allow you to have an enhanced relationship with your ex, affording great benefits to your kids.

Of course there may be times when you will need to have contact with your ex, and once you understand your particular dance, and take responsibility for your part in it, communicating will be much easier. You will have to learn how to control your emotions, keep the conversations short and simple, and not allow yourself to get pulled back in. I'll give you many more communication tools in the coming chapters.

One of the main reasons I wrote this book was to help women achieve the validation and the closure that their breakups didn't afford them. So let me repeat again: Most of you will not receive validation or closure from your ex-partner. And that's perfectly OK. You will receive it from me, and you'll receive it from the healing community. Now that that's been established, let's make a deal. Take some time and take some space away from your ex. The sooner you disengage, the quicker you will feel powerful, healthy, and wise. I know you can do this—and I promise you it is a huge leap toward recovery.

Many breakup books tell you that you must cease all contact with your ex. Clearly this is not always a realistic possibility. If you have children, you can never completely walk away. Your ex will certainly be in your life while you are raising them, which may mean for a very long time (think graduations, weddings, and grandchildren). In the next two chapters we'll look at breakups and divorces with and without children. I urge you to read both chapters, as there are many lessons here for all.

6

Breakups or Divorces *Without* Children

"I was thirty-six years old, determined to learn lessons and recover. I knew I wanted to remarry and have children. There was no place for my ex in my new life, and I purposely decided not to stay in touch or be friends. Two years later I met a terrific man, and we married and have two amazing kids. Today I realize how lucky I was that I got out of that marriage childless. It enabled me to fully move on and create a much better life." —*Tina*

Although all breakups are hard, women without children do have a less complicated course of healing. While you may not believe this now, your split actually affords you a valuable opportunity. You have the ability to cut the cord, turn the page, and completely move on. If you are not married, this is an added benefit to you. Most divorces are nasty, expensive, and time-consuming undertakings. And many people stay trapped in unhappy marriages for years if not decades to either avoid this unpleasant task or subject their children to the potential trauma of a broken home.

Additionally, being childless allows you to be selfish. You have the time to both take care of *and* get better acquainted with yourself, effectively process your breakup, and build an entirely new life. Kali, a teacher from Memphis, called off her engagement with this concept in mind. "Coming from a very traditional family, I was engaged to an anesthesiologist when I was twenty-four. I thought I was the luckiest girl in town, until several of my friends told me that Clem was doing a lot more then administering gas to his female patients!

I could have turned the other cheek and kept planning the wedding, but I didn't go that route. I decided to walk away, rejoin my friends, and start my life all over again. There was no divorce, no kids— and I eventually realized this was not a disaster, but an opportunity for me."

Now that you understand negative engagement, if you are involved in this behavior it's time to change course. If you keep going back to your ex because you are too hurt or afraid to move on, or still trying to achieve validation or closure, or attempting to be friends, you are putting yourself and your recovery in jeopardy. If you are able to break ties with your ex, now is the time to do it. Your healing phase will take longer and be more painful if you are still seeing or communicating with him. You are simply delaying the inevitable and wasting precious time—time that can and should be put into your mending. Your ultimate goal should be zero contact, and I am going to help you achieve it.

There is actually scientific proof for the premise that avoiding all contact with an ex is the right step. While researching her book *Why We Love,* anthropologist Helen Fisher set up an interesting experiment. To prove her thesis that the loss of love actually creates a physical/chemical reaction in addition to an emotional one, Fisher scanned the brains of those who had previously endured a breakup while showing them a photo of their ex. She discovered that the brains of these individuals lit up like firecrackers when they viewed the photo, plus they had intensely negative emotional reactions. And that was just from viewing a photo! So imagine what you're doing to yourself when you speak to and see your ex. And chances are you're going to obsess and agonize afterward. I can't emphasize this concept enough.

I do understand, however, that some of you may feel that completely breaking off all contact may not be possible. People generally meet and date from their personal sphere—which includes their job, social circle, college or grad school, or hobbies—or through mutual friends. Lily just ended a ten-year relationship and still belongs to the same gym as her ex, who regularly attends *and* brings his new girlfriend. Linda's ex works across the street from her apartment.

She runs into him on the street with some regularity and they use the same deli for their daily coffee. And Mackenzie had to see her ex for a full year after her breakup because they worked at the same company.

I fully understand the complications of these situations. However, I strongly suggest that your life will be easier if you can discontinue contact. If you can make certain modifications in your life, it will help you a great deal. These changes may include switching routines; avoiding visiting places your ex may frequent; briefly giving up hobbies you shared; not visiting restaurants, clubs, and other venues where he may be; and even creating new social circles. And that's only the beginning. Over time, you need to make other changes. It will be extremely helpful to your recovery if you take down his photos and delete them from your phone and computer, erase his number from your cell phone, stop reading and even expunge old e-mails, unfriend him on Facebook, and even consider blocking him from your phone, instant messaging, and e-mail. It's time for you to end most avenues of communication and put the extra energy into *your* recovery. I promise you, it's well worth it.

Can We Be Friends?

Many of you have a fantasy that you can be friends with your ex, and while I occasionally see this occur, it is not usual. Often we maintain this hope because we are not ready to let go. You may think that by suggesting friendship you are going to be able to keep him in your life in some meaningful way. When women attempt friendship too soon after a breakup, I see them repeatedly getting hurt. There are many reasons why your relationship ended, and there is a strong possibility that some of these factors will immediately leech into your friendship.

> "I had done a lot of work on myself after our marriage ended, and truly, Seth hadn't. He was very irresponsible during our marriage, which was one of the reasons we broke off, and that theme crept up a lot while he

was trying to form a friendship with me. I lost so much respect for him, and when the respect is gone, frankly, there's no need have a friendship. It wouldn't have been good for me, and it didn't feel authentic." —*Kate*

For evolutionary reasons, women's brains do take longer to disengage from love relationships. You are going to need time away from your ex to fully process your breakup. It's hard to do this work if your ex is still in your life. So please remember that the more space you have from him, the greater your ability to heal and move on. You may very well be able to be friendly with him one day, but it takes a lot of work and time to get there.

Working Together

It's a very natural thing to date someone from your office or industry. After all, this is where we spend the majority of our time and we have a lot in common with our colleagues. I actually met my husband through a job—he worked at a company that I did business with. This made for an exciting dating experience, because we had a lot of shared interests and knew a bunch of the same people. I never stopped for a second to think, "What will happen if we break up?" We worked in a small industry in a small city; it probably would have been awful for both of us if we had split up.

Several women I interviewed met their exes at their jobs, and for them, their breakups were especially treacherous. Having to spend hours at the same company, and at times, in the same room, with your ex can be agonizing. If you are either seeing him or hearing about him on a daily basis, how can you possibly recover?

A client of mine is currently in this situation, having worked alongside her boyfriend, a partner in their company, for more than a decade. Their recent breakup has caused her abundant heartache as she watches him move on with his life. He avoids her at work and she is being omitted from certain projects and meetings that she previously covered. This situation is keeping her stuck and zapping her energy, which is limiting her ability to recover. When I became insistent that she put her résumé in order and get out, she cried to me, "Why do *I* have to leave? Do I have to give up everything in my life? This job has been my home."

I'm not saying changing jobs or careers is easily accomplished, especially when you're feeling down. But seeing your ex every single day is going to make your healing extremely complicated. As difficult as it may be, I suggest doing all you can to either get a transfer or find a new job. It will do you a world of good to get away from this predicament and start afresh.

Is He in Your Social Circle?

Various women I spoke with described meeting their mates through friends. This is a very natural way of dating and it's great when you meet a boyfriend through a friend, or at a party. Today young people tend to date and hang out in large packs, and when that works out it's loads of fun. But what happens when there is a breakup? Who gets custody of that group? If you and your ex travel in the same social circle, chances are you are going to run into each other—a lot. You are going to need your friends now more than ever, yet it's going to complicate your healing if every time you go out you either run into him or hear about him.

Perhaps you need to take some time away from group events for a while. I understand this can feel isolating, and it's very upsetting to think that the social life you once valued is going on without you. Please remember your friendship formula—I'm sure there are other friends not involved in this group whom you can turn to for comfort, companionship, and socialization. And even though you may need to pull away from parties, concerts, and dinners that he may be attending, this doesn't mean that you can't reach out and see individuals from the group on your own.

There may be times when you will need to communicate with your ex over some logistical issues. If you recently broke up and there is a wedding that you planned on attending together in the near future, how might that play out? If you both signed on for a share in a summer house, who will go forth with that plan? And who will attend John's annual New Year's party? You have every right to say your piece and ask for what you need—just remember to be aware of your engagement dance when you do speak up.

Relocating

Breakups and divorces can certainly be catalysts for major changes in our life, and I have heard many encouraging stories involving relocation. Living in the same home—or even the same city—that you shared with your ex can be exceptionally challenging. It's hard to move on when you're constantly being reminded of him, sleeping in the bed that you shared, or running into him at the grocery store. Women without children do have an advantage here. If you are continuously bumping into or being reminded of your ex, perhaps moving or relocating is something to consider.

Olive was able to turn her life around once she moved from D.C. back to Boston, her hometown. She became reacquainted with a cluster of cousins, and truly felt as if her healing had finally come full circle when she arrived "home."

My client Charlotte, married for ten years, was subjected to a dreadful breakup when she discovered her husband's infidelity. Living alone in her marital home constantly reminded her of Jake and the life they shared together. We worked very hard in both her healing and understanding, but she was often frustrated by the slow progress of her recovery—until the day she decided to move. "It was a quick decision, but I knew I just couldn't stay there any longer with all those memories. It was too painful. I rented out my house and moved to a much smaller one in a different neighborhood. Once I pulled off this move, I was really proud of myself. It catapulted me into action and made me feel less like a victim. After that things did get much easier."

Although I generally suggest avoiding making major life changes immediately following a breakup, a move or relocation can be the right medicine if administered properly. However, finding a new home in your city or relocating to another state should never be taken lightly. If you are simply moving to avoid doing the work, you will find that your pain and sorrow may follow you in the U-Haul. Be sure to think this carefully through before packing any boxes.

Rules of Disengagement

Believe me, I understand how strong the impulse to engage is, but you will be so proud of yourself when you resist it. *Every single woman* I spoke with reported how satisfied she felt when finally taking control of this behavior. I know you can do this and I promise that you will feel relieved and powerful. Following these suggestions will help you break free.

When you have an urge to reach out, inquire, or spy:
• **Buy yourself some time.** Make a bargain not to engage for at least thirty minutes. As previously described, obsessions are reduced or eliminated if you simply make an agreement with yourself to delay your urge.

• **Create an affirmation.** I'm going to ask you to use this whenever you feel like reaching out, whenever the obsession/addiction is at its fiercest. Suggestions: "I am a powerful lioness—I can control myself"; "Stop the madness"; "This is the time to heal and be well." Repeat this chant over and over.

• **Remind and refamiliarize yourself about your negative engagement dance.** Chances are, no matter how you convince yourself otherwise, it will start up again the moment you reach out. And if you feel bad now, you're going to feel much worse once this gets under way.

• **Check in with your emotions.** What are you feeling right now? Are you feeling angry, lonely, anxious, sad? Process your feelings and turn your focus away from your ex and onto yourself. Use your bag of tricks to soothe yourself.

• **Move away from your emotions and into your intellect (try to switch from heart to head).** Honestly ask yourself, "What exactly am I trying to accomplish by calling him now? How has it felt in the past when this hasn't gone well? How will I feel if he doesn't respond, or if he responds in a form that is dangerous to my well-being?"

Instinctively you know that it is going to be distressing and it will set you back. It always does. Remember that.

• **Refocus your brain.** Change activities. Go for a walk, organize a room in your home, do physical exercise, cook, clean, write in your journal, read something from one of your inspirational/spiritual books, play some music, or watch a DVD.

• **Call someone from your support system.** Is there someone you can ask to serve as your "sponsor"? Someone who will agree that you can contact him or her whenever you feel like contacting your ex? Sign on a few sponsors and call them instead of calling him.

• **If you are in the midst of an engagement dance, pull away.** It is never too late to change directions. End the conversation. Walk away. Turn off your phone, electronic device, or computer.

• **When you feel like sending a letter, write one to yourself.** You need to express yourself (which is part of the reason you're engaging in the first place). Write it all down and take as much time as

---

If you are planning to see your ex at a work function or social occasion, or you think you might run into him:

• **Be prepared.** Prime yourself. Rehearse all scenarios in your mind before the encounter. Think through what might happen and how *you* would like it to happen.

• **Enlist backups.** If you're heading to a party and you know he'll be there, can you go with a good friend and inform her of the situation? If you know you are attending a work meeting or function and he will be there, think where you'll sit, how it may play out.

• **Remember you are always in control.** Even if your ex starts in on you, you can always walk away.

• **Refocus.** Try to find something else to focus on so you do not inordinately focus in on him.

• **Always keep a level head.** Watch alcohol intake. Many negative encounters are fueled by drink.

you need. Do not send this letter. It is for your own edification. It will help you explore and express your feelings and make your own discoveries. Make sure you are validating yourself!

• **Try a thirty-day cleanse (see p. 109).** Force yourself to stop engaging for thirty days—it will work wonders.

Rules of Engagement

I understand that there may be some times that you are going to have to speak to or see your ex. When this occurs, use these guidelines:

• **Familiarize yourself with your engagement dance and know your part in it.** If you push and prod, if you become emotional and cry, if you exhibit anger, he will (fill in the blank). Remember this every time you have to engage.

• **Buy yourself some time.** If your ex attempts to contact you, you do not have to answer immediately. Make yourself wait at least thirty minutes. If you take your time to carefully listen to his message or read an e-mail or text, it will give you time to think it through and create a strategy that best suits *you*. If you reply too quickly you are *reacting* instead of *acting* and may say something in haste that you will regret later.

• **When initiating contact (or replying) keep it simple.** What exactly do you need to say? Is it really necessary? If so, prepare yourself. Rehearse it. Keep your emotions in check. Be the grown-up. Don't get pulled into something you will later regret.

• **Be responsible for your own behavior.** Do not make sarcastic comments, play the blame game, be passive-aggressive, or guilt-trip. These actions will never benefit you.

Congratulations! You did it. You are going to feel so proud of yourself. You are really on your way!

Successful Disengagement: Linda's Story

I'm eager to share Linda's story with you because it's very representative of this chapter. I'm sure that many of you can relate to her struggles and be inspired by her subsequent recovery.

Linda had dated Scott for five years, and following their breakup, they stayed involved for an additional three years through a cycle of negative entanglement that kept both from moving on. This dysfunction occupied the majority of Linda's time, and most of her twenties.

Their relationship fell into trouble as Scott climbed the corporate ladder and became financially successful. Linda devoted much of her time to fulfilling his needs. This included making choices such as a relocation and career change, simply to please him. Scott became obsessed with work and work life, which included ample travel and entertainment. He worked late and partied hard. A naturally trusting and supportive person, Linda eventually realized what was happening. Scott was getting deeply involved in a "boys club" culture, and she suspected that he was making decisions that didn't serve her or their relationship's best interest. When she tried to talk to him about this, he would become indignant and belligerent (the prosecutor, discussed in chapter 5) accusing her of not understanding him or his job and threatening that her paranoia was ruining the relationship. *This caused the initial breakup.*

Linda, feeling extremely bereft and misunderstood, would spend considerable time obsessing about Scott. Because he refused to take any responsibility for his actions, there was no validation or closure. And worse, his prosecutorial style made her desire to reach out unquenchable. "Scott's cruel and blaming behavior made me even more determined to get him to take back his words."

Adding to the complications of the breakup, their social circle was incestuously intertwined, and Linda received regular updates about Scott's every move. She continually ran into him, which would fuel her rumination about how she'd been wronged. She'd hear songs that reminded her of him and visit restaurants that they had frequented. These factors all fed into the obsession causing her to continually reach out to him.

Scott always took her calls and the conversations were the same. Linda would explain to him what a good girlfriend she was, how he'd hurt her, and recite all the things he'd done wrong. Scott would start off sweetly stating, "You're right. You were the best thing that ever happened to me and breaking up with you was the biggest mistake." After that statement the conversation instantly became detrimental. "Then I'd ask him, 'So why won't you do anything to change your behavior so we could be together and be happy?', and that's when he'd always become vicious and turn on me. He would tell me I was crazy and say that I should never call again. Then he'd hang up. This made me *completely infuriated*—and that would be the fuel that would make me want to call him again and again. To insist that I wasn't crazy, and to prove that I was right and he was wrong."

After three years of this drama, which included brief periods of reuniting, Linda was completely worn out and sought my help.

She was motivated to break away from Scott, but was clueless about how to stop her negative engagement dance. We immediately got busy and simultaneously worked through healing and understanding, and she had many meaningful realizations and connections. While doing this work I continually encouraged Linda to not reach out to Scott, and slowly she did cut back on communicating, which always added momentum to her recovery. Here's a brief scenario of our work together:

• Linda was constantly on the go, thinking this would prevent her from sinking into a deeper depression, *and* that it would help her to disengage from Scott. In actuality it was doing the opposite. She was exhausted, running from her feelings, and not taking care of herself. I requested that she slow down and stay home a few nights a week.

• We put into place many of the tips and tools I present in chapters 1 through 4.

• Linda was spending too much time with the social group that she and Scott belonged to and the majority were married. This was constantly triggering Linda into thinking something else was wrong with her (remember Scott repeatedly told her she was crazy) because she was single. This would make her want to call Scott. Also, she received a constant news stream of Scott updates and antics. She spent too much time discussing him and the breakup with many willing people. I encouraged her to take a hiatus from this group and spend time with other friends—especially single females.

• During breaks from Scott, Linda would date a lot. Because she was still too attached to the notion that Scott and she belonged together, none of these relationships worked out. This made her feel as if Scott was the only man for her, and if they didn't get back together she'd always be alone. Because dating is most effective later in the healing process, I suggested she stop dating until she was fully recovered.

• I inquired into other triggers. Were there certain memories of Scott or times of days when she was more prone to calling him? We created a bag of tricks, and she started using them whenever she felt like engaging.

• Linda's apartment was located one block from where Scott worked. This caused her abundant anxiety. She was always on guard, afraid that she would run into him. Also, she had rented her apartment while involved with Scott, and memories of their time together haunted her while at home. It was agreed that when her lease expired she would move to a different neighborhood, which would be symbolic of a new beginning.

• In our talks, Linda had many insights that allowed her to better comprehend Scott's personality structure. This enabled her to have a clearer picture of why he behaved as he did in the relationship and the breakup. This new information gave Linda all the validation and closure that she needed.

Over time Linda was able to completely disengage with Scott. "Once I went a week, then two weeks, and then months without speaking to Scott, everything changed. I saw the relationship with so much more clarity. I felt so much stronger and proud of myself. Through working with Rachel I finally got the validation that I was craving—and realized that I would never ever get it from Scott. I was able to understand why Scott behaved as he did, and why *I* tolerated it for so long. Everything started making so much sense. I realized I wasn't crazy, and I was right. After that, I was on a whole new path—I was finally free."

Once Linda stopped contacting Scott, he unexpectedly started reaching out to her. And one night he showed up at her apartment with a teary apology—something she never expected. Scott still attempts to contact her occasionally and Linda remains strong and never takes his calls. Today she's doing great—she's in graduate school and planning on opening her own business. She's made many new friends and is focusing on her happiness. She's been learning how to trust and dating with a vastly improved radar. Linda's story illustrates that once you disengage, once you take back your power, wonderful things will happen. And they can happen for you, too!

7

Breakups or Divorces *with* Children

"At first I didn't want him in my life at all. I had no respect for him. He was not a person I wanted to be friends with. He became a man I didn't recognize. If we didn't have kids, I really would never have wanted to see him again. But I am a humane person. My compass said to me, 'Do the right thing.' And the right thing was to maintain a respectful relationship with him for the sake of our kids." —*Mila*

"I told my kids, 'He's your father. He'll always be your father. Whatever you feel now, you won't feel forever.' I begged them not to cut him off. I knew no matter how angry they were, and they had a right to be, they still needed a father in their life." —*Anne*

If you are ending or have ended your marriage and you have children, you do have a more complicated road ahead. As much as you may desire, you cannot completely detach from your ex, and many of you will continue to live in your marital home, filled with good memories of when you were an intact family, and other memories that may not be so fond. Focusing predominantly on yourself will be a challenge if you need to return to the workforce, or if working part time, you may need to increase your hours to pad your paycheck. And if you're already working full time, you are going to feel like a juggler with dozens of balls in the air. If you don't work outside the home, and many mothers do not, you may be having a difficult time filling your days constructively, and struggling to find more purpose in your life. And of course, added to these other stressors, there are children to raise who are having their own difficulties.

Now is the time to put your children's well-being ahead of your own. If your kids are subjected to you and your ex-husband's continued arguing, disrespect, and attempts at revenge, they are going to have a very rough time. And if you tell them your problems, or confide that their father is really a bad person/father/husband/cheater, you are going to expose them to information they cannot understand or process. Children do best in environments where there is stability. Divorce is hard on kids, but what is hardest for them is watching their parents argue, hurt, disrespect, or bad-mouth each other. Your children didn't ask to be born into this quagmire and they deserve to be raised in the healthiest way possible. Hostility after a divorce will undoubtedly cause them huge emotional scars. Of course there are going to be times when you get tripped up and fall into some of this behavior. But chances are you are not going to feel very good about yourself if you allow it to continue for too long. So please be smart, please be kind, and make a commitment to stop this behavior now.

Yes, life can certainly feel taxing and overwhelming. Raising kids with two parents is very hard work, and now here you are trudging along solo. If your relationship ended with acrimony, if your husband is not pulling his weight, if he is giving you a hard time, saying or doing inappropriate things, you are going to continually feel angry and hurt. And now you're going to get angry at me because I am going to spend the rest of this chapter giving you a variety of reasons why it's important (very important) that you accept your fate, make peace with your ex, and learn how to parent together. Yes, he may be impossible, completely uncooperative, and determined to make your life difficult, but hey, we are the stronger sex, and Yes We Can!

There are two types of divorces: immature and hateful, and mature and cordial. My job is to help you attain the latter. Some husbands are more helpful than others, especially if you share custody. But regrettably I hear too many stories of exes being available only when it's convenient for them. Other exes have no boundaries and think they have complete access to their kids and their marital home. I have a vivid recollection of being on a business trip when my divorced customer paraded me through his spectacular former marital home, until his ex-wife came home, became extremely livid, called him every name in the book, and threw us out (as she should have!).

I know of a woman with three kids who has been caught in a negative engagement dance for more than five years. Neither she nor her ex can agree on a divorce settlement and they are constantly battling it out inside and outside of court (several judges have literally thrown their case out). His full-time job is to make her miserable, but she cannot detach either. She is not a rich woman and has spent all of her life savings on legal fees—and they are not even divorced yet. Sadly, I have heard too many of these kinds of stories. Women running in and out of court, or fighting with their ex-husbands— for decades. Please don't succumb to this. I assure you, this is not how you want to live your life.

But the good news is that you are incredibly blessed. Although your family unit is no longer the same, it is still a family. You have produced beautiful, awe-inspiring children who will bring you a lifetime of joy. You will always share this bond with your husband, and even if you want to strangle him from time to time, *he is and will always be the father of your kids*. Acknowledging this fact, plus putting your children's needs ahead of your disappointment or anger, will allow you to coparent in a more effective way.

In my experience, the women who worked the hardest, who stuck with my program, were eventually able to take the high road and find a mature style of engagement. Even if their exes were nasty and problematic, they found that if they behaved calmly, respectfully, and appropriately, if they refused to fight or allow the negativity to penetrate their existence, life became easier, and they fully transformed. Women who didn't take any time to care for themselves, failed to heal and understand, continued with negative engagement remained stuck, exhausted, anxious, and depressed. They set poor examples for their offspring and had far fewer opportunities to create new lives or entertain the possibility of romance. If you commit to healthy engagement, you will set an extraordinary example for your children. You will show them that life doesn't have to stop because of divorce and that parents don't need to hate each other when a marriage ends. Moreover, if they see you in a new and healthier romance at the appropriate time, they will have a good relationship model to emulate.

Coexisting with Respectful Boundaries

I understand these predicaments of navigating boundaries and how exasperating they can be. You and your kids need defined boundaries in order to heal and recover from your ordeal. Your kids crave stability now more than ever, and if your ex is coming and going as he pleases or disrespecting your rules (or your life), it is not good for anyone. And if you are falling into your negative engagement dance every time he comes by, this is unhealthy and unsafe for everyone involved.

This is not a book on the laws of divorce and thus I cannot instruct you on your legal rights. But what I can tell you is that you have more of a voice than you may think. It's crucial that you learn how to effectively communicate with your ex so that you can get to work rebuilding your life as soon as possible.

Chloe, divorced for four years, has strived to maintain a courteous relationship with her ex, Patrick, who can be quite difficult. "Pat can be moody, controlling, and defensive. After we separated I knew I had to pull it together quickly for the sake of my young daughters. It was not effortless for me. I was very hurt and sad, and Pat was angry and had really poor boundaries.

"Pat missed the kids after he moved out, and was stopping by every day to see them. We were all trying to find our way, but eventually I realized that this wasn't good for me or our kids. It was time we started to adjust to our new circumstances—we were no longer a family that lived under the same roof. Also, I needed my space and time away from Pat so I could heal. I tried to explain this to him, and although he fought me, I held my ground, but without getting drawn into arguments—even when he provoked me."

A shy woman who deplores confrontation, Chloe struggled to find a way of engaging with Patrick about domestic matters. She understood their engagement dance ("I can be an avoider and he, a defender or prosecutor"), and was always thoughtful in her approach. "With simple logistical issues I stick to e-mail, and I am always respectful in my tone. There are times, however, when I need to have more difficult conversations with him if I feel he has said or done something inappropriate with the kids. When something like this happens, I rehearse what I want to say to him before I call. Then I *briefly* explain to him in a very calm manner, 'Pat I'm upset about A, B, or C.' If he argues or becomes defensive I say, 'OK, I just needed to tell you how I feel, but you can do whatever you want to do with that information.' I make it short and to the point, I don't argue, I refuse to allow myself to be drawn into something negative where I'll be upset. I want Pat to be a good parent, and sometimes it is my job to bring certain things to his attention and help him get there. Your kids are fifty percent their dad—and if you hate him or portray him in a poor way, what is that saying about them?"

I think Chloe, and all women like her, deserve our kudos for overcoming their obstacles and striving to be healthy coparents for the sake of their children *and* for their sanity. I know it's not always easy to make peace, and many of you are still in the earlier stages of healing where overpowering feelings are still raw. It's hard to behave like a mature adult and do "what's right," especially if adultery, lying, or mental (and physical) cruelty is involved. And even with a great deal of effort, some tell me that they still feel stuck and find themselves continually falling into old patterns.

How to Have a Healthy Conversation with Your Ex: The Art of Positive Dialoguing

Learning how to identify your personal engagement style and commit to brand-new rules of engagement is more than half the battle. Once you accept this concept, life with your ex does indeed become easier. There may still be ample times when he will act out and push all of your buttons. When that happens, I want to arm you with tools so you can avoid old traps, take charge of the conversations, and steer the exchange in a positive direction. Believe it or not, this is entirely possible.

Many women regularly complain to me that one of their biggest frustrations, even taking place years after a divorce, is their inability to have a normal dialogue with their ex without arguing. I realize you may think that it is completely impossible to have a healthy discussion if your ex is unwilling or unable to properly engage. I'm here to tell you that this is not true. He can be provocative, irresponsible, or impossible—but *you* have the power to turn the conversation around and change course. You just have to be prepared and understand some basic rules of positive communication. These rules are:

- Everyone has a right to say his or her piece (even if you disagree)
- Everyone has a right to be heard *and* validated

What this means for you is:

1. Never interrupt. It's disrespectful, and your ex will not feel heard, which may frustrate him and potentially cause an escalation.
2. Validate what he says, even if you don't agree, to keep the dialogue going in the right direction. This does not mean you have to agree with what he is proposing or saying, it just means that you have to show him that you understand where he is coming from, or what he is trying to say. A wonderful trick here is to simply repeat what he is saying. For example, if he says, "I haven't had time to pay that bill yet," you can say, "I understand that you're busy and haven't had time to pay the bill, but . . ." Repeating makes him feel heard and validated. It's easy and it works.

To prove my point, let me show you two samples of dialogues (with the exact same conversation) to display how this feat is accomplished.

The Wrong Way: Negative Dialoguing

He Says	You Say	Comments
Setting: It's Sunday night and the children are with your ex. It was agreed that he would bring them home by five p.m. He calls . . . "I'm taking the kids to a movie and I'll bring them home at nine tonight."	"What do you mean nine p.m.? That's way too late. You should know they have to be home at five. They still have homework to do, they have to clean their rooms, and get ready for school tomorrow. Why do you always do this to me?"	He's pushing the limits, but you've already lost your cool. The dance has begun. Your tone is angry and scolding when you say, "You should know," and you've become a pitier by saying "Why do you always do this to me?"
"What's the big deal? You are so damn controlling! You get so much more time with them than I do. They want to see a movie, and you never let them do anything fun. You—"	(interrupting) "I am not controlling. You just have to do things all the time to rile me up, don't you! How dare you say I'm not a fun mother. Do you know what my life is like since you left us? I have to do everything for these kids—and you slip in and out of their lives as it conveniences you! You left us and are the cause of all the problems!"	You interrupted, which frustrated him. You're being defensive and playing the blame game. You've started *dirty fighting* by bringing into the discussion the fact that he abandoned the family.

"I left you because you're a controlling bitch who has no idea how to have a good time. I'm so much happier with you out of my life. I'll bring the kids home when I damn well please!"

"I hate you! You are the most evil man." Tears. Hang up.

You are hurt, angry, and frustrated. You feel trapped, victimized, and unable to break free.

The Right Way: Positive Dialoging

He Says	You Say	Comments
"I'm taking the kids to a movie and going to bring them home at nine tonight."	You're prepared—he regularly does this. "I really understand your need to extend the evening. You must really feel bad when you drop them off on Sunday nights."	Good work. You are prepared, staying calm, and getting to the heart of the matter—that he does miss the kids and is eager to extend the weekend. You are speaking to him with respect.
"Yes, it's really hard. We had a great weekend—they're so much fun."	"I know, they're the best. We did raise wonderful kids, and you're a good father."	Great job. You complimented him. That always wins points, and better yet, it disarms him.
"Thanks, that means a lot to me."	"You know, John, Mondays are long days for the kids. Would you mind taking them to see a movie another time and dropping them off, say, six or six thirty tonight? Mary still has some homework, and their rooms are a wreck, and they need to pack their backpacks for tomorrow."	You calmly explain the situation to him. Then, you suggest a compromise—he can bring the kids home at six instead of five. If you can let him win something, that is helpful too.

"Come on, Natalie, why can't I take them to see a damn movie? They'll get all that done— what's the big deal?"

"I hear you, John, you want to extend the evening. I'm not saying you can't take them to a movie, I'm just wondering if you could postpone it—say till the next weekend you have them? I'm sure you'll agree that they need their sleep; it will help them have an easier week."

You are validating by repeating, which shows him that he's been heard. That will prevent him from further escalating, which he was starting to do.

OK, Nat, I hear ya. I'll bring them home at six. Thanks.

"Thanks so much, John. I really appreciate it. I'm glad the weekend went well. Have a good week, and I'll let you know if anything comes up over the next few days that you should know."

You are thanking him and promising to keep him in the loop. Excellent work.

May I suggest that you now take a piece of paper and write out a sample dialogue of your own. Pick a topic that you and your ex regularly disagree on, and transcribe it both ways. Now, study the "Right Way" dialogue, and commit to using this effective style of communication. You can certainly ask a support person to practice this new method by role-playing with you. Once you get this down, and you will, you can use it in all areas of your life (think conversations with your mother, kids, or your boss).

The Thirty-Day Cleanse

Here's a great story and useful tool for *any* woman, both with and without children. My friend Jenna had a rotten divorce. Cliff left her (midlife crisis) just before her eldest son left for college. They had been married since their early twenties, and by all accounts seemed perfectly happy. A stay-at-home mom, she was devoted to her three children, and to Cliff, who could be demanding and childlike. She was devastated by the ending of their marriage and Cliff's inept and erratic behavior following their separation.

Jenna was wounded, angry, and embarrassed. Their engagement dance immediately became mutually prosecutorial. Cliff took zero responsibility and blamed the failure of the marriage on her. During a last-ditch attempt at reconciliation via marriage counseling, he would bring up events from years past where he had been hurt by Jenna—and much of what he said was news to her.

Although she had recaptured her life in many ways, she continued to engage unconstructively with Cliff. Simple logistical e-mails turned into poison-pen tomes. Cliff loved a good fight, and would give it back to her in spades. At the end of each encounter she felt physically and emotionally beaten up. Turning to vodka, cigarettes, and other unhealthy behavior, Jenna felt her life being sucked out of her, and didn't see a way out.

One day Jenna and I met up with our mutual friend Chelsea, who had just returned from a spiritual journey that took her to India. Chelsea, divorced for four years, had ended her negative engagement dance within the first year of her separation. She has a great life, which includes a wonderful relationship with a dedicated and caring man. We met for lunch at a vegetarian health-food restaurant (in the spirit of her India trip) and the conversation eventually turned to Jenna's latest fight with Cliff. Jenna had written a seemingly innocuous e-mail to Cliff and received a spiteful reply. She was distressed and shaken, stating, "Can you believe he wrote this? How can he be so mean to me?" Chelsea and I both read the e-mail thread and identified that what Jenna thought was an innocent message was actually a passive-aggressive dig directed at Cliff. And in character, Cliff hit back hard.

Firmly, yet lovingly, I explained to Jenna what she had done to incite Cliff. I then insisted she put down her BlackBerry and stop engaging.

Jenna burst into tears, admitting her part in the destructive cycle. I had been active in her recovery, but at that moment I felt stumped. We had put so many great resources into her healing, what else could I do to get her to stop engaging? I looked around the restaurant, and sitting a few tables away was Deepak Chopra, a world-renowned author and teacher. Chopra has been preaching for years about the benefits of physical and emotional well-being, spiritual awakening, and love and forgiveness. Then I made eye contact with a woman at the table next to us, and she chimed in, "I've heard your conversation—I too had an awful divorce. Never lose hope. Today I have a wonderful life—my kids are grown and successful, I have a new career as a health and nutritional counselor, and this man here is my new husband. You've got to cut the cord. It's time to move on."

I looked over at Deepak for some telepathic guidance and this is what I imagined him saying: "Tell Jenna to wash that man right out of her hair!" Such wise words! I turned to Jenna and said, "I'm putting you on a cleanse—a thirty-day cleanse. You will treat your body like a temple, exercise, eat only healthy foods, stop drinking and smoking, and you will have extremely limited contact with Cliff for an entire month. And after that, you will be released from the intoxication of your negative engagement dance."

Jenna agreed on the spot. Similar to many other recovery models, we decided that I would coach her and we'd touch base every day. She promised that she would fully disconnect from Cliff for an entire month. She would only contact him if it was something important about the kids. When she did contact him, her messages would be short and to the point. There would absolutely be no negative engagement or commentary. She agreed, and we got to work.

I drew a chart for Jenna that had thirty lines and three columns. It looked like this:

Day	Inspirational quote	How do you feel today?
1		
2		

I instructed Jenna to fill out her chart daily. In the morning she would write an inspirational quote of her own choice, and before bed she would journal about how she felt each day without the negative engagement with Cliff. Jenna was a perfect student and finished the cleanse without one damaging incident. Today, several months later, she is on a completely different course and reports that she truly feels released.

Although this story sounds magical, it's not. Anyone can do this—you just have to want freedom bad enough. You may initially think that thirty days is an impossibility, but it's a blip on the screen. Think how fast a month goes! When you do this successfully for thirty days, then you can keep it going. One month turns to two, and two to four. This is how you recapture your life. This is how you become whole again.

A Few Last Words About Your Kids

There are wonderful resources available on parenting children through a divorce, and I encourage you to take the time to learn more about this topic. Although this is not a book about parenting, I worry that if you slip into too many bad habits, it will affect your recovery. Many women openly described to me their remorse over making poor choices when it came to their kids. So here are a few final points to consider, which come from me and from the community. Following these tips will help you help your kids, *and* help you disengage. You will feel so much better about yourself when you follow these simple rules:

• **Never, ever bad-mouth your ex in front of your children.** This includes when you are speaking to friends or family on the telephone and they can hear you.

- **Please remember that no matter what he has done, he is their father.** They are going to need to have a relationship with him, and if you poison them against him it will only damage them and backfire on you.
- **If you repeatedly bad-mouth your ex to family, friends, neighbors, etc., it will get back to your children.** Also, it will make you look bad.
- **Never use your kids as weapons or as messengers.**
- **Never make your children take sides.** You don't need them as your allies. This is not a competition.
- **If your children complain to you about their father, make sure what they are saying is valid.** Don't overreact. Sometimes kids want to placate you, so they will make him out to be a "bad guy," thinking that this is what *you* want.
- **Don't put your kids in a position where they have to defend their dad.** If you bad-mouth him, that often makes them feel sorry for him, which produces abundant guilt, and that's a complicated stew for all.
- **It is your job to protect your kids, and not the other way around.** They need to be carefree and enjoying their lives. Don't put them in positions they cannot handle.
- **If your kids are getting older and are having difficulties with their dad, teach them how to communicate their feelings and needs to him.** You can't always fight their battles. Give them the resources to do this.
- **Create an open space for your kids to speak to you about their feelings about the divorce and their father.** It's a huge opportunity for them to talk and heal, and for you to get closer to them.
- **You want your ex to be a good parent and sometimes you may need to help him be that.**
- **When you model good behavior with your ex, you are teaching your kids tremendous life lessons.** You want your kids to have healthy relationships. If you speak poorly about your ex, or men in general, this will not be good for your children.
- **Be very careful of anger.** It is OK for your kids to see you sad, but it's too scary for them to see you vengeful or out of control.

The Rules of Engagement

My dear friend Steve was left by his wife with little warning or explanation. He loved Nicole, was a devoted husband and father, and was both blindsided and devastated by her abrupt decision to leave. When he tried to reach out to her to inquire about the children or logistics, she was regularly cold and unkind. Other times she just didn't return his calls. Unknown to him, this dynamic was continually making him anxious and opening his wounds, which was affecting his recovery. Recently Steve and I were out with a small group having a great time. He had reported having several good days and I saw signs of his former self emerging. He was funny, engaging, and on his game. Plus, a woman who was interested in him had joined our group. In the midst of our merriment, his phone rang. He took it out of his pocket, looked at me, and said, "It's Nicole." Steve was about to pick up the call when I literally grabbed it out of his hand. "Don't you dare," I whispered. "You're finally having some good days, we're having a blast right now—how will you feel if you pick up and she's awful to you? It will ruin your night. You already communicated with her earlier—you know the kids are fine. Let it go." Steve looked at me as if I had just discovered the lightbulb. As he put the phone back into his pocket I observed his expression changing from angst to relief. "Thank you, Rachel. I didn't even realize I had that option. I'm going to use that strategy from now on. I guess I have to rethink how I communicate with her so it doesn't affect me so much."

Your life will be easier when you commit to these rules:

• **Accept the fact that your ex will always be a part of your life.** Acknowledge that concept and make peace with it.

• **Commit to healthy engagement.** Know your part in your negative engagement dance and make a pledge to stop it now.

• **Always take the high road.** Remain calm, civil, respectful, and in control.

• **During your healing phase, keep contact to a minimum.** Since the goal is to recover and move on with your life, too much communication with your ex can interfere with that. You need to see that you can make it on your own.

- **Establish ground rules around communications.**
- **If your ex is attempting to contact you via phone, text, etc., you do not have to pick up the phone or reply immediately.** If you are out with friends and enjoying yourself, or if you are having a difficult day, read or listen to the message when the timing is better, and then prepare yourself before you reply. It is perfectly OK to buy yourself some time. If there is an emergency with the kids, your ex will continue to call and then you'll know if something is really wrong. This will buy you some time, and then you can *respond* and not *react*.
- **If contact is required, think it through.** What do you need to say? What do you wish to accomplish? What is the easiest and safest way for you to contact him—phone, in person, text, e-mail? Remember to keep it simple. Role-play when necessary.
- **Prepare yourself.** Don't let yourself be baited into an argument.
- **Keep a level head.** Try not to let your emotions rule.
- **When communicating, keep it short and stick to the topic at hand.** Do not discuss your relationship. Do not bring up the past. Do not throw in little jabs. Do not try to get validation or closure. Request or suggest—never demand or reprimand.
- **Learn how to commit to positive dialoguing.**

Congratulations . . . you did it!!! Way to go, champ!!! You are on your way.

The Rules of Engagement: A Final Word

You've just finished reading and learning about one of the most complex aspects of healing—engaging with your ex. Once you agree to healthier ways of dealing with him, either total detachment or existing within defined boundaries, you are going to be in a much better place—and you're going to start having better days.

Before we move on, I'd like to share a final word on anger. As I discussed in chapter 4, "Navigating the Emotional Roller Coaster," anger is a perfectly legitimate emotion, and experiencing it may in fact help you through your healing phase. Now, as we're closing healing, and about to wade into the waters of understanding, I'd like to ask you to consider letting it go. I've made a case and presented you with abundant reasons why anger tends to complicate healing. I've given you ample tools and suggestions from myself *and* from the community to help you stop your negative engagement dance and commit to new rules of engagement. Now I'm asking you to briefly contemplate the *idea of forgiveness*. I know this may be a huge stretch for you. I'm just throwing it out there for you to consider. Toss it around if you'd like, or put it away for a while. We will be revisiting this concept in the future. In closing healing, I'd like to leave you with a saying from the Buddha, as interpreted by Jack Kornfield, one of the leading Buddhist teachers in America, and a favorite of mine.

The heart is like a garden.
It can grow compassion or fear, resentment or love.
What seeds will you plant there?
—Jack Kornfield

The Rules of Engagement
Tips and Tools

1. Although validation and closure are very important, accept that you may never receive it from your ex.
2. Commit to either total detachment from your ex, or learning how to coexist within properly defined boundaries.
3. Be mindful of your urges to inquire and spy.
4. Understand your part in the negative engagement dance and make a pledge to stop it.
5. If you do not have children, and your ex is intertwined in

your life, figure out a way to minimize or eliminate contact. If you have the opportunity for total detachment, please do so.

6. If you are a parent, learn how to coexist with your ex within healthy boundaries.

7. When it comes to kids, always take the high road.

8. Learn, practice, and commit to positive dialoguing.

9. Try the thirty-day cleanse. It's healthy, fun, and it works.

10. Create your own rules of disengagement and rules of engagement.

11. Find *healthy* ways to process your anger so it doesn't infuse your parenting or your relationship with your ex.

PART II

Understanding

An unexamined life is not worth living.

—Socrates

8

Grasping the Root Causes of
Your Breakup or Divorce

"I ran around for ages saying, 'He had an affair and it ruined our marriage!' That was definitely my line, my protective shield. But over time I realized I wasn't faultless. We were under too much stress and we weren't nurturing the relationship. Truthfully, there were many things that I did wrong, and I learned some hard lessons that have helped me be more present in my relationships today." —*Portia*

"I dated so many men who were emotionally shut down, committed to other women, uninterested in a relationship. I did a lot of things that really hurt me in the end. Eventually I realized I had to take some responsibility for making bad choices, then I had to figure out how to start from square one and get it right. I did the work, turned around my life, and finally got it right." —*Rachel*

I'm having a major déjà vu. Maya has brought her latest boyfriend into our session. He is about to break up with her, and I'm watching a train wreck. Today he is the most empathetic and articulate I've known him to be. Nick can be emotionally removed, impatient, and an intellectualizer, but for now he stays calm and describes why he's dissatisfied with their relationship and disillusioned with her. "Maya, you are so focused on our relationship moving forward that you simply can't enjoy what we have day by day. I just can't take the pressure any longer, or the constant nagging and fighting about what you feel I can't give you. I really care for you, but I believe the problem lies within you. You are so insecure, you misread so much of what I say or do, that you are constantly picking fights with me. Maybe I do have some commitment issues, but how can you expect me to think about us long term or propose marriage if we're always at odds with each other? It's been exhausting—and frankly, if you can't change your behavior, I've just had enough." I know Maya well, and Nick's comments, although hard to swallow, are not untrue. But there is still hope here and he is presenting her with a map—all the information she needs to save the relationship lies before her. Regrettably, she refuses to listen, acknowledge, or take the bait. Fighting back hard, she refutes his every statement with more skill than a seasoned litigator. Exasperated, they exit, and the session concludes.

The following week she's back in my office—alone, sobbing that he broke it off with her. However, it's as if she has no recollection of the previous week's session or anything that he said about her sabotaging behavior: "Why did he end it? I just don't understand. I was such a good girlfriend, and he didn't appreciate me. How is it that I picked another man who can't commit? What's wrong with me that it never seems to work out? I'm almost forty, I've had so many years of disappointment over men. I'm never going to meet anyone at this point. I'm just not lucky."

Truly, I feel her pain, but we've been down this road before. There is a definite pattern in both her selection of men and how she manages herself when she's involved. I would love to help her understand why her relationships fail, and I'd be delighted to do this work with her, but in the past she's felt too victimized, been too defended, and had little appetite for digging deeper into her core to sort this through. But today I see an opening and I prepare to slide in.

"Maya, I'm not so sure that luck has anything to do with your preference of men or relationship outcomes. Nick said some important things and I think we will miss a crucial opportunity if we don't honestly reflect and dissect. I think we can turn this thing around for you, but I'm concerned that if you don't open up and take a hard look at your own motives and behavior you are destined to re-peat these patterns again and again. This process, which is working toward *understanding* why your relationships end as they do, and what part you play in it all, will enable you to finally break free of these old habits and lead a much better life. Otherwise, I'm afraid there is little I can do for you." Maya becomes silent. She looks at me like a deer caught in the headlights. Will she run? Or stay, and finally get it right? This is a pivotal moment for her. Continued relationship failure or a brand-new way of dealing with love and life rests on the table. Like a wounded soldier who is finally ready to surrender, she nods her head, yes. "It's time. I'm ready. Let's figure this out."

Welcome to understanding, the linchpin of your recovery. I hope you are ready, willing, and open to beginning a new phase in your trajectory like Maya. If you've taken the time to read and do the work in healing, you are slowly regaining your strength and entering a more stable space. Healing takes time, and I encourage you to stick with whatever tools you have found useful thus far for the dura-tion of this book, *and* for as much time as you require afterward. I certainly don't have you on any schedule, so please continue to be patient with yourself and vigilant with your care.

You and I are going to become very well acquainted with each other during this portion of our journey. I will be open with you and explain how understanding once saved *my* life. But the ultimate goal of understanding is for *you* to become extremely familiar with yourself. By doing so you will acquire astounding information about your mate selection and relationship behaviors. Through the pro-cess of creating your personal love map, explained in chapter 10, you will have a blueprint to decipher where, when, and how early life events influenced and even predisposed your relationship path. Once we have this information, we can better comprehend exactly why your romance ended, and what part you played in it. It's like peeling an apple to find all the answers at its core. Or, as one woman I interviewed astutely described, "Have you ever seen those large rubber-band balls? Hard bouncing balls created with hundreds of tightly woven rubber bands? That was my relationship. At the center is the love I once shared with my partner, and each rubber band represents a layer of complication we added on over time leading to the eventual demise. To heal, you've got to take off each layer and examine its meaning—no matter how big or tightly wound it is!" Sounds fun? It will be fascinating, I promise. I'm sure some of you may be a bit skeptical right now. Fear not, there is a method to my madness, and it will greatly benefit you to have an open mind and keep reading.

One of the biggest recovery mistakes I regularly see is the elimination of this critical phase, and that is a colossal mistake. If you press fast-forward, you will endanger yourself to repeat unhealthy relationship behaviors time and again. Continuing with unexamined conduct makes absolutely no sense at all, and worse, it may lead to a life of constant heartache, abandonment, and depression. Understandably, many of you, like Maya, may initially be a bit hesitant to take on this project. It's difficult after a tragedy to step back and take a candid look at yourself in the mirror. Others may think, "*My* relationship choices? *My* relationship behaviors? I didn't do anything wrong!" In the beginning stages of a breakup we tend to focus on our personal suffering, ruminate about how we've been wronged, and struggle to find coping mechanisms to get us through each day. But total recovery requires an honest inventory of both your relationship and life history. It's about asking yourself difficult questions and being open to taking some responsibility. It is hard work, but very worth it. I'm going to do you a huge favor right now and give you the secret you've been waiting for all along:

> When you work through understanding in good faith, you will emerge with every question about your breakup or divorce answered; acquire complete closure; have a fuller knowledge of yourself; and be prepared to have healthier relationships in the future. These elements will enable you to fully transform your life.

The gateway to recovery is a skillful understanding and processing of your emotions. Massive chunks of information will emerge in understanding that will allow you to finally move past your heart-ache, and, if you so desire, into new relationships that are better, safer, healthier, and extremely fulfilling. It's all right here for you. I know that you can do this, and I know it really works.

The Story vs. the History

Although it is important to identify the basic reason(s) that your relationship ended, I'm going to challenge you now to dig even deeper. I want you to become very curious about yourself and your relationship. For example, many women lament to me that their relationship ended over an affair—a very common cause of breakups. And when I ask, "What exactly does that mean?", most fire back, "Don't you know what infidelity means? He cheated on me!"

Unfortunately, in my profession, I know all too well what infidelity means. But do you really understand the full reasons behind your partner's adultery? What I'm going to help you do is peel your apples (or rubber-band balls) to search for answers to these sorts of questions. Remember that each layer represents an unresolved issue in your relationship, and each layer holds clues for you to analyze. This exercise will prepare you for our deeper work on personal love maps in chapter 10.

Let's use the image of an apple to further develop this idea. An apple is a great metaphor for any couple. Your discovery that your partner is having an affair is, in your initial unexamined explanation, the exterior of the apple. It's the way you initially view the ending of your relationship, and it's what you allow the world to see. I call it "the story."

The initial unexamined explanation for your breakup is called the story.

Now we're going to start digging toward the core for what I call the history behind your ending. The core represents you and your ex as a couple and as individuals. The core is also the most important part of an apple. It contains the seeds that will produce, with tending, new, healthy crops. Obviously new apples cannot grow if you plant bad seeds. So you've got to really inspect the core to find the good seeds to plant. Examining the core and planting the best possible seeds is highly representative of you on your journey toward enlightenment!

The history is the *underlying cause(s)* that led to the story. It is extremely important to understand both the story and the history behind your breakup. Anyone can claim a story and hang their hat comfortably on it. But the real growth comes from dissecting and understanding the history. The history reveals how you and your ex handled various aspects of your relationship such as intimacy, life stressors, and conflict resolution. But it's also the historical behavior (including personal baggage) that you *both* carried into the relationship.

The factor(s) that led to the infidelity is called the history.

These are the questions that you will be asking yourself when you search for your history:

- What was going on in my relationship over the past *few months* that may have contributed to the story?
- What was going on in my relationship over the past *few years* that may have begun a pattern that led to the the story?
- What was going on in *my life* and my character, behavior, or psyche that may have contributed to the story?

- What was going on in my *ex's* life and my ex's character, behavior, or psyche that may have contributed to the story?

Let's go through an abbreviated exercise using Maya and Nick's scenario in order to uncover some history. The Story: "My boyfriend has commitment issues." During our deeper therapy work, Maya and I explored her earlier life to hunt for buried clues. This is what we uncovered:

When Maya was thirteen her parents, who rarely got along, went through an acrimonious divorce. Her mother, an insecure, impulsive, and perpetually immature woman, had an affair that finally ended the troubled marriage. Maya describes her father as a basically good guy ("I think he wanted to rescue Mom, but he couldn't"), who finally cracked under the pressure of managing his complicated wife. Maya recalls a lot of arguing during her childhood and she often felt afraid and unsafe. Immediately after their divorce, Maya's mother picked up her children and moved from Chicago to Dallas to be near her new boyfriend. She remembers this as a terribly unhappy time.

> "My entire life turned upside down. I felt as if I lost my mother, father, and all of my friends in the blink of an eye. I had to move, change schools, and start all over again. My mother was gallivanting around and was not involved in my life as I needed her to be. I didn't see my dad nearly as much as I would have wanted. He lived far away now and traveled a lot for work. I became very depressed and withdrew into myself. I felt that no one cared, so I started thinking that maybe it was my fault—that I was unlovable."

Maya did eventually adjust to her circumstances. She made new friends, excelled in school, and left home for college to study design. A beautiful and creative girl, Maya had no problems attracting men, but today she can see that a dysfunctional pattern developed in her late teens—she became attracted to men who were complicated in their own right (like her mother), and was determined that with her good love and nurturing, she could save them (like her father). Maya admits that she lacked confidence in her relationships and, on a subconscious level, she would press for a commitment to assuage her fears and insecurities about being abandoned. Adding insult to injury, also on a subconscious level, Maya regularly picked men like Nick, who had various complexities, and these relationships never worked out. The fallout from this predicament was that her already low self-esteem was further eroding, and she'd suffer tremendous anxiety and depressive episodes when these relationships ended.

When Maya and I started digging deeper into Nick's personality structure, many interesting facts emerged. Nick didn't see his parents' marriage as a happy one either. His father could be angry, demanding, and controlling, and he felt that his mother, a victim, was trapped. He doesn't remember them having any emotional or physical connection, and basically they lived separate lives under the same roof. Nick's conclusion was that he didn't have a positive association with long-term, committed relationships. Also, he dealt with his father's overbearing personality and parenting style by completely blocking out his angry and hurt feelings. Thus he never developed much emotional intelligence, and due to this, generally lacked empathy. So as you can imagine, when Maya became upset and pressured him for a commitment, he would become avoidant and completely shut down. Then a negative engagement dance would ensue where Maya would become the prosecutor, and Nick, the avoider. This regularly put their relationship in chaos, leading Nick to feel justified in his assessment that long-term relationships were not for him (his story). After months of this pattern, which neither of them had the capacity to understand, Nick ended the relationship.

Therefore, Maya's original explanation for the breakup, "My boyfriend refused to commit," was at the time her story. But as you can see, it is not the entire story. In order for Maya to get the full picture, she must be able to answer the set of questions I proposed on pages 124–25. During our continued therapy sessions as more information emerged, we peeled even deeper toward her core, and I gently proposed that she contemplate a second set of questions, which were these:

- Did Nick really refuse to commit, or is there more there?
- If there is more, what is it?
- When did you realize that Nick wasn't ready to commit and how did you deal with it?
- What was your role in this dance, and what might you have done differently?

Now, to show you the benefit of working your way to the end of the understanding phase, after Maya has completed both her and Nick's personal love maps, comprehended how early life events influenced their relationship patterns, and fully analyzed their personality structures, which determined how they interacted in a relationship, she answered the second set of questions, which started the process of creating her history (a precursor to our work on personal love maps):

- Did Nick really refuse to commit, or is there more there? "*Yes, there is more. Nick definitely had some commitment issues stemming from his parents' awful marriage and his controlling father, but my insecurities from my early abandonments caused me to pressure him for a commitment way before either of us was ready for it. I yearned for a commitment from him, or any man, so I could feel safe and loved. It was my mission in life to find someone who wouldn't abandon me to heal my old wounds—but I regularly picked the wrong guys for this. Although this makes no logical sense, I didn't know any better, and therefore I made this same mistake over and over again.*"
- When did you realize that Nick wasn't ready to commit and how did you deal with it? "*This pattern started after we dated for about three months. I would push for a commitment because of my insecurities, and he'd pull away. Or, because of his issues, he'd pull away and I'd sense it and become afraid. Then I would become frantic, nervous, and obsessive. I'd pressure him, get angry with him, and cause problems. To give Nick some credit, he did try to point out that my behavior only made him pull away further, but I just didn't have the capacity to listen to him or change at the time. I didn't realize I was doing anything wrong, and blamed him in total for our problems.*"
- What was your role in this dance, and what might you have

done differently? "*I picked men who definitely had emotional baggage and then pressured them to commit to me. If I'd had therapy or understood my patterns earlier on, maybe I would have realized that I had these issues and worked toward healing myself. Then I would have been in a better position to pick men who didn't have issues, and I don't think I would have pressured anyone nor been so afraid of abandonment.*"

Today, Maya's Core looks like this:

THE HISTORY:

First history reason—Maya's insecurities were initially caused by an early childhood abandonment: her parents' acrimonious divorce and subsequent events.

Second history reason—Additional insecurities were caused by unresolved issues stemming from her complicated relationship with her mother, who emotionally and physically disappeared after the divorce, and her perceived abandonment from her father after she relocated.

- These unresolved issues plus her other insecurities caused her to become involved with men who were emotionally troubled, thinking she could "save" them and cure her early abandonment.
- Then she would put too much pressure on them for a commitment they were unable to make.

Third history reason—Nick's parents had an unhappy marriage. His understanding of this situation was that long-term commitment was not a good thing. Also, because he was underdeveloped emotionally, he'd further hurt and alienate Maya during their negative engagement dance by being cold and withdrawn, and not displaying any empathy.

Finally, Maya's cohesive narrative (her fully integrated, honest autobiographical account) is this:

> "My parents had an awful marriage. They were constantly arguing or upset with each other, which affected the way they parented. I never felt I got the love or attention I needed. After they split up my mother completely disappeared. She was emotionally unavailable, and my father, although well-meaning, came and went from our lives. My self-esteem wasn't great (I suffered from depression for many years because of this), and to make matters even worse, I dated men who were emotionally unavailable. Whenever I was in a relationship, I was so afraid of being broken up with that I would act controlling and put pressure on my boyfriend to be more committed to me. Obviously this was a pattern that was doomed to fail, although I didn't have the emotional awareness at the time to understand it. I kept going for these kinds of guys, hoping one of them would finally give me the love and attention I never got from my parents. Also, because of my own insecurities and abandonment fears, I would become argumentative and defensive, which only made matters worse. I didn't allow myself to see what was happening and my part in it. It was too scary for me to dig deeper, so I always just felt like a victim and blamed it on everyone else—my lovers, mother, father—but never once did I stop to take a look at my own behavior in this mess. Once I put this all together and owned it, I finally was able to fully work on my own recovery. I have a life today that is radically different from where I started from. I feel whole and much more secure. Plus I'm involved with a man who is warm, nurturing, and supportive, and I now have the ability to be in this sort of relationship without sabotaging it."

Accountability

While interviewing women for this book and in my private practice, I regularly tell Maya's story. There are a few reasons why I'm so
drawn to her tale. As I mentioned, it's a solid example of what transpires at the core of many contemporary relationships. As illustrated,
most couples will find themselves in hot water when they allow their
history to tear away at the fabric of their connection. But there are
other lessons to learn too. Maya's ability to step away from her pain
and betrayal and take an honest look at the relationship and the part
she played in its demise is incredibly impressive. In actuality, taking
personal accountability for your part in your breakup is one of the
most important steps toward complete recovery. If you do not take
the time and do an honest assessment of your own performance, insecurities, bad habits, or emotional baggage, you are destined to get
too comfortable in the victim role, and even worse, replicate similar
patterns and potential mistakes in future love affairs.

I do feel quite strongly that we all play a role in the downfall
of our relationships. Even if that role is a minor one, to be whole
again, we have to know what part we played. I have sat through numerous sessions with clients who are unwilling or unable to take
any accountability—and it's not a pretty sight. They blame everyone (including me!) for their mishaps and walk away furious, bitter,
egocentric, and untrusting. These clients regularly stop counseling
immediately after the breakup—only to return several years later
in either newly problematic relationships, with more devastating
breakups under their belt, or after years of bleak isolation. The first
question I ask them upon return is, "Do you feel that you are ready
to do the work required to figure out what goes awry in your relationships and what role you play?" As with Maya, fortunately, most
agree.

But back to Maya for a moment. Over time she was finally able
to admit her role in her breakup and how her insecurities caused
sabotaging behavior. She realized that she put an excess of pressure
on Nick and relied too much on the relationship to fill her needs,

Keeping Hope Alive

If you recall, we discussed a stage of healing called hope. I have implored you to do all you can to keep hope alive, including fantasizing about what your life may look like when you complete your entire recovery process. One woman commented to me that she keeps an image of a buoy in her mind at all times. She eloquently stated, "I had to share a bed with my ex for months before we worked out our divorce agreement and told our kids. It is torture to go through that. I used a lot of beautiful imagery to get me through each day and night. I love the sea and I would imagine myself sailing or swimming with a big, beautiful red buoy at my side. That buoy represented my life raft. I remembered that there were supports in my life (including myself), and I would get through my nightmare. Never stop wishing for better days—if you believe they'll come, they always will."

which were at that time too vast to ever be filled by any man. Others I interviewed told me similar stories about their coming to grips with accountability. Hailey's marriage ended after one year due to her husband, Rob's, infidelity. She eventually came to realize that there were many signs she chose to ignore, and that her own timeline issues came into play. "Rob came from a divorced background. His father was a major philanderer and I don't think he ever really came to terms with what a committed relationship meant—and the responsibility that comes with remaining faithful to one person. Also his mother was very controlling, and ultimately he felt trapped in the institution of marriage. I ignored much of this because my family and community put much pressure on marrying young. I was on a mission to be married and have kids—all before thirty. My own requirements made me blind to all that was happening around me."

After your understanding phase is complete, you too will be able to make meaningful statements such as Maya's and Hailey's. Believe it or not, you will find that it is quite liberating to be able to see the whole truth and be fully honest with yourself about your own accountability for the breakup. It's another recovery breakthrough, and you'll be really proud of yourself when you get there.

I get it that this task is no easy feat. It can feel quite raw, revealing, and humiliating to admit that you played a part, even if it's minuscule, to hurt or destroy something you held so dear. And if you can be a bit defensive at times, like to be right, or need to seem perfect to the world, you may have to work harder than others. But I know you can do it, and as I've said, the payoff is well worth the toil. It you don't take responsibility you won't understand the entire picture—it's as simple as that.

There is a little catch-22 with accountability that I'd like to warn you about. Although I want you to be open to taking some responsibility in order to really figure out what really went wrong, I don't want you to become *overly accountable* or blame the entire breakup on yourself. That is self-defeating and will not get you where you need to go. I have sat with a variety of women who blame themselves *in total* for their relationship failure, and it's quite destructive. It will make you very angry at yourself, which may lead to a prolonged depression and an inability to fully complete our work.

I can relate to Maya's struggles, because when I was dating I had some issues that were similar to hers. I picked complicated men and suffered the consequences of my choices. And, fortunately like Maya, with a lot of work, I fully recovered and went on to create a wonderful life for myself. You'll learn all about my relationships mistakes and the profound lessons I discovered because I've laid out my entire story and history for you in chapter 11. Because I lived through many upsetting breakups, I completely understand how challenging it can be to step away from your relationship and evaluate it with full clarity, especially when you don't yet have the tools in place that enable you to do so. This is why I am introducing you to understanding, a crucial recovery phase, to teach you how to evaluate your breakup in a new and comprehensive way. This knowledge will release you from old patterns and present you with an opportunity to completely heal. Over the next few chapters you will learn everything that you need to know about your breakup. This information will release you from the past and allow you to create a new and beautiful life for yourself. It's right up ahead, so please read on.

~~~~~~~~~~~~~~~~~~~~~~~~

Grasping the Root Causes of Your Breakup or Divorce Tips and Tools

1. The story is the socially acceptable language that we use to describe why our relationship ended. It is the skin of the apple and is initially unexamined.
2. The history, located in the core, are the underlying causes that chipped away at your relationship causing the eventual demise.
3. Your relationship ended for reasons that are both story and history in nature.
4. Understanding and owning the full history of why your relationship ended is the linchpin of your recovery.
5. In order to fully understand all implications of your ending, you have to be open, honest, and curious. You have to look for clues to analyze and dissect. You must be willing to take some accountability as well.
6. Please keep hope alive through journaling, dreaming, and visualization.

~~~~~~~~~~~~~~~~~~~~~~~~

9

The Most Common Causes of Breakups or Divorces

"I guess the short answer is that we 'grew apart,' but over time I realized it was a relationship that was doomed to fail. Although we had some things we shared in common, overall we were extremely different, and as time passed, the differences became really pronounced. I think I was in a hurry to have a boyfriend and I overlooked a bunch of things." —*Jane*

"I was desperate to marry and start a family—my parents both died when I was young. He knew this, but when it came time to go there, he chickened out. He just couldn't make the commitment. This was such a rejection of me, of everything I stood for. I should have known this would happen. I loved him, but he was extremely immature, and in the end he couldn't come through." —*Elena*

Obviously there is no simple answer to what causes the millions of breakups or divorces that occur every year. Although there are hundreds of reasons why relationships come to an end, what we are concerned about now is discovering and assessing why *your* relationship ended. Understanding this is the first clue that we need to begin our detective work.

In this chapter, we are going to review several common reasons for breakups, which will add more dimension to your story and move you toward creating your history. Some of the most universal breakup categories that we will review include:

- Infidelity
- Financial and career difficulties
- Sexual and intimacy problems
- Addictions
- Disagreement over commitment
- Quarter- or midlife crisis
- Emotional and/or physical abuse
- Parenting stress
- Incompatibility, growing apart
- Falling in love with someone's potential
- Excessive arguing, dirty fighting
- Family enmeshment

I would like you to spend some time contemplating this list in preparation for the deeper work on personal love maps in chapter 10. This is a major step forward in your quest for answers and illumination. You may see yourself or your relationship in one particular category, or discover that there are details that you identify with in quite a few. Working through each category will:

- Provide you with ample validation that you are not in this alone. You will see firsthand that many relationships end similarly to your own.

- Allow you to have a deeper understanding about why your relationship ended, and what part you and your ex played in it.

- Enable you to take accountability. This brave step will add more clues toward discovering the genesis of your and your ex's history. And the more clues you have, the more complete your personal love map will be.

There are many books out there that will simply tell you that your romance was broken, that he's done you a favor, so move on. This is not my philosophy and it will not get you where you need to be. There are countless reasons why relationships fall short, and keeping one on track is extremely hard work. There are lots of moving parts, and sometimes I think it's actually a mini-miracle when we get it right. There is a strong possibility that there were many issues or events that led to your breakup, and it's important to understand them all. I will go into a bit of detail in each category and give story and history explanations to help you flesh out your thoughts for further scrutinizing. In fact, after reviewing this list, most women report that they identify with issues in several of the categories, including various ones they had never even thought about.

Some of you may stumble upon a depiction of your relationship behavior that really resonates with you (which is good), but is painful to admit. Please remember that I've strived to create an inclusive community, and I am an equal-opportunity writer. Although I lead in most sections with mistakes your ex may have made, it is your job to think about your own behavior as well. Perhaps your affair, financial or career difficulties, or addictive behavior was part of your history, which resulted in the ending of your relationship. If that is the case, perhaps you are thinking, "My God, I really messed this up. How could I have been so stupid?" Please understand that this exercise is not designed for you to become upset or angry with yourself. I will never talk in terms of failure or blame. We're talking about honesty, accountability, and wholesome curiosity. Trust me, we all make mistakes. What's more important is to learn from them so we can understand and change our behavior patterns. That's the definition

Beware of the Green-Eyed Monster

Jealousy has the capacity to thwart any relationship. If your ex is suspicious about your friendships (male and female), whereabouts, and is regularly checking your electronic devices, he may have trust issues that go quite deep. Healthy relationships are built on mutual trust. So be wary of jealousy and don't let it be an interloper in any future relationship.

of real growth and maturity. Hindsight is twenty-twenty, but I always say that it's definitely better to have hindsight than no sight at all!

Others may feel that these particulars don't fit your exact breakup experience, and although that may be true, it is important for you to have a broad overview regarding why relationships in general run into trouble. Also, you may find something that resonates for the future, and you can remind yourself to avoid that kind of man, or beware of that type of situation or behavior when you get back out there.

Let's get reacquainted with your goals:

• Begin to fill in your story and history break-up facts after reviewing each category.

• Validate yourself; you are not in this alone. You are part of a healing community. Thousands of relationships have ended similarly to yours.

• Look at your entire apple, both exterior and core, with objectivity, and then take accountability as needed.

• Once you take accountability, give yourself a big hug. Remind yourself that you are not a failure or a bad person. Everyone makes mistakes, and we're here to learn from them, not to chastise ourselves.

• When you see the part that you played in your breakup or divorce, start thinking about the root causes of your own behavior. We will cover this in more detail in the next chapter.

• Make a commitment to learn and grow from everything you have discovered from this chapter.

• Start thinking about healthier models of engagement to use for future relationships.

This is a great section to read with pen and paper at hand. After reviewing each category, please contemplate the following questions:

• Were there elements of this issue in my relationship? If so, what were they? Describe in detail.

- What was the part that I played in this particular circumstance?
- What part did my ex play?
- What lessons have I learned?
- What might I do differently in a future relationship?

The answers to these questions are of great importance to your understanding and recovery. Don't be shy, feel free to pry, and dig right in!

Infidelity

> "It's hard to even describe the mixture of emotions I felt when my boyfriend told me he had feelings for someone else. It makes you question everything in your life. If you really trust someone, and this is how they treat you—that's a huge statement."   —*Gail*

You cannot write a book about the pain of breakups without addressing infidelity. The discovery that your partner is either emotionally or sexually involved with another is one of the most shocking and devastating experiences one can live through. Being in a relationship carries many different definitions and implications, yet the desire that your partner remain sexually faithful seems to be nearly universal. Infidelity, and the baggage that comes with it, is an extremely difficult issue to move past, and it is one of the top reasons why relationships end. I've sat through many tearful discussions while women describe the shock, fury, and heartbreak that their exes' indiscretions caused them.

If you are reading this book there is a good chance that your relationship ended over some form of infidelity. If you were cheated on, you may have a more difficult recovery ahead of you. You will vacillate between feeling betrayed, astonished, ashamed, humiliated, despondent, full of rage, vengeful, and overly accountable. The deceit of infidelity can tend to go on and on, and many men lie for a long time before coming clean. From the moment you suspect your lover is involved with someone, until he actually admits and confesses the wrongdoing (and many don't), is an extremely distressing time. And if you know the woman who he is involved with, or if she is a friend, that double deception cuts like a knife. Some women recovering from the aftermath of infidelity describe having trust issues lasting quite some time. Trust is one of the cornerstones of any healthy relationship, and once that is shattered, we tend to question everything in our existence.

Many use infidelity as a catalyst to get them out of a relationship. They may be losing interest or becoming discontented with the relationship or themselves, but are not motivated to work toward a repair and are conflicted about leaving. Some don't know how to express themselves to their partners, are afraid of the actual breakup, and are scared of being alone. Others actually do worry about causing pain to their wives or girlfriends by expressing their unhappiness. Suddenly an affair can seem quite appealing to some who would rather venture into a new relationship instead of figuring out how to salvage or exit the old. This is a very problematic coping mechanism.

Figuring out the "history" causes behind your infidelity is going to take some extra assessing on your part. Not all men fully understand the implications behind their affair, and many are unwilling to give full disclosure and accounts. There are numerous explanations why people cheat. Some of the most common reasons are:

- Feeling emotionally disconnected and lonely in your primary relationship.
- A decrease in sex, or sexual dissatisfaction (including boredom).
- Commitment fears (feeling trapped in a relationship).
- Low self-esteem (needing your ego to be propped up by someone else).
- Feeling unimportant or undervalued by your partner.
- The joy of a conquest and challenge (especially for high-testosterone men).
- Sexual addiction (specifically if prostitution or multiple partners are involved).

• A personality disorder, such as narcissism, which makes cheating appealing and easy. Appealing because narcissists need constant ego-stroking, and easy because they don't feel much guilt and have a limited capacity for empathy.

• Feeling too constrained in one's life and needing to be reckless.

• Quarter- or midlife crisis (needing to know that others still find you sexually appealing).

• Career crisis. If your identity is wrapped up in your career and it's not going well, some look for a quick fix to feel good about themselves.

• Taking an emotional vacation from life's stressors.

• Coming from a family where a parent was a philanderer.

Scores of women internalize their ex's infidelity and blame themselves, which is a big mistake. Sadly I've heard too many women exclaim, "What was wrong with *me*? Why wasn't *I* good enough, pretty enough, sexy enough?" Please be careful not to go this route—it will accomplish nothing useful.

Financial and Career Difficulties

Everyone tends to have his or her own personal philosophy when it comes to finance, and it's not unusual for two people to fall in love with one being a "saver" and the other a "spender." Conversations about money can bring out the worst in folks. The person who is asking his or her lover to be more prudent with spending is often called "controlling" or "cheap," and a partner who enjoys carefree living is called "immature" or "irresponsible." Then there are the couples who jointly spend away, and eventually find themselves in whopping debt—putting intense strain on their relationship.

Prolonged unemployment and/or limited or reduced income can cause the loss of esteem, depression, substance abuse, emotional and sexual withdrawal, finger-pointing, fighting, and infidelity. Adrianna came to see me because her marriage was faltering due to her husband's job loss more than a year ago. She tearfully portrayed the toll it had taken on each of them and on their relation-

For Millennials . . .

As painful as breakups are, not all relationships are meant to last. In fact, the younger you are when you get married, the higher the probability you will divorce later on. You have to cut your teeth on a few committed relationships before you are ready to settle down. This will help you learn what your type is and what your relationship criteria are, and it will help you see if you have any history issues that need addressing. As you mature and really get to know yourself, you acquire a better dating radar *and* a greater capacity to be healthy in a love bond. That's certainly something worth waiting for.

ship. "I've gone through every emotion. I deeply feel sad for Jonah. He loved his job and got most of his esteem from it. He's looked for work, but hasn't been able to find anything. I fluctuate between empathy, helplessness—because I can't solve his problem—and fury. I'm working like a dog to support our family, I'm exhausted, and now he's very depressed, and that's influenced both his continued job search and our marriage. Some days I think, 'Well if you're home all day why aren't you cleaning the house or making dinner?', and if he catches me in one of those moods we really go at it. It has deeply affected our connection, and I'm starting to lose a lot of respect for him. Then I feel depressed too, and worse, trapped."

These days many women feel like Adrianna. Men put so much of themselves into their careers that if they are unhappy in or in jeopardy of losing their job, or questioning their career choice, or if their business is off, or if they're unemployed, they can go into a tailspin. When their ability to provide has been curtailed, it can send them to a really dangerous place, which can make them do all sorts of foolish things. Jennifer's husband abandoned her and their children when a downturn in his business led to a midlife crisis. He questioned everything in his life, and ended up leaving her to start all over again.

Without a doubt, financial and career stressors can take a heavy toll, causing much calamity and many new and/or older unresolved history issues to crop up. Getting through these problems requires a lot of hard work and dedication to the relationship by both parties.

Sexual and Intimacy Problems

We all think we know them: that fantasy couple that has everything, completes each other's sentences, and has continual hot sex. Now, welcome to the real world, where a high percentage of partnerships have sexual and/or intimacy issues. If you're exiting a lengthy relationship, you already know how challenging it can be to keep a sexual connection going strong year upon year. Sex can help keep a relationship alive and the lack of sex can burn it out.

Many individuals and couples who are experiencing sexual difficulties earnestly ask me why it's important to have a sexual bond with their partner. They often describe their relationship as "best friends," "familial," or "sibling-like," and tend to accept that attraction and sex wanes with the passage of time. Regrettably it is this philosophy that derails plenty of good unions. Sex really is an integral part of any romance. It's the one thing that unequivocally separates friendship from love. In difficult times you need some genuinely good experiences to share, and if you can see your partner as a source of pleasure, it's very positive. It's important to have sex—and even better to have good sex. Here's why:

- It helps you to feel more connected to your partner.
- It makes you feel cared for, attached, and comforted.
- It's a nonverbal experience that helps you communicate with your lover in an entirely different way.
- It's fun.

Some of the more common physiological or psychological sex issues that I see are:

- Low sex drive: when a partner has little or no interest in sex
- Erection or orgasm difficulties, or painful intercourse

- Complications caused by illness or medication
- Menopause
- History of trauma, such as sexual abuse
- Fear of intimacy
- Overuse of pornography (a biggie these days), masturbation, or sex addiction

These are generally treatable problems, but we are often ashamed, intimidated, or unaware of how to get help. And of course when you don't get help and let these issues fester, an individual problem suddenly becomes a major issue for the couple.

Other factors that can disrupt a sexual connection are:

- Incompatible sexual drives, which is extremely common— one partner wants it more than the other, or one partner wants more variety or experimentation than the other
- Losing physical attraction or respect for your partner
- Not making enough time for sex
- Letting life's difficulties—especially work, financial, or parenting stress—interfere with desire
- Relationship problems seeping into the sexual connection
- Infidelity

Sex strongly supports a love connection and for many couples it's part of the glue that holds them together. If you have sex issues and you work through them, it creates a collaborative model, which improves your sex life, communication skills, and your relationship. Conversely, if you lack a healthy sex life and begin to detach, it can be detrimental to your overall relationship.

Addictions

"Seemingly before my eyes my boyfriend turned from a casual drinker to an alcohol abuser. It was just terrible and caused havoc in our lives. I wanted to help him. I felt responsible. I eventually had to leave him, which was the right thing for me, but it was so hard." —*Nancy*

Addictions are ever present in our culture, and there are many things to get addicted to in today's world. Alcohol and drugs, although very prevalent, are not always the top dogs. Addictions to work, pornography, sex, gambling, and spending can also rip through a relationship, causing terrible repercussions. I've worked with quite a few women over the years who come for counseling due to their partner's addictive behavior, and it's a tangled web to sort through. Most addicts are steeped in denial, refusing to admit that their behavior is problematic. Often because of this a struggle ensues, causing the nonaddicted partner to feel powerless, hopeless, and furious. Many involved with addicts also lean on denial as their own coping strategy. Some described to me how they rationalized or compartmentalized their partner's behavior to avoid rocking the boat.

Nadia, the daughter of an alcoholic, found herself dating a man who was an addict himself. "I always knew that Sam drank too much, but I really thought that I could straighten him out. He'd been single for a while, and I convinced myself that a committed relationship would make him want to drink less. Sam used alcohol to both celebrate and unwind—and he just wouldn't give it up. We'd constantly fight about this, and I thought, 'If he really loves me, why won't he change?' I started feeling undesired and that messed me up. Eventually I left him and attended some Al-Anon meetings. I learned that my mom's problems with alcohol left me vulnerable to getting involved with an addict. I thought I could help Sam, and now I know that you can't make someone want to change. They have to have the motivation to do it themselves."

Recently much attention has been focused on sex and pornography addictions. Some addicts excessively use pornography, while others gradually move on to more integrated forms such as text, phone, or computer sex. Others become compulsive cheaters or visit escorts. Finding out that your partner is involved in this shady lifestyle can be as shocking as the discovery of an affair, if not worse.

Several women I spoke with described uncovering their partners' sex addictions as completely devastating experiences. Obviously the vast complications and implications of this situation throw any couple into crisis.

I see more and more work addictions these days, where one or both people are putting their careers and billable hours before everything, including each other. One disgruntled woman who lamented that her wealthy CEO husband was rarely at home told me that her sister remarked to her one day, "I would love to have your shoe collection—but I wouldn't want to be in your shoes."

Addiction takes a huge toll on the nonaddicted partners. On one hand they really want to help their lovers, and when they are unable to, they alternate between experiencing rage at the addict and, dangerously, anger directed toward themselves. If your partner's addictive behavior derailed your union, as much as I empathize with any woman's suffering, perhaps you dodged a bullet. Get the help that you need to understand the addiction and what part if any you played in it, and do your best to move forward.

Disagreement over Commitment Timeline

A common break-up reason for dating couples involves issues surrounding commitment. My paternal grandmother told me a story of how my grandfather, several years her elder and a confirmed bachelor, didn't want to wed, until he saw her dancing with another man. Men were traditionally known for attempting to avoid marriage. Today, however, I'm delighted to see many women also delaying marriage, instead focusing on their careers and themselves. Because of this trend, some women are marrying later, leaving men to push for a commitment, which is a nice role reversal!

Yet I do get a rash of women in my practice desperate for me to help them help their boyfriends "put a ring on it." Some of these relationships are potentially good ones, yet their mates have a commitment issue. These problems are varied and some are far more ingrained and deep-seated than others. It is very important to understand how serious these matters are, and whether your boyfriend has the desire and wherewithal to overcome them. Issues that are less entrenched and easier to surmount are:

- Peter Pan syndrome—wanting to hold on to youth for as long as possible
- Fear of loss of independence
- Not feeling secure enough in a career
- Greener pasture syndrome—is there someone better out there?
- Discomfort with monogamy
- Apprehension about becoming a parent

Other problems that are more psychological in nature can be trickier to tackle, especially if your partner is unaware of the root causes. Some examples are:

- Deeply affected by parents' bad marriage or divorce, leaving them with an aversion to commitment
- Early death or abandonment by a parent
- Having a past relationship end poorly (especially if adultery or deception was involved), which resulted in unresolved trust issues
- Fear of intimacy
- Insecurities, low self-esteem, general trust issues
- Selfishness—not wanting to give up too much for another

Unfortunately, what I regularly see is that couples (especially young ones) lack the skills to effectively discuss these issues, get to the root of the problems, and create effective solutions. Many of these troubles are solvable, but it does take patience, honest discussion, and work by both parties. A regular mishap I see is that many women tend to hyperfocus on a partner's inability to commit (without understanding the full ramifications of why), and pressure or threaten him to step it up. Paradoxically this scenario creates ample stress, incessant arguing, or avoidance—resulting in the already phobic male becoming even more phobic, thus losing the will to continue. I've often seen these relationships derail with the man saying, "I don't have commitment issues—we just have a bad relationship!"

A great commitment story was once told to me by a lovely woman, a photographer, whom I became acquainted with at my local nail salon. Jillian met Ben several years ago. They worked in the same building, noticed each other, and thought the other was attractive. One day, coincidentally, they were set up by friends. Ben was four years younger than she, and in no hurry to wed. "Ben and I really fell in love and had a great romance. I was thirty-three when I met him, and knew I wanted to be married and eventually have kids. But that was *my* problem, not his, and I was not going to rush something that was really good, or blame him for a commitment he wasn't ready for. After two years of serious dating I decided to discuss my feelings with him about our future. I said, 'Ben, I really adore you and could see spending the rest of my life with you. However, you have told me that you're not ready to get married, and that puts me in a bit of a predicament. I'm thirty-five, I really want children, and if you feel that you aren't ready to marry me by next year, as much as it's going to kill me, I'm going to have to walk away.'

"That's really all I said. I told him it was his choice and I was not going to bring it up again or pressure or blame him. This wasn't a trick or a ploy, but I knew I needed to be upfront and honest. If he couldn't get past his fears, I did need to move on—as difficult as it would be. I decided I would not bring it up again—the ball was in his court. I repeatedly reminded myself that I'd be OK no matter how the dice rolled because I had been true to myself."

I love this story and share it with anyone in this predicament. Jillian had enough security to let Ben work through his timeline issues, *and* enough self-worth to walk away if he was unable to step up. They eventually wed and now have two beautiful children, but that's not what's important because no matter how you spin it, Jillian was the winner.

If you were with someone who couldn't commit, and you tried in earnest to be supportive and patient and he couldn't move past his fears, you owe it to yourself to walk away. I know how hard this is, especially if there was love there. Unfortunately, I see too many women waiting for years and years for their boyfriends to commit, and this predicament has the potential to break apart any relationship. Generally what transpires is that the women become hurt and irritated, and their partners feel guilty and pressured—and a struggle commences. Many women internalize their partner's issues to mean that they're not good enough, and this takes a huge toll.

You deserve relationship happiness, and guess what, there are plenty of men out there who are not afraid to commit and would adore having you in their life.

Quarter- Midlife Crisis

It used to be just called "midlife crisis," but it's happening earlier and earlier these days. A life crisis is actually an identity crisis, and both men and women undergo them in profound ways. An older life crisis can be brought on by the fear or effects of aging, experiencing a milestone birthday, the death of a parent, and children leaving the nest. Younger people report them too, often brought on by various life challenges or a major stressor. These predicaments can cause one to take stock of his or her life and question if he or she should be in a different place (or with a different partner).

Alex noticed certain changes in her husband, who was turning forty. "He started working out, dying his hair, using Botox, and partying more. He was deathly afraid of aging, which I knew, so I didn't take it so seriously. Shortly thereafter he did start an emotional affair, which ended our marriage. I blamed it on myself for a long time, until I realized that this was his issue. *He* was afraid of aging, *he* wasn't happy in his career, *he* wanted to party more and not grow up. This was all a huge escape for him—and ultimately I realized that I'm better off for it. My mistake—I didn't notice earlier how insecure and unhappy he was. There were some signals, and I brushed them away. Next time around I will get involved with a real man. Someone who's not afraid of facing real life."

Symptoms of a life crisis can be:

- Looking for an adventure or escape from life's routines
- Feeling bored with people and events that may have interested you before
- Questioning choices and lifestyles that provided you with happiness in the past
- Sudden changes in mood or behavior
- Being more impulsive and less responsible
- Abrupt dissatisfaction with career
- Increased usage in alcohol and/or drugs

I've witnessed several men having life crises due to effects of the recent recession. Fear of job or income loss, or a downturn in business can make a certain type of man reevaluate his entire life. Often these reevaluations are not done with a level head and many perfectly good romances get thrown away because of this.

Life is hard, and in order to survive we have to create healthy coping mechanisms. That's what friends, therapists, and the gym are for! If your relationship ended over a life crisis and your partner didn't have the desire or the tools to see it through, well, try your best to turn your tragedy into a comedy. Truly, it's his loss, and quick fixes never solve anything—they always backfire.

Abuse

"I never would have considered my boyfriend abusive, but he was constantly jealous and always accusing me of flirting or cheating. He'd check my phone and my e-mail. He'd tell me that he couldn't trust me, that I was a liar, and he would never listen to my side of the story. We argued regularly over this. When we broke up I was a wreck. Then my friends and family all started coming forward and telling me that they thought it was an abusive relationship and he was an abuser. It took me a while to figure it all out, but once you go there you never go back—at least I certainly won't." —*Valerie*

Suzanne is sobbing in my office describing her latest breakup with her on-again, off-again boyfriend. "Roberto did it again. He accused me of cheating after he read a text on my phone from a guy friend. When I try to defend myself, to tell my side of the story, he twists my words around. After a while I don't even know my own truth and I start agreeing with what he says. Then he nails me, saying it's proof that I'm a liar. And here's the sick part—I end up believing him and apologizing. I feel so crazy—I don't even know what I'm doing any longer!"

It's extremely tragic that with all the information available about emotional abuse, women are still getting themselves involved in these dangerous relationships. Emotional abuse is described as a behavior that is used to control or overpower another human through the use of manipulation, fear, guilt, shame, control, force, or intimidation. Its spectrum ranges from blatant behavior—such as angry tirades (which can become physical), insults, threats, name-calling, and sexual demands—to more latent conduct such as constant criticism or disapproval, jealousy, and manipulation. Often the abuser insists he is always right, refuses to listen to your logic, and tells you that he's doing you a favor by giving you guidance, and if you listen to him, you'll be better off. Another problem is that abusive men can be quite charming and seem very confident in the early stages of dating. They wine and dine and shower you with gifts and affection, which really hooks you in. This changes shortly after they think they've won you over, and then the nightmare begins. This destructive syndrome often makes you feel brainwashed, causing an inability to decipher fact from fiction. These men slowly chip away at your self-worth, making you feel insignificant and afraid to leave. After all, he's told you that you'll never find anyone to love you like he loves you (or anyone at all for that matter)—and sadly, many women begin to believe this deception.

In actuality, most abusers are extremely insecure men with deep-rooted personality disorders such as narcissism or sociopathy. Many come from families where they were unloved, subjected to extreme criticism, abandoned, or abused. They have excessive fears of being deserted in relationships, and thus their main goal is to do everything in their power to prevent you from leaving. This is why they methodically chip away at your life and esteem—hoping to imprison you in the relationship.

Most women do not even realize what is happening around them and therefore get caught in their own unconscious dance of hanging on for dear life—hoping that their boyfriend/husband will change his behavior and return to the earlier days of their courtship when he was charming, loving, and attentive. Others tend to feel sorry for these guys and stick around trying to help them. These tumultuous relationships tend to have a lot of peaks and valleys, which include regular breakups and reunifications. And during the reunification period, the abusers can be on very good behavior, which hooks you in again.

Here are some of the most prevalent signs that you are involved in an emotionally and/or physically abusive relationship:

• Your partner may have a temper, and is controlling, critical, and jealous. He puts you down a lot, threatens you, tells you to dress a certain way, complains that you don't do a good job, that you're lucky to have him, and that you'll never find someone as good as him.

• He demands sex and humiliates you if you won't acquiesce. Or he tells you that you are lousy in bed, or makes you engage in sexual acts that you are not comfortable with.

• During arguments he curses at you, calls you terrible names, and brings up "awful" things you've supposedly done to him in the past.

• He's exceedingly jealous and looks through your phone, e-mail, and texts to catch you flirting, or having sex with someone else.

• You are becoming insecure, anxious, depressed.

• Your insecurities make you doubt your own abilities, and you really do start to wonder if you can make it without him, and if maybe he is right.

• You lose your voice and become timid, afraid of saying something that will cause an argument.

• You find yourself defending him to friends and family, or making excuses for his behavior. Or you completely stop talking about him to others.

• You keep hoping things will get better, and he'll return to his "nice self," or that you can help him, change him.

• You feel trapped and unable to leave the relationship.

• Your partner has physically hurt you—even if it only happened once.

If you see yourself or your ex in this description, you're going to have to figure out exactly what "history" reasons got you there *and* kept you in this sort of relationship. Your self-esteem is going to be extremely diminished and you're going to have to work hard to rebuild it and get back on your feet. Pay close attention when designing your personal love map discussed in the next chapter to figure out why your ex behaved as he did, but more important, how and why you became involved in this situation.

Parenting Stress

"Although we made a joint decision that I would stay home with our kids, my husband acted like I had 'The Life of Riley'—and it really pissed me off. I swear he changed a diaper maybe five times during our marriage. I tried to do it all, but I guess I was falling short. We argued a lot and became resentful of each other. He felt I put the kids before him and I felt he expected too much from me. Regrettably, this dynamic, which we didn't know how to improve, sunk us." —*Carolyn*

Last week I received a call from a lovely couple that I counseled several years back. I had helped them through some adjustments as newlyweds and they had completed their therapy in strong shape. I was on their e-mail list and received updates on their adorable daughter, born eighteen months ago. They had been exceedingly happy when they welcomed Ruby into their family, yet it was no surprise when they contacted me in crisis. Exhausted, both working long hours, with limited funds for child care, they were running out of steam and losing their connection. They were fighting over roles, playing the blame game, and becoming very resentful of each other.

They described a recent argument they had while rushing to a family event. He criticized her for not being on time and she fought back. "Why is it *my* responsibility to get everything ready for Ruby? I had to shower, get dressed, do my hair, pack her bag, make her lunch, and wrap the gift. What were you doing all that time?"

I work with many couples who come into counseling over the stress of keeping a marriage solid while parenting. They complain that their relationship has changed, feel disconnected from each other, and say that sex is often limited or nonexistent. The romance has disappeared and they protest that the love they once shared has been transferred to the children. They are eager to return to the connection and passion of their earlier courtship, but don't know how.

Many couples struggle over roles. Women regularly drive themselves batty trying to do it all. I've seen really great husbands who truly want to help out, but complain that their wives insist on doing everything themselves, or become critical if they don't complete tasks to their standards. These common problems do produce friction. It's no wonder that a brand-new study out of Ohio State University says when it comes to coparenting young children, couples argue less when the father is less involved in daily caregiving duties!

Predicaments arise when couples lack the communication skills to effectively articulate their feelings and create meaningful solutions to their issues. As you know from our negative engagement dance discussion, many couples communicate in ineffectual ways, causing minor problems to intensify. Often issues that are quite solvable can become overblown when we lack the ability, resources, or commitment to address them.

Some of the most common parenting stressors are:

- Different parenting philosophies
- Putting children before the marriage
- Inequality or issues over roles
- Working moms feeling resentful because they have too much responsibility for both the kids and running the household
- Stay-at-home moms wanting their husbands to help out more when they are home
- Husbands becoming resentful because they want more time, attention, and sex from their wives
- Lack of quality time, sex, or intimacy
- Stress over a child who has health, learning, or behavioral issues
- Putting career(s) before family

If your marriage was affected by parenting stress, try to really understand exactly what happened and why. When you grasp what went wrong it will help you to be a better parent, a better ex, and a better partner in future relationships.

Incompatibility and Growing Apart

"We started out like two peas in a pod, and with the passage of time, our connection severed. We shared the same bed, but there was an ocean between us. We grew apart for many reasons, some of them solvable, but we just didn't understand the repercussions of our behavior, and eventually it was too late—we had fallen out of love."   —*Carrie*

We all know the saying "opposites attract," but in actuality, successful couples need to have more in common than not. I've seen many adorable couples with major dissimilarities come together with a "you complete me" philosophy, only to eventually resent the opposing habits that they once thought were so cute. For these couples, issues of disparity can range from the mundane such as housekeeping or how to spend the weekends, to more serious ones such as different philosophies over career, extracurricular interests, child rearing, spending, religion, politics, and life goals.

Unless you are like Narcissus and fall in love with your own reflection, you have to make some compromises to be in any relationship. It is true that the more you have in common and share, the greater your chances at success. But healthy couples know how to make their differences work. Success comes down to compromise, good communication, and balance. I want couples to balance each other and accept the other's quirks and differences. Problems arise when we judge, preach, nag, criticize, or argue over these discrepancies. For example, I'm a "shoot first, then ask questions later" person, and my husband is a contemplator. He's clean, I'm neat. I'm a Pollyanna, and he has a tendency toward pessimism. At times these opposing behaviors conflict, but we've come to respect our differences and work with them. We focus more on where we connect than on where we disconnect, and that is certainly one of the key ingredients for any solid union.

All couples suffer some growing pains when their kids leave the house, but the ones that fare best have kept up their connection and embrace their mature years with vim and vigor. On the other hand, couples that have grown apart during child rearing may take a fresh look at each other and not like (or recognize) what they see. Fernanda, a fifty-year-old grandmother from Los Angeles, explained that by the time her thirty-year marriage ended she barely knew her husband. "John and I definitely grew apart. I was so young when I married him—what did I know? There were differences, which I either overlooked or tried to work with for many years. After raising four kids and spending almost half a life with each other, I realized we had so little in common."

Have I mentioned that relationships take work? If you put in your time, make sure you have plenty in common, respect the differences, and continually try to keep the friendship, intimacy, and sex strong, then you have a decent chance of success. But when the differences overwhelm the similarities, when we chip away at the foundation, it becomes too difficult to keep the love connection going for even a few years, let alone for perpetuity.

Falling in Love with Someone's Potential

"He always tried to get me to change, to be perfect. There was a real Pygmalion quality to our relationship. When we were first together, and I was young, I thought it was sweet. But over time I realized it was controlling and awful. I wanted him to accept me, to love me for who I was, not for his vision of what a woman should be." —*Christie*

Another tricky problem I see is becoming involved with someone and trying to get him to change. In other words, falling in love with someone's potential. We all know the saying "Behind every great man is a great woman" (which, of course, is true), and I do see many intelligent women fall for someone thinking he's a work in progress, or that if he only changed a little, he'd be perfect. That's all well and good if the transformation you're hoping for occurs, but what happens if it doesn't? It's one thing to go through his closet or make him buy new jeans or lose the cologne, but another entirely to get someone to shed his genuine nature. What does that really say to your lover? If you change, I'll love you, and if you don't, I'll leave you? This pattern is not beneficial, and worse, it's doomed to fail because you will be falling in love with something or someone who may not even exist.

Being in love with your lover's potential is really like falling for someone else. What often happens is that you desire to turn him into your ideal man, and in the process you overlook who he really is at heart and what he is or isn't capable of becoming. Danielle had a habit of dating very unemotional, rational men, only to think that the love of a good woman could bring out their cuddly side. This predicament caused her ample grief and disappointment. Yes, these men were brilliant and accomplished, but they were completely unable to provide her with the comfort, connection, and love that she craved. And not understanding her history or personal love map, she became entrenched in this pattern. She would repeatedly fall for this type yet regularly criticize them for all their "bad behavior." In turn, her boyfriends felt befuddled and insulted—they really didn't know any other way to engage and thought they were doing a good job until her complaints began. This resulted in much arguing and many breakups, which she chalked up to "there are no good men out there." Eventually she figured it out, changed directions, and started dating men who were more able to fill her needs.

Real love is not about trying to change someone. I want people to fall in love and accept each other for who they really are. If the bar is set too high and we're hoping for someone to change behaviors or characteristics—some that are quite innate—troubles arise. After all, you and your partner deserve to be loved for who you are, not for whom you hope the other will become.

The Bickersons

When I was a child, my family vacationed with another family whose natural style of engagement was arguing. The wife always had a scowl on her face and regularly barked orders at her husband. He in turn would bite back hard, and they'd be off to the races. This bizarre repartee was their natural style of communication. My siblings and I would howl with laughter as they turned a simple evening meal or a day at Disneyland into a wrestling match. We called them "The Bickersons," and I was not surprised to learn of their divorce decades later.

Over the years I've had many different incarnations of the Bickersons in my practice. These types of couples, who argue better than they get along, rarely see eye to eye. Someone always has to be right or needs to get in the last word. One partner is often hurt, sulking, or refuses to talk in order to punish his or her mate, and the other is generally pissed and making passive-aggressive (or aggressive) commentary. These couples can go days, weeks, and at times months, holding grudges and being infuriated with the other. Some actually do love each other, and for them this style of engagement is sport. In others there is a real dysfunction in how they connect, which can border on mistreatment and even abuse. When Bickersons fight, which they regularly do, they engage in harmful and injurious behaviors that I call "dirty fighting." Nothing positive comes from this type of negative engagement, and worse, it can cause irrevocable damage. My definition of dirty fighting is:

- Disrespecting, embarrassing, criticizing, or marginalizing your partner
- Name-calling, using insults, cursing
- Constant interrupting
- Refusing to listen or validate
- Becoming defensive or aggressive (losing your temper or screaming)
- Threatening
- Publicly airing grievances about your relationship and partner
- Bringing up events from the past that have nothing to do with the argument at hand
- Tit for tat ("You're mad at me for not cleaning the house? You never clean the house!")
- Button pushing, teasing, or imitating

Psychologist Dr. John Gottman, who has studied more than a thousand married couples, claims that there are four behaviors that will predict within 94 percent of the demise of a relationship. He calls these behaviors "The Four Horsemen of the Apocalypse." Most Bickersons engage in these traits, which are:

- **Criticism.** Repeatedly attacking your partner's personality or character rather than focusing on the actual behavior that bothers you and discussing it in a mature and effective fashion.
- **Contempt.** Attacking your partner's sense of self with the intent to cause harm. Openly disrespecting them. This includes name-

calling and cursing, hostile behavior or body language (eye rolling), and put-downs.

• **Defensiveness.** Needing to defend yourself whenever you perceive your partner is criticizing you. Always disagreeing with what he is saying, or rebutting his complaint with one of your own.

• **Stonewalling.** Withdrawing from the relationship, refusing to discuss something, or physically disappearing.

All couples have arguments, and that is perfectly normal. It is not the conflict per se that sinks a relationship, it's how the disagreement is handled. When conflicts are poorly handled and dirty fighting leads the way, this destructive behavior has the potential to cause great damage to the relationship and to the individuals involved.

I spend a lot of time teaching my clients how to fight. If you identify with any of these traits, you'll be doing yourself a huge favor when you figure out why you engage this way and make an agreement to ameliorate the behavior. Doing so will enable you to be more successful in all relationships—not just romances.

Family Enmeshment

Another common predicament I see, especially with younger couples, is the inability to set healthy boundaries with their family of origin. If you consider your mother or sister your "best friend," how do you prevent that relationship from fusing into your romance?

For example, Zoe initially described her husband's relationship with his family as the story behind their divorce. And upon further scrutiny, she discovered the history. "Graham considered his father and brother his best friends. The majority of our free time was spent with his family. We spent every single summer weekend at their house, and whenever I complained, he'd be like, 'What's the matter? You hate my family!' I didn't hate his family, but I wanted some time alone, and he would never grant me that request. Then I did start to resent him—and them. They were just as bad as him, and never realized that a young marriage needs time to develop and grow. I suspect that they were all insecure and needy people, and because of this they had no concept whatsoever of healthy boundaries."

It's wonderful to be close to your family, and when you grow up in a loving household it gives you a better chance of happiness and success in life. However, when couples join and form mature romantic unions, it is important to examine the status of the relationships they have with their families. When we enter into a serious commitment or marriage, family roles and statuses may need to reverse. What that means is that the couple now becomes each other's *nuclear family*, and the family of origin turns into the *extended family*. This fresh setup allows for the new couple to become each other's main confidant and it fosters intimacy—important components in a healthy relationship.

Most of these problems can be worked through with good communication and compromise. If this resonates with you, you'll be doing yourself a world of good if you start to reevaluate your definition of healthy boundaries in all relationships.

What Does Your Core Look Like?

After reading this chapter, quite a few of you have probably drawn apples that could easily fill an entire shopping cart—and that's a good thing! It means that you are putting together all the pieces, analyzing what worked and stopped working in your relationship, and being honest with yourself. Upon reviewing their apples and deciphering the story and history behind the ending of their relationships, most women inform me that they actually feel enlightened *and* lightened. I hope you were able to see and comprehend aspects of your broken relationship that you didn't previously grasp. Perhaps you were even able to take some accountability and think about what changes you may need to make in the future. Doing this work will definitely help you to move forward, examine old habits, and enable you to engage in enhanced relationships in the years to come. Remember that hard work always pays off. I guarantee you it will.

The Most Common Causes of Breakups or Divorces Tips and Tools

1. There are countless reasons why relationships end. There are lots of moving parts, and keeping a relationship intact takes a great deal of hard work.

2. It's important to have an education about why relationships in general end. It will help you to analyze what went wrong in yours, and to think about what you want or don't want in future relationships.

3. The lessons you will learn by understanding why *your* relationship ended will inspire you to change behavior, change course, and engage in much healthier relationships in the future.

4. Validate yourself—you are not alone. Millions of relationships have ended with similarities to your own.

10

Why We Love Who We Love

Understanding Your Personal Love Map

> "My father was an alcoholic and my mom, an enabler. For over twenty years I dated alcoholics, repeating that same pattern. It felt so normal to me that I didn't even stop to think that I had other choices, or there was another way of living my life." —*Angela*

My mother's parents had a very complicated relationship that included a divorce and remarriage to each other—way before that was fashionable. Although equally special, together they were like oil and water. Several years after my beloved grandfather's passing, I recall asking my grandmother a question that I had always pondered. "Grandma," I said, "why did you fall in love with Pops?" Well into her eighties, she paused, smiled, and replied, "Your grandfather, he was *so* handsome."

During my interviews for this book, I asked every woman the same question. "What made you fall in love with your ex?" No matter how bereft or angry these women were, no matter how many years had passed or tears had been shed since their split, when the question was posed, they stopped and let their minds wander back to a place that they will never forget. Answers ranged from "he had the bluest eyes," "his curious mind," "his infectious smile," and "he made me laugh," to "I admired his ambition," "he was kind," and, "he was a great dancer."

The mind is a funny thing. Not one person replied, "he was controlling, like my mother," or, "he was a philanderer, like my father."

No one said, "My father never paid attention to me, so it makes complete sense that I fell for someone who was emotionally removed." Not a soul muttered, "I need to rescue people because my sister died of cancer," or, "I grew up rearing my siblings, so it's no wonder I fell in love with a man-child."

Over the past thirty years, women in the United States have become nearly autonomous when it comes to making relationship decisions. We are earning our own money, enjoying our independence, and many are delaying (or eliminating) marriage and childbirth. We are freer today than we've ever been to make our own choices regarding career, lifestyle, and love.

One would think that with all our self-reliance and awareness about healthy relationship behavior, picking the right partner would be easier than it's ever been. Still, time and again remarkable women tell me stories about making extremely poor matches and being devastated when these relationships fail. Many bemoaned, "I knew from the beginning that something was wrong," or, "I am guilty of purposely ignoring signs." Others remarked, "It was over years ago, but I hung on hoping he would change, or that it would get better."

Paradoxically, with all of our newfound independence and relationship knowledge, the divorce and break-up statistics remain quite high. Each year one million women will divorce in the United States. In addition to that staggering number, there are 600,000 annual separations from cohabitating partners, plus millions of breakups from nonmarital relationships. Exposing what lies underneath this disparity was a large part of my motivation for writing this book. In my own dogged hunt for clues I pondered the following questions:

• What is the magic formula in our psyche that determines why we love who we love?

• What takes place in our love drive that makes so many smart people make relationship choices that aren't necessarily in their best interest?

• What makes us incapable of reading the signs and viewing our behavior, our ex, our love union, and our breakup with greater clarity?

There are many ingredients that go into determining who sparks our interest and ultimately who we pick as partners. Love, attraction, and pheromones are certainly key components, but there are countless others that dictate the choices that we make. This chapter is about fully exploring what life events transpired that both formed you and led you to pick your ex as your love partner. I will show you that from the beginning of your life, countless little nuances merged together, which led you exactly into the arms of the man that you are currently mourning. There are many coincidences in life, but few coincidences in love. You might have met him by chance, but there is a reason you chose him among others, and there are other reasons yet that determined the trajectory of your relationship, breakup, and grieving process.

In order to figure out where and how all these mechanisms fit together, we are going to need some very good detective work. Based on the last two chapters, you are getting quite skilled at looking for signs. If you've created your apples, examined the story and the history of your breakup, and taken a bit of accountability, you are halfway there. Now it's time to go even deeper and examine what genetic/biological, social/cultural, and psychological factors from your earlier life influenced your partner selection, romance, and grieving period. I call this exercise "creating your personal love map."

From the moment you were born your personal love map was formed. This map contains data that are unique to you, and deciphering it holds the remainder of the information that we have been searching for. Through the process of creating and interpreting your personal love map, you will finally have the complete story about every aspect of your relationship. This will include:

- Interpreting how important events from your past influenced your individual personality structure and relationship behavior
- Understanding why you picked your ex as your love object
- Comprehending exactly what went wrong in the partnership

- Grasping what part you played in the relationship breakdown
- A better knowledge of your ex's personality structure and relationship behavior
- Finally, an understanding of how your personal love map also determined your break-up conduct and mourning process

Decoding this information is one of the most critical components in your recovery. After finishing this chapter, you will have a nearly complete tool kit that will enable you to continue repairing and rebuilding yourself in the upcoming transformation phase. You will feel so much better when all of the pieces of the puzzle come together and you finally get the answers you've been searching for. The information here will help you not only in your recovery, but in every single aspect of your life. This will be your "aha" moment.

Using Your Breakup as a Breakthrough

While interviewing for this book several women questioned my break-up credentials. As you may have figured out by now, I am a married woman who recently celebrated a milestone anniversary. I am wed to a wonderful man, and although we've had our share of bumps in the road, we have a deep connection and a very solid union. Talk is easy, but as a relationship specialist, I work very hard to walk the walk. Keeping a long-term relationship intact takes a lot of commitment and endeavor, but it is entirely possible if you select the right mate, stay on track, and take responsibility for your own behavior. These traits, which are so ingrained in me today, were completely illusive in my earlier life. From my late teens into my twenties I dated emotionally unavailable, narcissistic, or commitment-phobic men. I made decisions that weren't always in my best interest that chipped away at my underdeveloped self-esteem and that kept me in a state of suspended melancholy. Never once did I stop to evaluate my behavior or see that there were other ways to live my life.

One day a close male friend sat me down and said, "Rachel, you are such a great girl and have so much to offer. I scratch my head wondering why you are constantly dating toxic men when so many nice guys ask you out. I really hope you can figure this out, because I am worried about you." I trusted this friend—he was kind and mature (the type of guy I *never* would have dated back then) and we really understood each other. I had recently graduated from college, and although I was on a terrific career path, I suspected that I had some issues that needed tending when it came to romance. That conversation was the catalyst for what eventually would become my change and growth.

I strongly believe that anyone can alter undesirable feelings and behavior and completely turn his or her life around. You simply need two components: the wish for change and the motivation to do something about it. Sometimes it takes a crisis to contemplate the opportunity for resurrection, and that's how it happened for me. I committed to figuring out what was interfering with my ability to have a successful love connection. I immediately stopped dating and spent a solid year in counseling meticulously examining my entire life to search for answers. As difficult as this work was (and believe me, it was tough), I trusted that it was a huge chance for me to come to a place of great understanding, strength, and growth. My work eventually paid off and I was finally able to see what had transpired in my earlier life that was driving my less-than-stellar dating track record. From that moment on, I fully committed to an entirely new way of dating—and living.

This experience completely changed my existence and enabled me to rejoin the world as an emotionally intelligent and confident young woman. I started living my life as a conscious being with a very sharp antenna. By the time I met my husband several years later, I was a force to be reckoned with. We easily fell in love and began a delightful courtship that even today fills me with joyful memories and continued optimism. Optimism because I was in such a low place and I succeeded in my recovery. By the way, there is nothing particularly unique about me—I was a girl with some baggage and a broken heart. I made a decision to put time and effort into rebuilding, and guess what? It worked. So I'm here today to tell you that you can do this work and have a full recovery. You can move past your distress and discover what really makes you tick. You can create a fabulous life for yourself that includes deeper and healthier love. Trust me, if I did it, so can you. Later on in this chapter, I will demonstrate the concept of interpreting your personal love map by further discussing my story. If my blunders, discoveries, and remedies can help you, I am happy to provide material for growth! To really heal and move on, you have to fully understand where you've been and what you've been through. You have to be able to write your own autobiography—that complete narrative which explains it all. These are the keys that you've been searching for. It's this knowledge that will set you free from past confines and propel you into an entirely new way of dealing with life and love.

The Theory Behind Your Relationship

We are now going to begin the process of creating your personal love map. We are going to map out the most substantial events in your life that served as a blueprint for how you regard and respond to love.

For you to properly complete this project, we will review a small bit of psychological theory and discuss how we grow and mature, attach to others, pick our mates, and handle abandonment. These essentials are the foundation of your love map. Although I don't want to completely throw you back into the classroom, understanding these concepts will be very useful for you. Once you become familiar with this material, I know that you will find it very meaningful in your self-discovery process *and* in the evaluation of all types of relationships for many years to come. A bit more detective work, ladies! So here we go. . . .

An individual's personality is the complex mix of various characteristics that makes one person unique from another. With the advent of psychiatry and analysis in the late 1800s, Freud and others hypothesized about human emotions, behavior, and motivation, yet in somewhat of a vacuum. Analysts studied the individual patient and mostly focused on their dreams and fantasies. "Nurture"—that our personalities are 100 percent created by how we are parented—was the predominant theory at the time and not much attention was paid to the patient's genetic imprint, cultural perspective, or personal relationships outside of the therapy room. By the 1950s and 1960s psychology had gravitated toward the study of people in relationships. That's when the fun started. Ideas were first presented on the importance of human attachment and it was surmised that our earliest relationships set the tone for later romantic partnerships. This concept was considered revolutionary and the analytic community did not completely accept it.

Over time credence was eventually paid to "nature," which proposed that inherited traits and behaviors run in families, and not everything is rooted in how you were raised. Later it was discovered that both the culture in which one was born plus social factors impact individual development. Finally, over the last decade fascinating information has emerged about the science of love. Family therapists, anthropologists, and neurologists have joined with others in the mental health community to scan brains and conduct cutting-edge research into discovering what actually transpires in relationships and love. Bodies of knowledge are emerging validating earlier theories that say we humans are designed to be attached and interconnected with others through mutually loving and healthy relationships, and that we are wired to suffer when these relationships come apart.

Today it is widely believed that our personalities are formed through the influence of three separate yet interrelated components: biology, psychology, and socialization, and this is called a "biopsychosocial" perspective. This model assumes that individual maturation is never limited to one realm of experience. As we grow, our personality forms from a variety of domains including the biological (genetic), psychological (emotional experiences), and social/cultural influences.

Designing an accurate personal love map requires an understanding about how all three spheres influenced your development. Although each piece holds many clues for you to review, the predominant component is psychological, and for this reason

I have switched around the order, and we will spend the majority of this chapter piecing together your psychological profile. Thus, biopsychosocial will be explored as:

- Biological
- Cultural
- Social
- Psychological

Through evaluating and understanding how your personality was formed, you will be able to have a much clearer picture of your relationship motivation and behavior, *and* be more proficient in conducting a fuller assessment of your ex's motivation and behavior. The more you acknowledge and understand, the more you can grow, and the more you can grow, the faster you will reach a full recovery.

Let me take one more moment to fully lay it out for you:

Living a psychologically honest life is a major stepping stone toward complete happiness and full recovery.

Creating Your Personal Love Map

I am now going to introduce several concepts of personality development that will finally enable you to fully understand all aspects of your relationship and breakup. Please use your journal during this entire section. Taking copious notes will help you process and prepare you for your autobiographical exercise at the end of this chapter.

The following page contains a diagram of the important areas that make up your personal love map. As you read ahead, I will give you much information and ask you numerous exploratory questions. As we go, draw your own map and place your notes and answers in the designated areas. After you've completed and interpreted your map, create one for your ex as well. This exercise will give you a complete understanding of the factors that influenced the behavior of you both during the relationship and during its ending.

YOUR PERSONAL LOVE MAP

Factors Affecting Your Personality Development

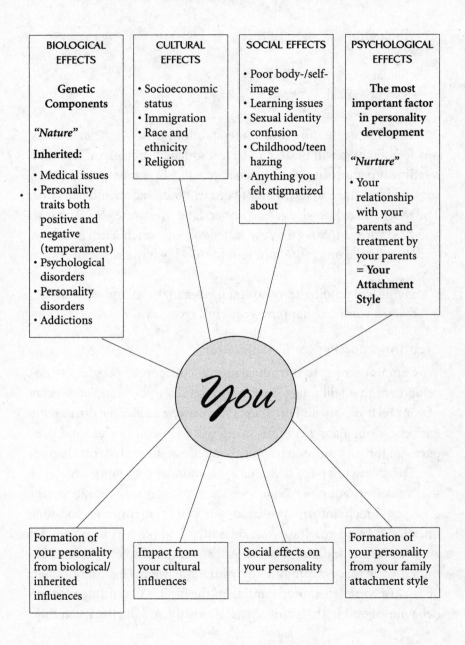

BIOLOGICAL EFFECTS

Genetic Components

"Nature"

Inherited:

- Medical issues
- Personality traits both positive and negative (temperament)
- Psychological disorders
- Personality disorders
- Addictions

CULTURAL EFFECTS

- Socioeconomic status
- Immigration
- Race and ethnicity
- Religion

SOCIAL EFFECTS

- Poor body-/self-image
- Learning issues
- Sexual identity confusion
- Childhood/teen hazing
- Anything you felt stigmatized about

PSYCHOLOGICAL EFFECTS

The most important factor in personality development

"Nurture"

- Your relationship with your parents and treatment by your parents = **Your Attachment Style**

You

Formation of your personality from biological/inherited influences

Impact from your cultural influences

Social effects on your personality

Formation of your personality from your family attachment style

Biological

The biological piece is the inherited genetics in your personality. It's the "nature" in the equation. From a medical perspective, a biological component could be a chronic physical or mental problem that affected you or your family. For example, in childhood I had two very good friends who were diagnosed with juvenile diabetes. Back then this illness was considered grave and it was not expected that one would live a long life. This diagnosis greatly affected both of them and reformed their personalities. Neither ever felt "normal" again and this determined their relationship path. Both avoided intimate romantic connections, and consequently, neither had a long-term relationship or married.

Millions of individuals suffer from depression, anxiety, OCD, bipolar disorder, ADD, phobias, and addictions that originate in their brains and affect the way they function. Many of these conditions are passed from generation to generation. For example, Monique has abundant anxiety (as does her mother), and her anxiety manifests itself as an overwhelming need to have control in all aspects of her life. This didn't bode well with her ex, who had a strong desire for independence, and that disparity caused their breakup.

Often nature and nurture intersect. Angela's father and sister are alcoholics (biology) and her mother is the quintessential enabler (psychology). Angela found herself repeating her mother's patterns by dating many alcoholics and desperately trying to cure them of their disease, yet always falling short.

Biology is also the temperament you were born with and personality traits that you have inherited from your lineage, and it's worth examining how they contributed to you being you. You may have your mom's nose or your dad's build, but you also have similar brains. Often, this is a good thing. For example, my husband has a math/science proclivity, and the majority of his left-brain family are engineers, doctors, scientists, accountants, and math teachers. In comparison, my right-brain maternal grandmother played piano by ear and spoke fluent French, as do my mother and brother.

Other inherited personality traits are less desirable. Some families are very shy, withdrawn, or even reclusive. Some cannot handle stress and have no patience. Others are type A and perfectionists. Some have anger-management issues and are downright mean. Others yet are mellow or even a bit lazy. Some are overly analytical, unfeeling, removed, and cold.

Knowledge about how your genetics affected you will enable you to have a deeper understanding of your personality formation, your relationship behavior, and what, if anything, requires modification. Please think about yourself and your nuclear and extended family, and ponder what traits—both favorable and unfavorable—formed who you are. Then do the same exercise for your ex. Here is a list of questions to ask yourself so you can start filling in your map.

- Were there any chronic or critical medical problems that affected you or your family?
- Were there any genetically based psychological issues such as depression, OCD, ADD, anxiety, or phobias that might have had an effect on you?
- Did you inherit some personality traits such as right-brain creativity or left-brain math/science logic? And if so, how did this affect you?
- Were your parents type A personalities or perfectionists, and if so, how did that affect you?
- When you were a child, what was your temperament like? Were you serious or comical, shy, anxious, or fearless? Were you emotional and intuitive? Or were you stubborn or easily frustrated? And, of great importance, what was your parents' response to your temperament? Were they supportive and encouraging (as they should be), or dismissive or lacking in coping skills?
- What else may you have genetically inherited from your lineage, and how has it affected you?

Cultural

The cultural piece in biopsychosocial is the society, ethnicity, or religion in which you were raised, or your socioeconomic status. Please contemplate what lessons were taught to you by your parents and grandparents, based on those components. What themes ran along those lines? All of these are important factors to consider because they are part of how you were created, and who you are today.

Culture and psychology often intersect. Maria was born to immigrant parents who had to work multiple jobs to support the emerging multi-generational family. Although she felt loved, her parents were rarely home for fun or emotional support. Maria followed in her parents' footsteps and became a workaholic. Overly responsible and generous to a fault, she willingly gave much of her income to her parents and younger sisters, leaving little money or time for herself. It's no wonder that when she met Alejandro, a handsome doctor from Spain, she jumped the first plane out of town. Maria became engaged, married, and moved to a foreign country within four months. Divorced yet fully healed today, she openly discusses how her cultural identity plus low self-esteem caused her to make a spontaneous decision that didn't turn out as she had hoped. "My parents weren't poor, but our Puerto Rican culture was all about how hard work pays off. The combination of my overworking for so many years plus my parents' absenteeism as a child worked against me when it came to love. I never had the confidence I would have liked to, and that correlated to not always making the best romantic moves."

How might your cultural upbringing have influenced your personality development and relationship behavior? How about your ex's? Go through the following points and see how they might relate to your upbringing and fill in your map.

• Were there religious or ethnic factors that influenced your upbringing?
• Were close family connections deemed important or not?

- What kind of values were you taught?
- Were females as valued as males?
- How did your socioeconomic status impact your life?
- Was immigration or prejudice a factor in your upbringing?
- What kind of economic values were you taught? What was your parents' work ethic? Did they both work? How was work and career regarded?
- How was education valued?
- Did you have to date within your culture or religion?
- Is there a certain age that marriage is considered appropriate or necessary?
- What messages did you receive about sex?
- How does your culture view breakups or divorce?

Social

Over the years I have worked with wonderful men and women who come from very loving families, yet their esteem was severely compromised by childhood/teen social problems. If you had a weight problem, acne, were not very athletic, didn't do particularly well in school, weren't "popular," or had a learning disability, you may have suffered social consequences that had an impact on your confidence, and in turn, relationship behavior. Kids can be so mean and the effects of schoolyard bullying can last a lifetime.

Steven grew up impoverished. He has vivid memories of wearing hand-me-down red pants to school and being called a clown. His poverty affected him so much that he desperately strove to be wealthy to prove to the world that he "made it." Thus he became all about the flash and not the substance. Bills went unpaid so he could splurge on foreign cars and designer suits. His wife had no access to his money, and had to take public transportation and clip coupons so he could uphold this phony lifestyle. Steven's poor self-image drove him to make many foolish choices that eventually led his naive wife to smarten up and walk out.

If you are gay or lesbian, coming to terms with your sexual identity is a good example of how the crossover of cultural and societal norms affect how one will fare. Sandra was one of eight children hailing from a staunch conservative Catholic family from the Midwest. She didn't reveal to her family that she was a lesbian until her thirties. This negatively affected her in many ways. "I never really felt like I fit in at school. Then as I got older, I was really scared of telling my family because I thought they'd reject me because of their religious beliefs. I had trouble connecting in relationships because I was so ashamed of my sexuality. I felt like a freak, and you can't have a healthy relationship when you don't feel good about who you are."

Might social issues have affected your development and relationship behavior? How about your ex's?

• Did you have any physical inadequacies (real or perceived) that may have affected your self-esteem such as weight, height, acne, or physical features that you were unhappy with?

• How was your sports ability? Did it influence your competitiveness or lack thereof?

• Did you have any medical or physical disabilities that embarrassed you?

• Were there any memorable social events that affected your esteem or confidence in a negative way, such as lack of friends or boyfriends?

• Did you have any difficult situations with friends that may have hurt or embarrassed you?

• Did you have any learning issues?

• Were you anxious or shy?

• Were you teased about anything?

• Did you realize you were gay or grapple with your sexual identity?

Psychological

There are many fascinating theories backed by research describing how childhood development predisposes how we behave in all relationships. One of the most comprehensive theories in psychology today is called attachment theory, which states that the emotional bond between a parent and child has consequences that last a lifetime.

Much has been expanded upon the reputable work of the British psychiatrist John Bowlby, and Mary Ainsworth, an American developmental psychologist, who extensively studied the attachment styles of parents and children. According to their research, a young child needs to develop a secure relationship with at least one primary caregiver for social and emotional development to occur normally. This attachment provides the child with the safety, security, and protection required for healthy growth and positive esteem. Without this secure love a child can have psychological and social impairments that will undoubtedly affect how she feels about herself, who she chooses as romantic partners, how she operates in relationships, and how she mourns her losses. Thus we form adult attachments and act in ways that are similar to the original bond we had with our earliest caregivers.

In the 1960s, Ainsworth wrote about various styles of attachment. If we have a secure attachment to our parents, we proceed into young adult life as healthy, confident beings who view relationships and love through a positive lens. Alternatively, if one falls into the less-secure categories it influences the way in which we pick love partners, handle ourselves in relationships, and process our break-up experiences. Additionally, individuals with the least secure attachment are predestined to have more complicated relationships and suffer "abandonment depression" once a relationship terminates. Although it is quite essential to acknowledge how biosocial schemas contributed to your personality development, the understanding of who you are psychologically and how you attach is enormously important, and I'd like you to spend some time contemplating this.

Using an attachment-theory model, I will now walk you through three different attachment styles and explain how each affects us in extraordinarily powerful ways. Identifying your attachment behavior is extremely noteworthy because it will provide critical information on how you both deliberately *and* unintentionally pick partners and conduct yourself in relationships and breakups.

The ABCs of Attachment, Selection and Abandonment

Attachment

Still listed under psychological, we're now going to explore attachment theory. As mentioned, our human brains are developed to attach to others in interconnected relationships. According to neuropsychiatrist and attachment researcher Dr. Daniel Siegel, our attachment system was developed more than two hundred million years ago when we became mammals. Today, there is much research, including a thirty-five-year project, the *Minnesota Longitudinal Study of Risk and Adaptation,* which clearly demonstrates time and again that we are all profoundly influenced by the treatment ("attachment") we receive by our parents during our childhood. Thus, for the purpose of designing your personal love map, we are going to evaluate your relationship with both of your parents in terms of three A's:

- Assured attachment
- Ambivalent attachment
- Avoidant attachment

You may see aspects or themes that are identifiable in more than one category, and that is perfectly normal. Our childhoods and parental relationships fall alongside an intricate spectrum. Also, you may discover that your bond with Mom was assured, but with Dad it was ambivalent. If this is the case, and it very well may be, try to dig deeper and ask yourself about that or other inconsistencies. Taking a step back to evaluate all particulars from your earlier life will have many positive consequences in the long run. I certainly understand that gaining perspective can be very challenging work. We spend every waking minute with ourselves and sometimes become too comfortable in our own heads with our private script. Learning how to decipher fact from fiction takes time, patience, and a bit of bravery.

Although this type of work is extremely necessary, it is revealing, and not without some risk. Many of us are afraid, especially after a breakup, to revisit the past. A lot of us tend to be uncomfortable tracing family patterns and feel that there is no point in blaming our parents for historical events that were beyond our control. Many hold on to grudges for dear life and become too comfortable in the victim role. And countless people know they have issues, yet never stop to think about where they originated, or how they affect them and others. Believe me, I am not here to ask you to rake your parents over the coals. Nevertheless I have often said throughout this book that deep exploration is quite useful, and that using your past as an educator is a major component toward living an honest and emotionally healthy life. If you don't take time to think through how your relationship with your parents affected you, both good and bad, you are putting yourself in jeopardy of making and repeating missteps in all of your relationships. This includes friends, children, colleagues, *and* lovers.

I'm now going to provide you with descriptions and scenarios describing all three attachment styles. Please pay close attention to see where you fit in and what is meaningful to you. Remember that there is a huge correlation between the attachment style that you had with your nuclear family and how you view and conduct yourself in romantic relationships.

By the end of this chapter I would like you to emerge with new information about how your relationship with your parents affected and influenced the formation of your self-esteem, and your relationship and break-up behavior. Once you are finished with this chapter, go back and repeat it for your ex. Knowing how he was raised and how experiences from his childhood affected him will help you to better understand his relationship and break-up behavior.

After you have read through all three styles, please rate where you feel you best fit in on the attachment spectrum with both of your parents, and then do the same for your ex. Then create an attachment spectrum on your personal love map and write down all the attachment qualities representing your relationship with your parents and how they affected your upbringing.

The Attachment Spectrum

1	2	3	4	5	6	7	8	9	10	11	12	13	14	15	16	17	18	19	20

Assured	Ambivalent	Avoidant

Assured Attachment. If you hail from an assured family you are extremely fortunate, and as you may already know, life's ups and downs will be a bit easier for you to cope with. If you rate your family one to five on the attachment spectrum, you have a close and caring relationship with both of your parents and there was ample love, attention, and comfort during childhood and later years. Because of this you will have a fuller capacity to form loving and trusting relationships.

In assured families:

• Your parents wanted to have children, attended to you, and willingly reacted and responded to your needs. Although no family is perfect, these families generally form the securest bonds with their kids and are usually intact and harmonious clans.

• Family comes first and everyone works together for the greater good of the unit. Kindness and respect are valued and your parents tried to the best of their ability to take excellent care of you.

• Your parents also strived to encourage you to try new things, take some risks, and made you feel important and special—especially when you weren't feeling your best.

• Your parents have an ability to communicate, express affection and empathy, and in turn, so do you.

• Assured-style families make a huge attempt to roll with life's myriad problems and function as a team even during challenges.

• Your parents understood and accepted your temperament and knew how to work with it. For example, if you were an anxious or nervous child, they gently and lovingly encouraged you to explore new situations to help you become more confident. And if you angered or frustrated easily, they provided comfort and taught you how to self-soothe.

- Furthermore, assured parents generally have good marriages, which serve as excellent role models for their children to emulate.

Jesse is a wonderful example of an assured attachment. When I asked her to describe the bond she shared with her parents, she immediately replied, "Unconditional love!" Jesse explained to me how her tight family prepared her for life, love, and a bad breakup. "My parents were just wonderful people—everyone loved them. They were strict, but they were fair. They made things enjoyable for us. They valued us and our opinions. They never judged us, and always made us feel special and secure. And they also had a wonderful marriage. Family was very important, and we were expected to be home every Friday night for dinner, which as teenagers we rebelled against. But my mother encouraged my brothers and me to invite as many friends as we wanted. That dinner became famous in our town and everyone clamored for an invitation."

Having a secure attachment will undoubtedly help you pick a decent guy and perform well once in a relationship. It does not, however, always predict the outcome. Jesse met her boyfriend Will in college and they dated for five years. She described him as a "great guy from a good family," and credits her positive attachment style with helping her make a good relationship choice. "Will and I were very serious and talked about a life together. We were discussing marriage in our midtwenties and then something happened and he panicked. I think he just wasn't ready to settle down, but didn't have the maturity to fully understand this, so he made some bad decisions that really hurt me. The night we broke up, I called my parents, who were away on vacation, and told them Will had left me. The next morning at five a.m. there was a knock at my door. My father had flown all night to get home to help care for me."

Jesse reports that the breakup was very difficult for her; however, she always held on to her optimism and had no doubt she would recover. This is usually the case when you are raised in a family with an assured attachment—you realize that although breakups are hard, in time you are going to be fine. Jesse and Will were so young when they met, and apparently their relationship simply ran its course.

This doesn't mean that she picked the wrong guy or made any major mistakes. When I asked her about accountability, she professed to being "too optimistic, too young, and too naive." Also, she came from a very traditional family (culture), and many of her friends and relatives married young.

Another benefit of an assured attachment is the outpouring of affection you'll receive post-breakup. "The love and mega-support of my parents and two brothers really saw me through. Of course I was upset, angry, embarrassed, but I knew I would be OK. You know, after I recovered, those years that I was single again were some of the best of my life. I did a lot of living back then—things I wouldn't have done if Will and I stayed together and married so young. I look at my breakup as a blessing because I eventually met my husband, and he is the best guy in the world!" Jesse's assured attachment style helped her through her challenges, and continues to guide her today when the going gets rough. "My parents unequivocally loved and valued me, so that assured attachment was there. I would rate my mom's style a two, and my dad's style a four. But I'm happy to round it out and say I'm lucky that I came from a three!"

If you were raised in an assured family:

• Although there may be biological or social issues that you or your family grappled with, you will have self-esteem on the positive side because you know you were loved and cherished by your parents, and because of this, you are in the best possible position to enjoy healthy adult relationships.

• Assured adults can fully participate in intimate relationships, generally do not have trust or abandonment issues, are comfortable seeking out social supports, and have an easier recovery path after a breakup.

• Once in transformation, they pick themselves up and eventually date because they enjoy relationships, and picture themselves involved in one again in the future.

Ambivalent Attachment. If you had an ambivalent style of attachment with one or both parents, there were definitely some issues that interfered with their ability to be fully devoted and effective parents. Ambivalent people do not attach, connect, or feel intimacy for others as easily as assured folks for a variety of reasons that fall along the biopsychosocial spectrum. Your parents may have loved you and had good intentions, but at some point something affected the way they raised you, treated you, or paid attention to you. Perhaps one or both were challenged insofar as showing affection, understanding, patience, or even love.

Ambivalent attachment can occur if:

• Unemployment, poverty, or economic stress was a factor.
• A parent was an overworker and not home much.
• There was a chronic or critical illness or death in your immediate or extended family.
• A parent suffered from a mood disorder such as depression or anxiety, anger issues, or a personality disorder such as narcissism.
• A sibling required an inordinate amount of your parents' attention.
• If your parents had a disconnected, unhappy, or hostile marriage there is a good chance that it affected their parenting ability.
• If a divorce occurred, even a "good divorce," it will have an effect on your attachment style.
• If a parent is controlling or demanding or unreasonably strict
• If a parent is overly critical
• If a parent is too needy and insists on love and attention
• If a parent repeatedly threatens or guilt trips you
• If a parent has no boundaries, uses you as their therapist, or allows you to do as you please

These types of conditions will most certainly affect your parents' ability to give you the love, attention, and devotion that you undeniably deserved.

Sofia's parents had a problematic relationship and she rarely remembers them getting along. "My father was very demanding and had a temper, and I think my mother felt unloved and under-appreciated. They would fight and my mother would go for weeks without speaking to him. She was the queen of the cold shoulder. My sisters and I had wagers about how long their fights would last. Although they both loved us and tried in their own way to be good parents, it was nearly impossible because they were never on the same page. One of them was always in a bad mood, and if there was tension in the house, which there often was, we had to stay away from them. They eventually split up, which we all knew was the right thing, but even afterward their fighting continued—money, visitation, etc. We'd go for weeks without seeing our dad, and my mom was so overwhelmed and stressed all the time. As a result, my sisters and I have all suffered in a variety of ways. We've all had our challenges in relationships, and I only recently came to see that it was mostly because of my parents' lousy marriage and their inability to put parenting ahead of their own drama. Also, we never had any role models to see what healthy relationships looked like."

Often I hear stories about families that appear to be inordinately close and devoted, but on further scrutiny one or both parents is actually quite controlling and passing decrees about what constitutes love. Carly was from one of those families. "I considered my mother my best friend to the exclusion of all others. At the time I didn't understand how it was negatively affecting all of my romantic relationships. My desire to be married finally drove me to therapy, where I eventually came to see that my mother had some issues with anxiety. Her message to us kids was 'No one will ever love you like I will'—but the flip side of that message was 'No one will ever love you!' Therefore, I had a hard time letting go of her and being intimate with a man. Also, if I got too close to a boyfriend, she'd start to guilt trip me about not spending enough time with her. I felt so torn!"

To the outside world Carly's family can look like an assured attachment style, but in actuality it is quite ambivalent. In this instance, her mother was insecure and deeply afraid of abandonment, and therefore she brainwashed her children to believe that nuclear family love is the only love that counts.

"How can I complete my love map? I have a hard time remembering facts about my childhood."

This is something I often hear. Some of us have much better "working memories" (the actual term for memory recall) than others. And others block painful memories as a coping mechanism. If this describes you, try jarring your memory by looking at old family photos, reading old letters, or even looking through yearbooks or listening to songs that were popular from your youth. You'd be surprised how those exercises can help put missing pieces together.

If you have a parent who demands love and attention, who is needy and insecure, who requires an inordinate amount of care or attention, and who guilt trips you if you don't play it his or her way, this is not the definition of unconditional love. Healthy parents work themselves out of a job. They want their children to become mature adults and leave the nest.

Here is how an ambivalent family relationship might have influenced you:

• If you were raised on the ambivalent scale you may be very successful in some areas of your life, yet have a more difficult time in emotionally intimate relationships.

• If your parents had a poor marriage, you may not have had any role models to emulate.

• You may be prone to abandonment issues if a parent had a life-threatening illness or died.

• Ambivalents run the gamut. Many desperately yearn for connection (because they didn't fully get their needs met during their childhood) yet don't fully possess the skill set to navigate healthy relationships. Others can have lax boundaries, be a bit codependent, try too hard to please, and find themselves extraordinarily disappointed and hurt when their love connection severs.

• On the other hand, some ambivalents have a hard time getting close, expressing emotion or affection, or feeling empathy.

• If you are from an ambivalent family, your confidence may not be as good as you would like it to be. Due to this you may engage in "people-pleasing" behaviors, and require a high level of approval or responsiveness from your partner.

• Coming from an ambivalent family increases the probability that you may suffer from anxiety or depression.

• You may have some jealousy and/or trust issues.

• On the other hand, you may expect too much from your partner, be overly critical, defensive, put too much pressure on the relationship, feel generally dissatisfied, and think that you put more into relationships than your lovers do.

Avoidant Attachment. If you were raised in a family with avoidant attachment, there is a strong likelihood that your childhood and/or teen years were filled with disconnection, conflict, or chaos. Since this is the lowest level of attachment, there is a good chance that either one or both of your parents had fairly severe issues that halted their ability to be effective parents.

Here are some facts on avoidant parents:

• Many avoidant parents are compulsive, controlling, impulsive, inconsistent, irresponsible, and have limited coping skills. Some are childlike, self-involved, do as they wish, and cannot handle the responsibilities of parenting.

• Others are emotionally void and have no ability to display affection or feel anything at all.

• Many regularly suffer from a severe mood or personality disorder, or an addiction. Some are involved in illegal activities, are habitual cheaters, or are downright liars.

• Others are emotionally, physically, or sexually abusive.

• Some range between volatility, hostility, total enmeshment, or complete detachment, neglect, or abandonment.

- There may have been a lot of fighting or drama in your family, or an abundant amount of criticism or even cruelty.
- Since avoidant parents don't have great relationship skills, there is a high probability that your parents had a terrible marriage, or a terrible divorce. Or you may have been raised by a single parent due to the physical absence of the other.
- The odds are generally pretty high that an avoidant parent is the product of another avoidant parent—this is definitely something you should spend time contemplating.
- Severe stressors that are biopsychosocial join to create an avoidant person. I've heard umpteen stories of women raised by parents who were traumatized by poverty, orphaned, raised by drunkards, survived a war, or suffered some form of abuse. Believe me, these types of circumstances can easily turn any individual into an avoidant, and sadly, the implications of such are often passed from one generation to the next.

As previously mentioned in the biology section, if you come from a family or had a parent with a history of drug or alcohol abuse, there is a very good chance that it seriously affected your upbringing, and in turn, your attachment style. If you are an ACOA (adult child of an alcoholic) you may find yourself trying to save the world, needing total control, or drawn to men who are addicts themselves. There is a chance that you too have had problems with addictions.

If you were raised by a parent where there was emotional abuse it will undoubtedly affect the way in which you view and behave in relationships. Emotionally abusive parents do not love unconditionally (or love at all), and even worse, because they are so miserable themselves, they chip away at their child's self-worth, attempting to break or destroy them. When you grow up feeling unloved or even unliked by your parents, if your childhood is so unstable that you can't trust or feel safe, the effects are extremely far-reaching.

Giselle describes her mother as a "rageaholic." Clearly an unstable woman, she had a flair for drama and flew off the handle at any given moment. "You never knew what would set my mother off. One

day it was OK to practice my piano, and the next[...]
crap out of me for playing while she was on the phon[...]
divorced when I was young, and my father moved awa[...]
saw him. Mom was a 'love addict.' She had a succession of lov[...]
her mood was very much determined by how her latest boyfr[...]
was treating her."

Giselle, in turn, told me how she too floated from one bad relationship to the next. "I kind of raised myself, so believe it or not,
I had *some* esteem, and I was able to get good jobs and hold them.
But I was always mildly depressed and mostly felt lonely and unloved. I went for real low-life kinds of guys—I didn't think I could
get anything better. I was deathly afraid of anger or conflict, because
of my mother's temper, so I let a lot of men get away with really
bad behavior. I never stuck up for myself—I was too afraid of being
broken up with. I have a recollection of feeling completely suicidal
when a relationship of a few years ended when I was in my twenties. I went into such a tailspin of depression. I was smart enough
to eventually get some help and sort through it all. My mom is still
a mess, but I have developed empathy and forgiven her. She was
abandoned by her mother when she was very young, raised by her
elderly grandparents. She never learned how to love—or how to be
a mother."

There are many unfortunate consequences from growing up in
an avoidant family, such as:

• If your upbringing was unstable, erratic, or abusive and in
turn you grew up feeling unloved, depressed, anxious, unsafe, or insecure, the domino effect is that you may face abundant challenges
in relationships.

• Many avoidants possess a diminished self-worth, and others
acquire an overly inflated sense of self (narcissism) to bury their
insecurities.

• Some desperately search for love to fill the emptiness inside of
them from not feeling loved, and others have severe trust issues that
impede their ability to bond with friends or lovers.

spectrum there is a good chance
been somewhat problematic and
ing.

at you were involved in a romance
ly Bickersonian, or codependent.
mily increases the probability that
r depression.

love connections fall apart. They
physical anguish and tend to have
r exes. Many distance themselves
from others and do not seek the help they need and deserve. Others
lean too hard on their support system because they do not know
how to care for themselves.

If this attachment style resonates with you, I have so much empathy for the pain that you undeniably have endured. Every child deserves love and safety, and it's extremely unfortunate that life handed you this challenging bill of goods. Never lose hope and please remember that I am giving you the support and tools to help you heal yourself, fully recover, and get more satisfaction from your life.

Now that you've read through all three styles of attachment, you have a greater understanding about the correlation between how one is raised with one's self-esteem and relationship behavior. Your personal love map is really expanding. We will continue exploring this concept through the remainder of this chapter.

Family Love Maps

What I'd like you to do now is create the personal love maps of some important family members. As I've said, understanding your parents' and grandparents' love maps holds many important clues for you to further investigate.

1. Draw a family diagram (genogram) of your nuclear family and include your grandparents. You are welcome to add extended

family too. The more members you include, the more patterns and trends you'll identify.

2. Describe the personality structure of your parents and grandparents. You can add others if you'd like, but those are the most important relatives for you to study. Discuss what elements of biopsychosocial formed each one's character.

3. Now describe their psychological profile and rate how they attached to others and to you.

4. Finally, please interpret their love maps. Stop and think—where did everything originate? How do you suppose all these elements merged to form your personal love map? How has this all affected how you feel about yourself and romance, and how you perform in relationships?

Repetition Compulsion: Choosing One Bad Relationship After Another

"All of my lovers disappointed me—I was always looking for 'more' and could never find it. Finally I traced it back to always feeling disappointed by my parents. They were never there for me emotionally. I didn't realize it at the time, but I was repeating my childhood themes in my adult relationships. I picked men who also couldn't be there for me emotionally, and I'd get so hurt when those relationships inevitably ended. But anyone can change, you know. It's frightening to go back there and do the work to heal your past, but it works. Once you do that you can get involved in much better relationships." —*Nadia*

We're getting very close to putting the final pieces of the puzzle together. I can sense the excitement in the air! I've just shown you that our personalities are formed by intricate forces that are biological, psychological, and social in nature. Plus, there is a huge correlation between early attachment styles and their influence on how we perform in adult relationships. In keeping with that theme I'm now going to explain to you how the convergence of these elements also predetermines whom we choose as lovers.

The majority of us have some level of awareness regarding how our upbringings and relationships with our parents affected us, and after reading about attachment styles, you now have a greater understanding about this. But what you may not fully comprehend is how certain messages you received at an impressionable age integrated into your being and caused you to instinctively select partners based on those messages. Some of these messages are very affirmative ones. If you come from an assured-style family, you have a greater probability to pick assured partners and engage in predominantly healthy relationships, and your recovery path will be less complex after a breakup. Someone like you will look for lovers who value and possess similar positive characteristics to one or both parents. In other words, as we grow up we develop an orientation to *new* attachment figures, both friends and lovers, who have remarkably comparable personalities or traits to our original caregivers.

Alternatively, if you were raised in a family that was ambivalent or avoidant, you will have a more challenging time finding healthy love matches. Moreover, there is a high probability that unconsciously you will pick men with similarities to the parent *you have unresolved issues or traumas with*. This behavior is called repetition compulsion, and it means that you unknowingly have a compulsion to repeat themes and behaviors in adult relationships based on your unsolved childhood schemas—over and over again.

Repetition compulsion is completely paradoxical. Understandably, we are drawn to seek love, yet curiously we search for someone who resembles one or both of the parents whom we had problems with. Once this love partner is found, and we become involved, we expect him to fill our unmet needs from infancy and childhood. Therefore we search for the parent we had issues with, find him, and then expect him to be completely different and provide us with what our parents simply couldn't. And of course he can't do that because he has the same character defects as the bad parent(s)!

The fallout from this behavior is extremely damaging. For instance, if your mother was critical and emotionally withdrawn you may find yourself attracted to partners with identical qualities and behaviors, yet this dynamic is completely unrecognizable to your untrained psyche. Consequently, you may surprisingly find yourself falling for a man who never appreciates your strengths and inordinately focuses on how you are disappointing him. The repercussion from this destructive pattern is that it keeps you stuck in a hopeless cycle while you desperately attempt to please your lover in the same way you tried to please your mother, but failed.

Why, you may ask, would someone willingly participate in this behavior? First, this behavior is not willing—in fact it is not even recognizable to you. Second, it feels normal. Mom was critical, so your experience with a critical partner seems very familiar and even comfortable to you. And last, on a subconscious, unexamined level, you are unwittingly trying to get your lover to tell you that you matter, that you are remarkable, because Mom never did. Unknowingly, you are desperately determined to get the love or missing ingredient from your romantic relationship that you never deservedly acquired at home. You are yearning to get this void filled by your lover thinking that it will heal your past unfulfilled parental relationship, and because of this, you deduce that it will finally make you complete.

As described, a compounded problem with repetition compulsion is that the men we pick to fill these voids within us are never good matches, and that's because they have qualities similar to the problematic parent. I'm going to give you some examples from the healing community to flesh out this point, which is so important. I will also tell you that every single person I interviewed who previously suffered from repetition compulsion eventually stopped the insanity and turned her life around, including me.

• Allison was the eldest child in a large divorced family. Her mother, a cold, detached woman, put a lot of responsibility on her to help run the household and raise her siblings. Unknown to her at the time, she grew up with many insecurities because she was continually trying to please her mother, who never showed her any appreciation. What little esteem she developed came from "mothering," and as a young woman, she continued helping her parents, her siblings, *and* eventually their children—emotionally and financially. In college she fell in love with David, a damaged man/boy. The youngest in his family, David suffered a trauma when his father died when he was a child. Consequently he was overparented by his mother and siblings. He met Allison, a mother figure, and easily attached to her. Effortlessly, they fell into a mother/child dynamic that lasted ten years and produced abundant conflict. Allison was always trying to get David to act like a man, and he rebelled by acting more and more like a boy. She did everything for David, and felt underappreciated by him—as she had by her mother. She finally identified her issues, took responsibility for her part in the dynamic, wised up, and ended the relationship.

• Noreen was adopted. Although loved by her adoptive family, she never entirely got over the initial abandonment by her birth family. Desperate to marry and have children to create a natural family of her own, she fell for Ryan, a successful doctor who cared for her but had selfish and narcissistic traits, along with ambivalence about marriage and children. Noreen hung on for dear life for many years trying to get Ryan to marry her. She subconsciously presumed that if she could change him, it would heal the old wound she carried with her due to her adopted status. This dynamic was destined to fail, and it eventually did. Her breakup was unbearable.

I have worked with women who come from assured families, but still participate in repetition compulsion, which can be quite perplexing to them. They are really stumped about the origination of their behavior, and protest to me, "I came from a great family, and I'm close to both of my parents, so why do I get involved with bad guys?" Although the majority of repetition compulsion sufferers do come from ambivalent or avoidant attachment styles, this syndrome can also occur if you come from an assured family but had other factors that were biological, psychological, or social that impacted your esteem, or colored how you view men and relationships.

For example, Barbara shared an assured attachment with both of her parents, yet grew up with poor self-confidence due to her continual battles with body-image issues. "I was very heavy when I was in grade school, plus I had big frizzy hair, and it left a lasting impression on me. In turn I grew up never feeling good about my appearance and always feeling like I had to prove myself." Thus Barbara repeatedly got involved with men who had girlfriends or commitment issues, thinking if she could win them over it would make her feel good about herself. When these relationships ended she'd be extremely depressed and self-loathing.

As you can see, repetition compulsion is an enormous problem that many unfortunately suffer from. Truly, if we are looking toward another person to fill an emptiness or an old wound inside of us, that relationship is doomed to fail. And when it fails, you are destined to suffer a double abandonment—the old wound that never healed from your earlier life, plus the new one as well. Breakups are so much more painful when this condition is involved.

The entire point of this book is to get you well and whole again. It's vitally important that you ask yourself if repetition compulsion has influenced your partner selection and relationship track. If so, turn toward your love map and family genogram to figure out where it originated. Once you understand what you are dealing with you can make a plan to break the pattern. This work involves identifying the original wound, healing it, and most important, completely rebuilding your self-esteem. In phase 3, "transformation," I will give you ample information on rebuilding your life and creating new relationships with men who are kind and respectful. Men who appreciate who you are and value you, because you are amazing and special. I promise, there are plenty of nice guys out there, and you can learn to fall for one of those!

Abandonment Depression

"After I learned about abandonment depression, I was like 'Yes, this is me.' It's more than depression, it's a terrible emptiness. I always went so out of my way to help people—to be a great girlfriend—and if those friendships or relationships ended I'd fall to pieces. I'd feel so rejected and so awful about myself. Then I realized that these feelings went so far back, they were ancient. I felt such strong rejection because both of my parents were completely self-absorbed. I never got any support from them. I didn't put it together back then, but I knew I suffered more than others after breakups." —*Susan*

Abandonment is a raw and complex emotion, and many of us naturally suffer some degree of it when a relationship ends. Breakups can trigger awful feelings of dejection, yet some of us are more susceptible to experiencing intense abandonment grief than others.

Many issues factor into how each of us will respond to our loss, which include the conditions behind the split, the length of the relationship, *and* our past history with "emotional abandonment." As I've previously described to you, pain and disappointment in our earliest relationships with our parents determines how we pick our partners, behave in relationships, *and mourn our losses.*

You are now aware that if you came from a close and loving assured-style family, your parents were there to help you develop, and your needs were mostly met. Because of this your self-worth developed on the positive side, you were less emotionally dependent on your ex, and although your ending was sad and challenging, in time you will pull yourself together and move on. You have internalized valuable memories of how you were loved and treasured in your earlier life and those recollections give you strength and guide you through your darkest moments. Therefore during your breakup you are experiencing *only one loss*—the loss of your current romantic relationship, and nothing more.

In contrast, if you came from an ambivalent or avoidant family, for a variety of reasons that we discussed, your parents were not completely emotionally or physically available in your life. This doesn't necessarily mean they were bad people or didn't love you, but there was interference in their ability to unconditionally love, support, and attend to you. As a result most people come from families rated high on the attachment spectrum are catapulted into adulthood with a bit of emotional baggage in tow. And this baggage gravely affects how we deal with our breakups and recoveries. Let me explain this important connection to you. When we are so young and innocent and experience hurt or rejection from our parents, it is agonizing. In actuality this is our first experience with loss, and we call it "emotional abandonment." Because we are children and don't know how to deal with this, we disassociate ourselves from those awful feelings and push them deep down inside of us. Of course we don't understand any of this behavior on a conscious level, so we find coping strategies to deal with those uncomfortable feelings.

For example, in order to manage our earlier pain or lack of esteem, some of us may have turned into perfectionists in order to feel good about ourselves. If that is the case, we fully define ourselves by our accomplishments, and can tend to be very hard on ourselves *and* our lovers. Others may feel a persistent need to be in control at all times in order to feel safe. Some have a relationship with alcohol, food, shopping, or substances that may be too cozy. Many are constantly searching for love, unknowingly attempting to fill an emptiness inside of them. Some become overly dependent, needy, and deathly afraid of abandonment while ensconced in relationships. Others yet have a very difficult time trusting or connecting, and therefore become too self-reliant, commitment phobic, or avoidant when it comes to love. A common denominator is that when you come from an ambivalent or avoidant family, or if you had past circumstances that negatively influenced you, until you do the work to heal yourself, you carry a void inside of you that feels like it can never be satiated. Most of us are not even aware of these feelings let alone the origination of them. But they are there, hidden away, and will crop up in curious and, at times, detrimental ways until they are uncovered, dissected, and eventually repaired.

If you suffer from early emotional abandonment and are not aware of it, there is a good chance that you instinctively searched for someone to adore you and take care of you, which you unconsciously deduced would heal your old wounds and finally fill that void inside of you. This seems to make sense, of course, except there is a very good chance that that special someone has a few qualities or quirks that are uncannily similar to the parent or situation you have unresolved issues with (remember repetition compulsion?). Thus the stage is now perfectly set for you to really fall apart when this relationship backfires, and it generally will. Whatever strategies you had previously used to cope with your past pain suddenly no longer work and you are primed to suffer a horrific *double abandon-ment*—the old unresolved loss from your emotionally abandoning parents *and* the brand-new abandonment from your current lover. Thus, your old wounds that have been pushed aside for many years are now ripped open, fully exposed, and your buried pain comes spewing up like a geyser.

This experience—which is an intense, visceral reaction to the ending of your romance—is called an "abandonment depression." Discovered and named by psychologist James Masterson, abandon-ment depression is a deep and prolonged despair that produces powerful feelings of abandonment, depression, fear, helplessness, and emptiness that is rooted in your earliest experiences with emo-tional abandonment.

Although all breakups are painful, I can tell off the bat when working with a new client whether she is afflicted with abandon-ment depression. If she broke up with her boyfriend five years ago and never dated again, that is abandonment depression. If her mar-riage ended three years ago and she is still angrily embroiled with her ex, that is abandonment depression. If she is ferociously and desperately dating, well, that too is abandonment depression. And, if she is stalking and trying to win back her ex as if her life depended on it, you bet, abandonment depression.

You may be vulnerable to experiencing an abandonment de-pression if you identify with some of the following characteristics:

• An attachment style that is rated as ambivalent or avoidant
• A parent(s) who physically abandoned you
• Unresolved issues stemming from the death of a parent
• Parents who divorced, especially with acrimony
• Having felt unloved or unvalued as a child and thus suffer from low self-esteem

• Biological social, or cultural factors that negatively affected your self-worth
• A strong fear of abandonment
• A personality that is predisposed to depression or pessimism
• Extreme sensitivity to criticism or rejection
• A tendency to be a perfectionist
• Participating in people-pleasing behavior
• Having a propensity to be codependent in relationships
• Having a tendency to be untrusting, suspicious, or jealous in relationships

Furthermore, symptoms of abandonment depression include:

• Suicidal or self-injurious behavior
• Repetitive suicidal thoughts or fantasies
• Partaking in any addictive behaviors
• Using drugs (prescription or illegal) or alcohol to mollify your pain
• Desperately trying to win back your ex
• Using sex to lure back your ex
• Intense preoccupation with your ex
• Completely cutting off your ex and refusing to participate in any form of break-up discussion or closure if it is offered
• Engaging in any type of stalking behavior, which includes compulsively calling, sending texts and e-mails, or showing up at his apartment, office, or places and events because you know he will be there
• Obsessively discussing the breakup with anyone who will listen six months or more after the breakup
• Taking 100 percent of the blame for the failure of the relationship and becoming extremely self-loathing
• Refusing to acknowledge that the relationship is over six months to one year after the breakup
• A deep and persistent (not occasional) depression lasting six months or more after the breakup
• Having no optimism about the future, which continues one year after the breakup

• Refusing to date or even consider the possibility of romance one year after the breakup

• Feeling that you can never trust again and that all men are bad, one year after the breakup

• Still being furious with and wanting revenge on your ex one year after the breakup

If you feel you are suffering from early abandonment pain and abandonment depression, acknowledging and healing your old wounds is of extreme importance on your journey to recovery. Completing your personal love map and genogram will afford you the opportunity to deeply contemplate what went on in your parents' lives that didn't allow them to care for you in ways you indisputably deserved. You are going to have to work really hard to make those connections, and then work even harder toward healing yourself from both your old wounds *and* your current breakup. Healing entails making a commitment to understand and make peace with your earlier life, rebuilding your self-esteem, learning how to trust again, and pledging to a new and healthier future. Reconciling the past and forgiving yourself and others will release you and lighten your load in unimaginable ways. Then you will finally have a clean slate enabling you to fully heal and recover from your breakup.

Understanding Your Personal Love Map Tips and Tools

1. Our personalities are formed through the influence of three separate yet interrelated components: biology, psychology, and socialization. This is called a "biopsychosocial" perspective.

2. A young child needs to develop a secure relationship with at least one primary caregiver for social and emotional development to occur normally. Without this secure love, children can have psychological and social impairments that will undoubtedly affect how they feel about themselves,

whom they choose as romantic partners, *and* how they operate in relationships.

3. Our childhoods and parental relationships fall within an intricate attachment spectrum that encompasses three distinct styles:

   • Assured attachment
   • Ambivalent attachment
   • Avoidant attachment

4. Identifying which attachment style best describes your upbringing holds many clues that will explain why you picked your ex as your love partner, how you performed in the relationship, and your break-up behavior.

5. As we grow up we develop an orientation to *new* attachment figures, both friends and lovers, who have remarkably comparable personalities or traits with our original caregivers.

6. When we search for partners who have comparable *unfavorable* traits with the parent(s) that we had an ambivalent or avoidant relationship with, and then hope to change them to fill emotional voids in ourselves—this is called repetition compulsion.

7. If you participate in repetition compulsion and have early unidentified abandonment issues, you are primed to suffer a horrific *double abandonment* during a breakup—the old unresolved loss from your emotionally abandoning parents (or other painful past unresolved circumstances) *and* the brand-new abandonment from your current lover. This is "abandonment depression."

8. If you feel you are suffering from repetition compulsion and abandonment depression, acknowledging and healing your old wounds is of extreme importance on your journey to recovery. We will discuss this in more detail in the upcoming chapter, "Letting Go."

11

My Story

Writing Your Autobiography

I have given you enough information to enable you to complete your personal love map and begin the process of fully analyzing and evaluating it. I believe you have made many new connections and now have all the facts you will ever need to answer questions regarding why you picked your ex as your lover, your relationship conduct, why your relationship ended, and your break-up behavior. You have even learned a few things about *his* background and character formation too.

As a final exercise I am going to ask you to put all the pieces together by writing your autobiography. This is a comprehensive narrative that lists the most important events in your life leading up to your relationship and subsequent breakup. Everyone has a unique story to tell, and re-creating it is one of the most potent ways to discover who we truly are. Writing is so illuminating and cathartic, and even if you feel by now that you know yourself and your story, I assure you that a few new particles of data will flow from this creative project.

I completely understand that this is not an easy exercise, because I have just concluded it myself. Frankly, I did not want to include my own story in this book. Although I have given you a few tidbits about myself, I can be a private person, and am not prone to airing my dirty laundry. As a therapist, I am more comfortable listening to or telling the stories of others than revealing my account, but in this case I think it will help you to see an example of an autobiography before you write your own.

Although I have not lived through the end of a lengthy marriage, I have personally experienced ambivalent attachment, repetition compulsion, and abandonment depression. I also picked up the shattered pieces, completely healed, and went on to create an amazing life for myself. It is solely for this reason that I have chosen to share my story with you. If my narrative can help others, then I will challenge myself to do something for you that is uncomfortable for me. My payback, by the way, is your promise for a complete recovery.

My Story

I'd like to begin my story by introducing you to both sets of my grandparents, and I suggest you do the same when writing your autobiography. The more generational information you attain, the more connections and associations you'll be able to make. If your grandparents were already dead when you were a child, or if you have few recollections about them, this would be an opportune time for you to inquire among family like an investigative reporter in order to gather facts. It is very helpful to have this data, especially if you suspect that your attachment style is ambivalent or avoidant.

Several years ago I was working on a school immigration project with my daughter, and we discovered some profound details about my paternal grandfather that no one else in my family, including my father, knew. This newfound information enabled me to make many discoveries.

My Grandparents

My Maternal Grandparents

My maternal grandparents were interesting and extraordinary people and they greatly influenced my life. My daughter is named after my beloved grandmother, and rarely a day goes by where I don't think about or miss them. I feel so fortunate to have had them in my life, especially as an adult. However, they had a rotten marriage, which gravely affected their parenting of my mother.

My grandfather Jack was one of seven children born to impoverished Hungarian immigrants in New York City. He and his six siblings grew up in a two-bedroom tenement and had no education above seventh grade. He was handsome, charming, and smart—over six feet tall, olive skin, green eyes. He was a dead ringer for Clark Gable. He came from a colorful family that also was slightly crazy. They were known as yellers, and there are some famous stories about raucous brawls and neighbors trying to get them evicted due to their volume problem. My grandmother swore that one of his sisters was a paranoid schizophrenic who went through her drawers whenever she visited until my grandmother put a note in every drawer saying, "Gertrude, stay out!"

My grandfather worked very hard to climb out of poverty and make a life for himself. He was known to have an awful temper, was rumored to be a womanizer, and hated parting with money. I remember him as very funny (he constantly used puns and played with words), extremely bright, and somewhat of a cynic. He was pessimistic, didn't trust many people—but he adored me. He was an emotional man who came to visit me at my first big-shot job in a fancy New York City office building—and openly wept out of pride for my opportunities and accomplishments. Look at what a difference two generations make in America! I would rate my grandfather's attachment to his parents as ambivalent, and I believe he suffered from abundant stressors that were biological (he had a bad temper, as did his parents), psychological (ambivalent attachment/ he also suffered from depression), and social/cultural (poverty and prejudice).

My grandmother's childhood was quite the opposite. According to her, she hailed from a calm and peaceful family and I'd always assumed she had an assured attachment. She was close to her parents, especially her father, and cherished her brother and sister. Her father was a tailor and they were considered well off for the times. She was a spectacularly beautiful woman and kept her looks through her years. I never remember her becoming cross or saying an unkind word about anyone. She was a wonderful grandmother and my siblings and I would eagerly await her weekly visits. Out of her grandma bag she pulled delicious homemade cookies, cakes, and intricately sewn Barbie clothes that she created with love. She played the piano and loved the arts. Although smart, she was not an intellectual like my grandfather, and preferred to pamper herself and spend time with friends than keep up with politics or current events. She was an eternal optimist.

As I already mentioned, their good looks drew them to each other. My great-grandmother warned my grandmother against marriage, stating, "Sara, they are *meshugganah* [a Yiddish word meaning extremely insane], his people. You must stay away!" Even in the 1930s, who listened to their mother? Although they definitely had a love for each other, I think their marriage was doomed to fail from the start—they didn't have that much in common and fought bitterly over their differences. My grandmother was a slowpoke and a clean freak. She could literally spend hours dawdling and dusting—and this drove my grandfather bonkers. In turn, he was really cheap and controlling with money, and my grandmother, who liked clothes and jewelry, didn't always acquiesce to his demands. They struggled financially, and fought over money all of their married life—including on my wedding day.

I was devoted to my grandparents, as they were to me, and I shared a deeply assured attachment with them. They were extremely "with it" and throughout my twenties, when they were still healthy, I would meet them for dinner or we'd see foreign films together (they took me to my first indie movie when I was in high school). I could easily converse and connect with them, and our relationship was always effortless. Their love was absolutely unconditional, and when I was growing up they were my anchors.

Regrettably, my mother's relationship with her parents was very different from the one I enjoyed. Her earliest memories are of them arguing. Their fighting upset her so much she would literally vomit out of fear. An only child who was on the bookish side, she would retreat into her own world to deal with the constant ruckus. When my mother was eight her parents decided to split up, which was extremely rare in those days. After heading to Reno for a "quickie divorce," my grandmother had to get a job to support herself and my mom. My grandfather owned a bar, worked long hours, and was rarely around. Apparently my grandmother could not work full time and care for a child, and consequently my mother was sent away to boarding school. Now mind you this was no fancy boarding school—it was a shoddy operation for kids whose parents couldn't care for them. Apparently she was miserable and treated poorly. A skinny girl, she was forced to eat, and if she refused, she was isolated and severely beaten. She felt cast off, hated her parents, and would hide when they came to visit. My heart breaks as I write this to think about my mother as a little girl separated from her family— frightened and alone. My mother never forgave her parents for this abandonment.

However, just five years after their divorce was finalized, my grandparents got back together and remarried! As the story goes, my handsome grandfather became engaged to a much younger woman and called my grandmother in hysterics begging her to save him, which she did. So at thirteen my mother left school and returned home to live with her parents. I do think those were more favorable times and things had turned the corner financially.

While writing this chapter I began to contemplate my grandmother's relationship with her parents. If it was really assured, why would she have picked my grandfather (other than the fact that he was handsome) and then remarried him? The obvious answer is that times were hard, they were poor, and a single woman with a child had limited options. Still, it made me think. My mother and grandmother had a complicated relationship, and I recall that my mother displayed anger and was guarded and defensive when in her company. While I certainly understand the difficulties they endured, I wondered (digging to the core), was there more? I remembered my mother telling me that she did not like her grandmother, and that she was selfish and critical. And I believe my mother once intimated that her grandmother should have taken her in rather than allow her to be sent away during her parents' divorce. Then recently, out of the blue, a cousin of my mother's contacted me. She was very close to my grandmother and told me many wonderful and heartwarming stories. But she also echoed what my mother had said, and added that my grandmother's mother was not a particularly nice person. These important clues led me to wonder if my great-grandmother was a selfish person and a critical parent to my grandmother. And in turn, could my grandmother have been critical toward my mother? After studying these leads, and knowing how my mother parented me, I came to believe that my grandmother's attachment to her mother was actually ambivalent, and not assured as she had believed. And the repercussion of this was passed on directly to my mother, and then via her parenting, to me.

My Paternal Grandparents

Although lovely people, my paternal grandparents lacked the panache and vibrancy of my other, more exotic grandparents. They were conservative, proper, and traditional people who were kind and loved their grandchildren very much. My father's parents were very family-oriented, and when I was a child we spent most Friday evenings at their home with various other relatives. Those are happy memories for me.

My grandfather was an immigrant from Romania who arrived at Ellis Island when he was just four years old. He emigrated with his father and three siblings. His mother had died during childbirth when he was two. Life for my grandfather was unbelievably difficult. Like my other grandfather, he was extremely poor. His father worked several jobs in order to care for his children, but could barely make ends meet. My great-grandfather could scarcely survive without a wife and as a result he remarried a woman several years his junior. Shortly thereafter they had a few more kids. Allegedly, this stepmother was not the kindest of creatures and had no interest whatsoever in her new husband's children from his previous marriage. Hence, when my grandfather was thirteen and his brother fifteen, they were sent far away from home, and his two sisters were put into foster care. I did not know any of this until two years ago when researching that school project along with my daughter. My father and his sister did not have a lot of information about their father's childhood when I asked them. They suggested I contact their cousin Doris, who lives in Rhode Island, and whom I had met maybe twice in my life. Sure enough, good old Doris had tons of information that blew my mind and helped me put some missing pieces of my personal love map together.

Apparently my grandfather was sent on the "Orphan Train" to the Midwest to work on a farm. According to Doris, from the late 1800s to the early 1900s, an estimated two hundred thousand children who were orphaned, abandoned, or homeless were transported across America on trains. My grandfather and his brother, Doris's father, were among them. Some went to new homes and others went to work. My grandfather and his brother literally lived as orphans and were separated from their family for many years. Like prisoners, they labored for long hours, had few freedoms or pleasures, and were treated very poorly. I can only imagine how dreadful it was. Several years later when World War I broke out, they escaped and headed back to the East Coast. My grandfather eventually made his way to New York City with many stops and odd jobs along the way. Upon arrival he secured a position in a garment factory repairing steam irons. As this tale goes, my grandfather was a smart and industrious man who quickly figured how to take apart and rebuild irons and other electrical equipment. He then studied at night to become an electrician, becoming one of the first licensed electricians in the state of New York, and subsequently started his own company making steam irons that were used in the garment business. The company he founded is still in business today.

I remember my grandfather as quiet and serious. He was a formal man who regularly wore a tie and lived by a certain code of conduct. He was a staunch Republican and had very defined views of the world. A man's man, he could be a bit rough and liked to drink Wild Turkey. He did have a gentle side, which came out in his later years and was mostly reserved for his grandchildren. He was quite generous and financially helped his sisters and several of my grandmother's sisters when they required assistance. He had a strong belief in education and insisted on paying for all of his grandchildren's college so we could experience what he hadn't been able to. I do believe, however, that he was an austere father with a mean temper who could not connect emotionally. Could you blame him? The man was brought up with so much abandonment, disappointment, and abuse (avoidant attachment) that he never properly learned how to be in an intimate relationship. At heart he was a good man and at times a sentimental one. But he was damaged from his earlier experiences, and sadly he didn't have much ability to demonstrate love or affection to his wife or children. He was impatient with my grandmother, and I recall several incidents where he was downright disrespectful toward her.

Just like my other grandmother, my paternal grandmother came from a loving home. I recall hearing that her mother had been a real matriarch. Estelle had one brother and four sisters and they were a very close family, so close that none of her four sisters ever married or moved away from home. My grandmother, who was the youngest, was the only daughter to leave the nest. My great-aunts were all wonderful women—they were smart and resourceful, and became career girls, which was fairly unheard of back then. One even ran the Math Department for the Department of Education in New York City. The closest I ever came to discovering why they all remained spinsters was when one great-aunt disclosed to me that their mother could be, well, a bit anxious and controlling, and didn't exactly encourage her daughters to leave.

My grandfather was thirty, a confirmed bachelor, when he met my grandmother. A petite but buxom blond with green eyes, Estelle fell for him and convinced him to change his ways. I don't know how she did it—both persuade him to marry her and get out from under her mother's thumb—but she did! They had an extremely patriarchal marriage. Arthur did things his way, and my grandma always submitted. Due to his avoidant upbringing, I doubt that he understood women or love relationships in any meaningful way. My grandmother, although a lovely woman who was so well intentioned, was a Nervous Nelly, just like her mother (biology/temperament). She suffered from anxiety and occasionally drove everyone in the family nuts. She could also be insecure and demanding of attention and affection. Although I loved her, I experienced her to be needy and overwhelming. Thus, from what I understand about her mother's parenting plus my own observations, I speculate that her attachment with her mother was less assured than she professed it to be, and more toward ambivalent.

I loved all of my grandparents, and individually they were outstanding people. I really do believe they tried to be the best parents that they could with all the hardships they had to endure. There were limited resources to teach people how to be good partners, let alone good parents, and everyone flew by the seat of his pants. They did, however, strive to be excellent grandparents, and thankfully, their love and support was the backbone of my young existence.

It's easy to write about those who are gone yet remain in our minds. It's more challenging to tell you about my parents and upbringing. My parents are still alive, and today, I am close to them both. Sadly, this wasn't always the case. Creating a relationship with them took a lot of endeavor and understanding on my part. It's nearly impossible to do that kind of work without having the insight or compassion for the adversity that they suffered in their earlier lives. For this reason I am urging you to conduct a detailed survey of your grandparents' lives. Through this exercise you will uncover substantial information that will help you understand how your parents' personalities were formed, how they behaved in their marriage, and why they parented you as they did. This work will eventually lead you, as it did me, toward understanding, acceptance, and, if needed, forgiveness. These stepping stones are part of the process that will enable you to fully understand your relationship and its ending, and lead you into transformation and eventually toward full recovery.

My Parents

My mother, who was brilliant and beautiful, resembled Audrey Hepburn. She shared her father's intellect, sense of humor, and interest in liberal politics, and her mother's passion for the arts. She was a serious student, a voracious reader with an unparalleled vocabulary, and a skillful pianist. She attended a local college and excelled. At nineteen she met the man she would marry at a dance. He was tall, blond, and quite attractive—an upcoming lawyer and the son of a prominent judge. During their first dance he announced that she was dancing with her future husband. She fell deeply in love with him and they married shortly thereafter. My grandmother told me he was a wonderful man and a devoted husband and son-in-law. Apparently he adored my mother. I think the two years they shared together, until his cancer diagnosis, were exceedingly joyful ones for her. Sadly, though, he passed away, and my mother became a widow at age twenty-one.

My father was the firstborn male and was unequivocally fawned over by his mother, her four unmarried sisters, and his maternal grandmother. There was a lot of estrogen in that house and I don't think he liked that one bit. I believe he found his mother to be a worrier and overprotective, and in response, he learned to do his own thing to escape from her. And he could do his own thing because he was definitely the prince in that family. Like his father, my dad was also a real boy—he was very athletic and loved sports and hanging out with his buddies.

Due to their limitations, my father wasn't deeply bonded to either of his parents, and thus I propose his attachment style was on the ambivalent spectrum. His father was simply unable to intimately connect, and his mother, because of her anxiety, needed too strong of an attachment (enmeshment). Consequently, he became a very independent man with guarded psychological perceptions. Also, because of his father's parenting, plus the model of his parents' marriage, his ability to demonstrate love or affection was compromised.

My parents were set up on a blind date by their two mothers, who were acquaintances. I cannot initially say that it was a match made in heaven. My mother had moved back into her parents' home after the death of her husband, and my father had recently returned from the Korean War. I certainly can see what my father saw in my mother—she was stunning, smart, and cultured. She was also a widow for only one year, and tragically battered by life. My mother, who did grow to love my father dearly, said he was very intelligent and he made her laugh. Her mother told her that he was from a good family, and he'd be a good provider.

My parents wed, moved to the suburbs, and soon had three children. Similarly to my father's upbringing, my parents' marriage was wholly patriarchal. My father called all the shots and my mother always complied. Mothering strategies, alas, eluded my mother. Coming from such a dysfunctional childhood, she had no script to follow and few coping skills. As was common in those times, my father expected her to raise us kids and she often felt alone, unsupported, and overwhelmed.

Mom had many great qualities. She was very funny, loved to laugh, and enjoyed a dirty joke. She was hip, chic, played the guitar, and sang like Joan Baez. She had a huge social conscience and dragged us children around to peace marches during the Vietnam War. When she was in a good mood she could light up a room. But emotionally she was pretty closed up. She was beaten down from her avoidant childhood and the subsequent tragedy of her first husband's death. What few resources she had went into her marriage, which left very little space for us. My father, a traditionalist, liked things a certain way and expected a lot from her. He never fully understood her limitations, and I think she often frustrated him. Dad, like his father, had a temper (biology), and regularly lost it with her. I believe she found pleasing him a full-time job. But she wanted to be a good wife—to be successful at something. This became her life mission, and she regularly told me that my father came first. Running a household and parenting three children was just too much for her. She was frequently annoyed, overstressed, and in turn, as her father before her, she developed a temper (biology). As a result she rarely showed us any physical or emotional affection or took care of our emotional needs in any substantive way. Her gas tank was perpetually on Low.

I do have a lot of joyful childhood memories and many of them involve my siblings. I was the eldest with a sister and brother in tow. From a very young age I took on a motherly role with both of my siblings. I think my parents were grateful for this because neither of them were even a tiny bit maternal. And from that time forward there was an unspoken rule in our house that anyone with emotional needs went to see Rachel (my therapist training started at a very young age).

My father is at heart a very good man. He is honest, has never been unemployed, pays his bills on time, loves to pay taxes, and is not a philanderer. If you asked him, he would say he was an outstanding father and husband. He worked hard but also played hard. He was a businessman who took his job very seriously, and was well respected by his employees, associates, and friends alike. He was very generous and a good provider. He definitely loved his family, but because of his ambivalent attachment, and as his father before him, he had difficulties expressing his love. He could be impatient, had a fierce temper (biology), and I was afraid of him. He was old-school and believed that "children should be seen and not heard." Our house was not a democracy—he was the rule maker and rarely gave us a chance to express our views once a decision was made. Since childhood he'd always gotten his way, and he wasn't about to change that just because he became a husband and father. He had high expectations for his children, and I believe we continually disappointed him.

My Siblings and Me

We weren't the easiest kids in the world. We were extremely social, brought home lackluster grades, and were not intellectuals like our parents. I believe they found us to be unimpressive and mediocre—and had no problem about telling us so. My dad was a better parent when we were little. He enjoyed playing with us, and could connect with less effort on that level. However, as we grew up a huge generation gap developed, as was quite common in the '60s and '70s, and we just didn't relate to each other. I believe he really didn't understand girls, and my sister and I were 100 percent girly girls—emotional, dramatic, fashion forward, and boy crazy. And my baby brother, who was sensitive and artistic, was not a manly man. Truly, my dad just didn't get us.

When my sister went through puberty a severe change occurred. She became moody, stubborn, and volatile. She had a real mouth on her, and didn't like to be told what to do. She regularly pushed back against my father, and he didn't like it one bit. Thus the adolescent and teen years in my household became a perilous and chaotic time. She regularly acted out with both of my parents, and a great deal of tension and fighting ensued. This was a terrible period in the history of our family. To deal with this angst, plus my own deep-rooted feelings of inadequacy from my parents' challenges expressing love, pride, or support, I needed to create survival tactics. As a result, my coping mechanisms became work and boys.

Like my sister, I didn't like to be told what to do. I found my father's parenting conditional and controlling, and similar to him, I developed an independent streak of my own. Thinking back, I realize that I had to become self-reliant if I was going to outlast my teen years. I needed to figure out how to take care of myself because I felt I wasn't getting what I needed from my parents. This trait really helped me survive and has served me well my entire life, proving that opportunities to learn and grow can come from one's struggles.

Things became progressively worse at home and my father and I regularly clashed. When I was fifteen years old, he was so fed up with me that he insisted I get a summer job so I could support myself. This and convincing me not to drop out of college were the best gifts he ever gave me. So off I went into the world of work. I got my first job waitressing at a truck stop on the intersection of two busy roads in our town. I applied with my two girlfriends and we were all hired. By the end of the day I was the last remaining—they had both been fired. I was all alone with the meanest boss, maybe the meanest person, I had ever known. I was terrified of him and would weep in the bathroom when he yelled at me, which was a regular occurrence. But I refused to give up. I persevered. I was a quick learner and a hard worker and over time that mean boss took me under his wing and taught me everything I needed to know about the restaurant business. He appreciated my work ethic and came to admire me, as I did him. He threw me a huge party when I had to return to school at the end of the summer—something he had never done for any of his prior staff. Work made me feel confident and valued. It enabled me to shine on a larger stage. This was the summer of my awakening. From that day forward I have never stopped working. It is very much part of who I am and it continues to bring me joy and esteem, and allows me to feel accomplished, especially when the chips are down. Equally important, that boss became a mentor to me, and from then on I learned to search out and rely on mentors for teaching, nurturing, and support—a great resource that continues to guide me today.

My other coping mechanism was love, and unluckily, I was less proficient in this area. I was a pretty and outgoing girl who enjoyed fun and laughter. I had a strong network of friends, which was another important escape for me. I regularly turned to my friends, and then eventually, to boys for support and attachment. However, as time passed, instead of focusing on my female relationships, or school, or sports and hobbies, like a normal teen, I became overly interested in romance. Boys responded to me, and I remember that it made me feel important. These were new feelings for me because I felt unloved, unheard, and misunderstood by my parents. At sixteen I had my first serious relationship, which lasted two years. We shared a mature connection and were very devoted to each other. I recall needing that relationship like the air that I breathed—it made me feel safe and loved.

When we amicably parted ways an interesting pattern developed. I became a serial dater, and never felt happy or fulfilled unless I was involved with someone. Obviously there were many problems with this behavior. As I have explained, when we look toward a romantic partner to wholly get our needs met, to make us feel confident, to fill our void, we are setting ourselves up for trouble. Of course I was completely unaware of this at the time and just thought I was a normal girl who was boy crazy.

During the summer before I left for college, I fell hard for an absolutely gorgeous guy from the wrong side of the tracks whose heart belonged to someone else. We dated irregularly, yet I became completely infatuated with him. He was bad for me on so many levels, but I was hooked in and just couldn't let go. On a deeply unconscious level I was determined (no—make that frenzied) to make him love me and forget about his ex-girlfriend. If I could only do that, I deduced, I would feel special. I would be important. I would actually matter. My psyche cried out, "Please choose me!"

But of course it never happened and ridiculously, I hung in the game for well over a year. He was the son of an alcoholic who drank too much, had low self-worth, and couldn't commit to anyone, let alone me. We eventually broke up, and I remember suffering terribly. It was a pain like I had never felt, and today I understand that it was my first abandonment depression. I have a vivid memory of walking around on a beautiful summer day asking myself why I felt so absolutely lousy and wondering if I was ever going to feel any better. It's been more than thirty years since that breakup, and I can still recall that frightful feeling. Regrettably this was a pattern that went on for several years.

Emotionally I floundered during my college years. I missed my high school supports and did not have the esteem to excel. I regularly felt depressed and vulnerable. Hence, I turned to my healthier coping mechanism in order to survive. Although financially I didn't need to, I worked in various jobs all through college, which enabled me to feel grounded and secure. As was my pattern, I made bosses my mentors and flourished under their tutelage. I was offered a big job during my sophomore year of college, which prompted the conversation with my father where he literally begged me not to drop out, stating that it would be a decision I'd regret for the rest of my life—and he was right.

With regard to dating, I continued with my unhealthy behaviors. Although many nice boys asked me out, I had no interest in them. Sometimes I would try. If they were kind and paid attention to me, it just felt incredibly foreign and I couldn't respond. I broke a lot of hearts in this way. I continued to be attracted only to men who for one reason or another had no idea how to treat a woman or could not commit. If you were sexy, detached, or screwed up, you were my kind of guy! You even got extra points if you were in a rock band or loved drugs or alcohol more than me. I was a stubborn little thing and I didn't give up easily—probably to avoid the break-up pain that I was already familiar with and always feared was just around the corner. Thus, my story at the time was that I mostly felt unlucky and blamed myself (self blame = depression) and my parents for my unfortunate circumstances. I did not have the ability at the time to examine my core and create a history.

But today, looking back with perspective, all of these men had major intimacy issues and came from ambivalent or avoidant families themselves, but of course I didn't understand any of this at the time. And because of my own ambivalent upbringing, this behavior seemed natural to me. These were the boys I fell hard for and it never dawned on me that I was doing anything wrong or had alternatives. I was so desperate to find love and, sorry for the cliché, but I was certainly looking for it in all the wrong places. And because you are a good student and have paid attention to the last chapter, you understand what this behavior signified. Yes indeed, I was steeped in repetition compulsion and saw no way out. And every time one of these relationships ended, I would experience an awful abandonment depression, which only fueled my obsession to get back out there and find someone new to take away that pain.

I repeatedly dated men who really didn't care about me, who were narcissistic, emotionally detached, or commitment phobic, and you probably know why:

1. It felt completely normal and comfortable to me. I didn't feel loved by my parents so this type of attachment (or I should say "detachment") was familiar to me, and honestly, I didn't feel I deserved much more.

2. Although I had some self-confidence from my achievements, I had very little *relationship* esteem, so having someone mistreat me was par for the course.

3. I was frantic to find someone to love me because I had a huge emotional void and I surmised that it would be filled by the love of a man.

4. I was picking men who had character flaws similar to my father and mother and was desperately trying to get them to notice and love me. But I was choosing men who had attachment issues, and ridiculously expected them to heal me, subconsciously hoping it would cure my old wounds from my perceived early abandonment. Thus, I experienced the paradox of repetition compulsion.

Eventually I started to realize that this behavior really wasn't working for me. I was walking around feeling dejected a lot of the time. I had just broken up with a guy I was pretty crazy about. Truly, he was mostly a good soul—a jazz lover who wanted to be a DJ. But guess what? The entire time we were together he had another girlfriend. We weren't adulterers, mind you—this was a situation we had all preapproved! I even knew his girlfriend. I thought I loved him, and was therefore willing to accept a situation that completely wasn't in my best interest. But I stuffed those feelings away and pretended it was all very modern. He was a year older than me and the day he graduated from college he capriciously announced that he was moving away to start a new life with his other girlfriend, who happened to come from one of the wealthier families in America. I was devastated by this news (what was I thinking?) and described my wounded feelings to a good friend. This friend was the one who finally confronted me. He said he believed I had some issues that needed tending and suggested that I would benefit from counseling. And as I've already explained, this conversation was the catalyst for my life change. My jazz-fanatic boyfriend was the last unhealthy relationship I ever had.

Everyone loves an upstart, and just like my two grandfathers before me, I was determined to climb out of my emotional poverty and create a new life for myself. My friend had given me the name and number of a therapist and I wasted no time making that phone call. Starting my own process of healing and understanding was very scary, but I knew it was time. It's a real challenge to reveal our deep-seated fears to one another, but I knew I needed to create supports for myself and I suspected that adding therapy to my system was a good move. Intuitively, I knew I had only two roads ahead of me: a life of continual heartache or one that I suspected could be healthier and much more fulfilling.

Starting the process of therapy is like being an excavator on an archaeological dig. Each time you uncover a new buried artifact in your psyche, you meticulously wipe it off with a very small brush (not a sledgehammer) in order to examine the fine details. My therapist was a warm, wonderful, and maternal woman who patiently and gently led my excavation. Without a doubt, her guidance and support changed my life.

Even though I had never been in therapy, I attained a bit of self-awareness. Psychology had always fascinated me. I was quickly able to describe my patterns to her. Although I had some inkling as to where my behavior originated, I was clueless about how to stop it. We spent a great deal of time discussing how my parents' personalities were formed, their marriage, their complexities, and how it all affected my development. She described healthy attachment, unconditional love, and expressed that in her opinion, I didn't get the emotional support that I needed to thrive. I cannot describe to you how liberating it was to hear this. I had walked around for so many years feeling as if there was something wrong with me. For the first time in my life I felt validated and, as you know, validation is such an important component in healing.

My therapist also made it possible for me to see that I was actually extremely resourceful and entirely healthy in many ways. I had used my relationship with my grandparents, my friendships, my first boyfriend, and my jobs to keep me glued together. I realized that these components helped me develop independence and confidence, which ultimately gave me strength and kept me moving forward. Once I acknowledged that, she insisted that I had the resources to break my dysfunctional dating patterns. Together we set out to do just that. Discussing my childhood and the alienation I had felt was very painful, and this sent me to a pretty dark place. Still, I hung on to hope and plowed ahead. So many people are afraid to do this work (and believe me, I get it), but you really can't fully heal until you roll up your sleeves and dive in. When we bury our sadness deep inside and refuse to acknowledge or examine it, it sets us up for a lifetime of unconscious living and, worse, chronic dissatisfaction.

As my counseling neared completion my healing and understanding were well under way. I was feeling more hopeful and starting to emerge from my black cloud of sadness. Curiously a new emotion emerged: anger. As I've explained, it's very important to get in touch with your anger, yet we have to be careful to not let it get the best of us. With my newly discovered awareness, I contacted my parents to tell them that I had determined that they were not so great at parenting—and perhaps they shouldn't have had kids. As you can imagine, this didn't go over very well and we went into an unpleasant period of playing the blame game. My father and I can both be prosecutorial, and these conversations accomplished nothing other than making me feel pretty awful. I soon discovered that our negative engagement dance was not doing either of us one bit of good. And perhaps you'll also recall that I've remarked that we rarely get closure from those who have hurt us. Closure comes from our supports, and closure comes from ourselves.

A major turning point for me was when I began the process of exploring my parents' upbringing and started to feel some deep empathy for them. I came to understand that due to their own childhoods, plus the tragedies in my mother's earlier life, they really did the best that they could with the equipment that they had. Over time I realized that my parents actually did love their children, they just found it hard to love us in the way we needed to be loved. Maybe they were afraid, maybe they didn't know any better, maybe our temperaments (biology) didn't match, and maybe they themselves hadn't been loved as they needed to be. These concepts gave me a lot of perspective. Once I understood this, I was ready to forgive them and move firmly into my own personal transformation.

I remained in counseling for more than a year. I was developing enhanced self-confidence, getting my groove, and I tried not to let anything interfere with this. I had graduated from college, was working, making new friends, and starting to come into my own. Around this same time my brother and sister had left home for college and my parents experienced a turning point in their lives too. With their children nearly grown and their parental responsibilities lessened, they became more content, and their marriage improved. My father was more successful in his career and started slowing down. They traveled, enjoyed their lives, and were more accessible. My mother even got some help herself and sought out treatment for depression, which she credits for changing her life. Also, unexpectedly, my father started recognizing and acknowledging me. After I spent a few years in the workforce, he told me that I impressed him. He admired my success and competence so much, he even offered me a position in his business. My own personal growth, plus my parents' new interest in having a relationship with me, was the perfect combination for my complete metamorphosis. I had finally turned the corner.

Those next few years were much happier ones for me. I began dating again when I knew I was fully transformed and able to make better choices. I started going out with nicer guys and experiencing mutually fulfilling relationships. At first it did feel a bit awkward and, truth be told, I did miss my "bad boys" a tiny bit. But I was absolutely determined not to go back to that lifestyle. After the initial discomfort passed, I actually started enjoying being with men who respected and valued me and sought out commitment. This was the final icing on my already-baked cake—it felt so good to be involved in good relationships with proper men! And guess what? When these relationships ended for one reason or another, I was perfectly fine. I did not suffer abandonment depression, and even if the breakups were sad, I brushed myself off, took care of myself, and focused on the things that I loved in my new life.

Several years into my recovery I met my husband. We were set up by default. My colleague Becky and I were bitching to my boss, Kathe, about being single, and she said she had two guys to introduce to us. I was meant to be matched up with a very upper-crust man named Frank, who hobnobbed with the Kennedys, and Becky was supposed to meet Gary. It took Kathe a while to pull these dates together, and as time passed, Becky and Frank had moved on and met others. "I just don't see it," Kathe protested. "Gary is too rock-and-roll and I don't think you'll like him. But I guess I could set you up with him, if you insist." I insisted. Hesitatingly she did, and we've been together ever since.

Although Gary and I bonded quickly, he had to pass a lot of tests in order to achieve serious-boyfriend status. I needed to know that he was normal, healthy, and that he was real. Over time I discovered that he came from a great family and was very close to his mother and three younger sisters. Finally—a man in my life who had a well-developed emotional side and respected women! He had no childhood traumas or dramas, he was easygoing, and he treated me very well.

In the end, I made a good pick. Gary is a wonderful husband and father, and we've worked hard over the years to keep our marriage strong. We are a very good match and complement each other. We appreciate our similarities and respect our differences. Although I was already in a very good place when I met him, falling in love with a good man and participating in a healthy relationship completed my recovery.

The path to accepting my childhood, forgiving my parents, and working on my personal flaws was a long and winding one. As time passed I too was willing to accept responsibility for the things I did to hurt or frustrate my parents and I am fully accountable for my less-than-perfect early relationship performance and break-up behavior. If you are determined to do this work and keep an open mind, life will continue to bring you little gifts. Upon the birth of my daughter, my father turned into the "world's best grandpa." He was, and continues to be, extremely devoted to his only grandchild. He would spend hours playing with her and planning fun adventures. I recall watching one of these scenes with his sister, who had a bemused look on her face. When I asked her about her expression, she turned to me and blurted out, "He never played with you kids like this!"

Two years ago my mother was diagnosed with a rare degenerative disease and is gravely ill as I write this. My father completely stepped up and is doing an extraordinary job caring for her. To watch my mother—who endured so many hardships—have life sucked away from her in her early seventies is a tragedy of huge proportions. Yet to observe my father—who always lived life on his own terms and had others at his beck and call—embrace the role of a selfless caretaker, something completely foreign to him, has profoundly changed the way I look at him. Although our relationship was strained for many years, today I am proud to call him my father and I think he feels the same way about me.

I think there is always something to learn from every woman's story and I hope that you found some value in reading mine. Even if you were raised in a family with assured attachment and had minimal biological, cultural, or social stressors; even if your personal love map looks entirely different from mine, breakups can be agonizing and so difficult to transcend. We all have questions that require honest answers, and a looking back at your earlier life holds many clues. Creating your personal love map (and doing so for your ex) and writing your autobiography will really help you put the missing pieces together. It will also make you feel as if you've accomplished something concrete when so much is in flux. And it's cathartic!

Life is full of challenges, and I continue to reinvent myself and attempt to be the best I can be. At a young age I refused to become a victim or allow myself to remain trapped in a life of dysfunction and unhappiness. I worked so hard to heal, understand, and transform—and I encourage you to do exactly the same. Anyone can recover from her earlier circumstance and/or break-up experience and recapture her life. You just have to want it and be brave enough to strive for it, even if it's grueling. In writing this book, I am giving you the validation, support, and tools necessary to do the work and make these changes. It's fully possible to get back on track—and I really believe you can do it, because I did it myself.

12

Letting Go

"When you're in a bad marriage, you feel absolutely hopeless. But when you get out of that, and you move on and you let go—I mean really let go—you are fine. You get to feel hopeful again. Hopeful about the future, about your life. Hope will keep you going." —*Helene*

"I used to think I'd take him back under any circumstances—no questions asked. But today, a year later, I wouldn't even consider it. He humiliated me and broke my heart. I'm a completely different person now, and only surround myself with positive people. I'm so over him—and it feels fantastic!" —*Vanessa*

It is extremely apropos that I am writing about letting go today, which is exactly eighteen months from the day I put pen to paper and started conceptualizing *The Breakup Bible*. So many women I interviewed told me that eighteen months was their magic number. It represented the point when they were finally ready and able to completely say farewell to their past and embrace their new lives.

For me, letting go of my old relationship behavior happened in fits and starts. Even as I began creating and interpreting my love map, I still made mistakes. Mentally I was putting my puzzle together, but it took time for my heart to catch up with my head. I was afraid that I didn't have what it took to meet a nice guy or participate in a healthy relationship, and that fear would sporadically sabotage my prospects. Occasionally I did revert back to some of my earlier conduct. I remember feeling stronger, more pieced together, so I decided to test myself to see if I could now handle situations that were previously difficult for me. I'd engage with an old boyfriend to see if I could get my say in or deal with him more effectively. On the subject of infidelity, which I mentioned earlier, one notorious weekend I even visited an ex in another city, subjecting myself to a complete catastrophe that would actually make a great scene in a comedy. Luckily, I can laugh about it today, yet it did warn me that I was jeopardizing my progress. On occasion my recovery path felt slow or too arduous for me. I'd become impatient, frustrated, lose focus, and, at times, lose hope. One of these periods prompted a conversation with a friend who was several years older than me, and who had overcome some real obstacles in her own life. I sought her guidance one evening when I was feeling especially blue. I remember crying to her that I wanted to change, I wanted to be "normal"—but on that particular night I felt like romantic happiness was beyond my reach.

I vividly recall her words, which were both soothing and wise. She told me, "Rachel, what concerns me is that you're allowing some old emotions and behavior to hold you back from something you really want to do. You're hiding behind the image of your former insecure self who was afraid of feeling her feelings and lacked the tools to change course. And because of this you are not allowing yourself to see your new growth or feel the power of who you are becoming today. Maybe it's time you consider letting go of whatever you're still holding on to, and believe in yourself enough to break these old patterns. If you fall down, I'm here to help you. But if you fall down and I'm not here, trust in yourself. I know you can handle this or any challenge, and when you own that, it's the very best lesson in life."

Erica's patience and guidance helped me see that I actually was making some good progress, and after our talk I did get back on track. I refocused with a renewed sense of purpose, and as you already know, I eventually let go and wholly recovered. It's hard for me to explain the fear and joy I experienced when I finally turned the corner and grew into my new self; the exuberance I felt as I finally pushed past my confines and really let go. As I discovered my brawn, the image of my former self became smaller and smaller.

Beginning to Let Go

It takes a vast amount of insight and courage to change the way we look at things and consider another perspective. We tend to hang on to old feelings and beliefs like our childhood teddy bears, and letting go is a very intimidating prospect. Yet we always benefit when we find kernels of truth hidden within ourselves and bravely decide to change course. When we take the time to listen to our gut, to follow our newly sharpened instincts, as scary as it may be, transformation is right around the corner.

We've traveled a great distance on our journey together. You've worked so hard, and continue to test your mettle in remarkable ways. I have absolute faith in you and am so impressed with how resilient you are becoming. Timing is everything, and I believe you are ready to tackle some new challenges once again. For this reason, I am going to suggest that it's time for you to begin the process of letting go. As scary as that prospect may be, letting go will allow you to start moving with greater intention away from the past and firmly into your new life. Letting go is about liberation. Letting go is about

Acceptance

Accepting that your relationship has finally come to an end and preparing to let go is one of the hardest things that you are ever going to have to do in your life. We women are optimistic beings who don't give up so easily. We like a challenge and will go full speed when we know what we want. Knowing when to walk away from a harmful or hurtful situation takes a great deal of fortitude. It also takes time, wisdom, guts, grace, and determination.

freedom. Letting go is about discovering a brand-new type of love—the love of yourself. Believe me when I tell you, this is the greatest love you will ever experience.

I fully understand that a lot of you are still smarting from your breakup, and I've described to you that full recovery takes endeavor, and it also takes time. Please continue to be patient with yourself, especially on difficult days. But I am hopeful that by actively participating in healing and understanding, especially now that you've completed your and your ex's personal love maps, you are starting to have some better days (maybe even some great days) and can finally see the light up ahead. Even though I've plied you with so much information and encouraged you to stay the course, I've never lost sight for a moment that you are all still sorting through the rubble, and it can be so daunting to move on and create a brand-new life for yourself. Please don't forget that even at this stage in the game, progress is still two steps forward and one step back. But this will change and the path ahead will soon be crystal clear.

I now have some good news *and* some bad news to share with you. Here it is:

Good news: This is the last chapter where we will be discussing your breakup or divorce and your ex.

Bad news: This is the last chapter where we will be discussing your breakup or divorce and your ex.

I believe these statements are probably among the most exciting and terrifying ones that you have read thus far! Once we get into the "transformation" section (phase 3), we will be closing the door on your past and preparing to walk strongly and proudly into your new life. But first, in this chapter we will be discussing the concept of letting go. I will give you a variety of suggestions and anecdotes for contemplation.

We all respond to new challenges in a variety of ways. Some of us confront them and dive in headfirst, and others hide under the covers or head toward the hills. Letting go is a challenge and it is a choice—and it's one I hope you accept with dignity. We all know people who hang on to their pain, their fury, their indignation, and wear it as a badge for the world to see. I recently heard a story about a woman who talks incessantly about her divorce to anyone who will listen—and her marriage ended more than a decade ago. Sadly, I occasionally see this too. The broken-down soul who refuses to understand, acknowledge, take responsibility, forgive, or let go. The woman who is encapsulated for an eternity in bitterness and grief. Who goes through the motions without ever taking chances or being open to creating a new life or discovering love. I implore you, never let this be you.

Letting go is indisputably one of the hardest things I will ask you to do. Although I know you are all desperate to recover from your ordeal and move forward, we do tend to hold on tight to our pain, our memories, and our old love feelings out of familiarity and habit. Saying good-bye to that mind-set can be very scary. Often we get too comfy with our sorrow, our nostalgia, even our anger. Many of us are afraid to let go because it means we have to fully accept the fact that our relationship is over and there are more challenges ahead. Our tendency is to fight for what is comfortable, ironically even when it's most uncomfortable. But you know that old saying about one door closing and another opening—think of this new stage with that wise proverb in mind.

Letting go enables you to explore the world from an entirely different perspective and see how vast and exciting it truly is. It prepares you to rediscover yourself, and, in the process, determine what you really want from life. Letting go allows you to write your own script where you are the leading lady as opposed to a bit player. It gives you permission to create the existence you've always fantasized about, which will enable you to discover your true essence and fulfill all of your dreams.

Saying farewell is heartbreaking in its own right, but as you already know, the heart is a pretty strong muscle, and it does heal. Parting with our past is a crucial aspect of the recovery process, and as hard as it is, it needs to be accomplished. But fear not. As I promised, I'm going to fully coach you through. Together we'll explore various concepts and rituals of parting, and you will emerge with even more tools—from me and the community—to ease you along this last leg of understanding.

A Meditation

Let's take a moment to do a meditation together. When you are ready, please light a candle and allow it to symbolize the hell that you've been through: the sleepless nights, the loneliness, the self-doubt, the grief, the anger, the obsession, and the relentless fear. Now tell yourself it is OK to let these feelings go. Give yourself permission to heal and be whole again. Visualize your sorrow going skyward with the smoke. Let your pain be carried away by the wind. Let your anger wash out to sea. Let the guilt and remorse dissipate into the universe.

Now replace those old feelings with new and joyful ones. Picture yourself firmly in the new life that you will create for yourself. The one that you will build with your own blood, sweat, and tears. Tell yourself that the worst is over and that you are going to be fine. Prepare yourself for elation. Allow yourself to embrace silliness, joy, and laughter. Out with the old, and in with the new. The time to let go is now. Blow out the candle, take a deep cleansing breath, and let's get to work.

Treat Yourself!

Letting go is challenging! Try not to push yourself too hard and please don't get frustrated. If you're feeling stuck, as I often did in my recovery, take a break and give yourself a "mini treat." Some of my favorite simple treats are:

- A girls' night out
- A flavored latte
- Something sweet (a cupcake always cheers me up)
- A festive cocktail with a splash of champagne or passion fruit shared among friends

Healing Old Wounds

"I knew I had to let go of my old childhood resentments and to stop blaming in order to be able to start
loving." —*Alicia*

After reviewing chapter 10 on personal love maps and reading my
story in chapter 11, I hope you understand that full recovery from
your breakup may entail healing some pain from your past. For most
of us the ancient pain I speak of comes from our parents, but for
others it could be a sibling, grandparent, or other important person
in your earlier life who may have hurt, mistreated, disappointed, or
abused you. Some women said that their breakups reminded them
of past love affairs that had gone wrong, and how unexpected and
upsetting it was to relive an old heartbreak when trying to heal from
a new one.

This old pain I refer to can also originate from our own insecurities about real or perceived personal disabilities or limitations.
Letting go of your present relationship pain does entail healing
those wounds too. Once you begin the process of repairing, you'll
be pleasantly surprised how much insight, perspective, and strength
you develop. Suddenly, when the old wounds are healed, and you
take responsibility for how they affected you and your relationship,
letting go of your ex and your unpleasant thoughts and emotions is
a much easier transition. Alternatively, if you continue to hold on to
these old resentments and feelings, it's going to make your recovery
so much harder because it will complicate your ability to move on
in both life and love. I know you'll agree that this makes complete
sense.

As I explained in my personal story, acknowledging and healing my old wounds regarding my parents was the catalyst for my
growth. I could not have broken my patterns and changed my life
if I didn't understand where my problems originated and how they
affected me, and more important, committed to repairing and rebuilding. The repair I speak of consisted of understanding why my

parents raised me as they did, and eventually realizing that they did the best they could with the skills that they had. And, in my circumstances, I had to forgive them in order to truly let go. This work freed me up to rebuild myself and complete my recovery.

If you feel that certain issues from your past interfered with your relationship choice, performance, and break-up behavior, today would be a great day to begin the process of letting go of your old wounds. The very best way to do this is through a thorough and honest examination of your personal love map. The devil is definitely in the details. Go back and observe your genogram, and reread your personal autobiography. Think hard about how the person(s) who hurt you may have been damaged themselves. How were they raised and what obstacles did they have to undergo in life? What trauma, addiction, illness, personality disorder, or temperament were they afflicted with, and what interfered with their ability to love you as you deserved to be loved? And if you discover that you have unresolved past issues due to a poor body image, prejudice or racism, or learning or social issues, now would be the time to work on healing that pain too.

If there is someone in particular who hurt you in your past, and if this person is still alive, you may still be entwined in a negative engagement dance. You may be trying to get him to acknowledge his wrongdoing, take responsibility for his transgressions, notice you, apologize, or make amends. You may still be furious with him and continually attempting to hurt, shame, or cause him harm. Although that behavior may feel natural to you, it will not benefit you at all. It will cause you to continually be opening your old wounds—and living with that incessant sorrow, disappointment, and anger is mentally and physically draining.

Proper healing is about pushing past this very old pain. It's about having the good sense and maturity to finally understand what transpired in your early life, acknowledge how it affected you, and make a conscious decision to let it go. And, if you played a part in the equation, it's about taking responsibility for that piece, and forgiving yourself.

Here's a great story that's very representative of this concept that

I'd like to share with you. Sharon has been with her partner for more than a decade. She credits discovering him and their wonderful romance to her personal journey toward healing her old wounds.

"My father died when I was young, and my mother remarried a man I hated. We were 180 degrees different, my stepfather and I, and we butted heads continually. He was controlling and ultraconservative. I deplored him, and blamed my mother for marrying him and ruining my life. Holding on to that anger, that rage, really affected me—and I suffered in relationships because of this. I was unhappy and bitter and I attracted the wrong kind of people. I eventually realized that I wanted to change. I could see how my behavior and the person I had become were negatively impacting my life. I had a temper. I was angry. I was really pessimistic. So I started reading books on Buddhism and forgiveness—and a lot really resonated with me. I decided to deepen my spirituality by going away to a meditation retreat, and something amazing happened. Suddenly I felt compassion for my stepfather, for my mother, and for myself. We were all in a bad situation together and none of us knew how to figure it out. After that experience I called my stepfather and said, 'You're my friend. Let's get past this and get on with our lives.' Shortly after that I met my partner, Joel. He is a very gentle and spiritual man, and I don't think he would have had any interest in me—or I in him—had I not gone on this journey and let go of my anger and resentment from my past. It takes so much energy to stay angry at someone, so you've got to let it go. That doesn't mean you have to be best friends,

A Relapse Can Actually Be a Good Thing!

If you find that you've taken a few steps backward, which is perfectly normal, gather new data and then stop to evaluate. Ask yourself what triggered the return to an old behavior. What tools need to be put more firmly in place? What exercises do you need to revisit? Return to your love map; it will always help you find your way!

or accept poor treatment, but you have to let go. If you can't let go or forgive, you can't grow, and if you can't grow, you can't move on."

I couldn't have said it better myself.

Letting Go of Anger

"Letting go of anger is the hardest thing to do in the world. It's very hard to release it, but make no mistake—you must!" —*Jaci*

Various women I spoke with described a profound struggle with anger after their breakups. As I've described, it's very important to feel all of your feelings, and anger should be experienced, processed, and eventually released. Holding on to anger for too long is like allowing a rabid beast to live in your home. It is an extremely powerful force, and if given the opportunity, it will eat away at all that is valuable, leaving you and your loved ones in shambles. Anger uses a lot of energy, and if left to fester, it will take up too much space in your precious life. Believe me, the more anger perpetuates, the more damage it will do.

Beth, a divorced woman and breast cancer survivor, described her dance with anger to me. "We all hold on to our anger—it's very hard to release it. You think you want to release it, but if you are honest with yourself, it kind of feels good. You think it means you have control, but in actuality, it's the furthest thing from control. You end up hurting yourself physically and mentally. I started doing a lot of yoga after my cancer diagnosis, and I noticed that much of my old anger and resentment was coming up during my practice. My father was so annoying when I was growing up, and I was so angry at my mother for a million reasons. I was continually upset and frustrated with my ex. One day I asked myself what would happen if I let go of this anger. I realized I had a lot to let go of. Once you start to accept that we are all imperfect—that maybe your parents or your ex didn't know any better—it's a whole different experience. Today there is absolutely no room for anger in my life."

I urge you, please do not allow yourself to be defined by your anger. If your life is guided by rage, you will not have the resources to work on yourself, and this will hold you back in many ways. Try to get a better understanding of your struggle with anger, and use the abundant tools I have given you to make peace with it and finally let it go.

Letting Go of Fear

"I was thirty-seven, childless, and petrified that I'd never meet anyone. What was I thinking? I was successful, smart—I had two master's and a PhD, and I was attractive. But fear does get the best of you and it plays destructive tricks." —*Vivica*

Running a close second to anger, fear is unequivocally an emotion that every woman struggles with after a breakup. Many of our fears are perfectly legitimate ones, and others come from old tendencies or the temporary loss of confidence stemming from our experience with loss. The top fears women describe to me are:

- The fear of being alone
- The fear of dating again
- The fear of never being able to meet someone and have another relationship
- The fear of not being able to have children
- Financial fears
- Being fearful for the mental health of your children, yourself, and even your ex

For some lucky souls fear is a motivator, but for most of us fear is a demon. It can cause paralysis, and paralysis is extremely problematic, especially now. In order to complete the tasks I'm going to request of you in the next section, you're going to have to seriously consider letting go of your fears. I know this is easier said than done, but fear will categorically derail our work if you allow it to.

Please be very mindful of your friendship with fear, and do not allow it to brainwash or hinder you in any way. Remember that you are already busting through your fears every single day in both small and grand actions. Take comfort in that thought, and remind yourself that you have what it takes to let go of what scares you and create a brand-new life for yourself. I'm so proud of myself when I push past my fears, and I know you will be too.

Letting Go of Old Habits

"Getting used to eating alone . . . that was a hard one to conquer. That, and sleeping alone. But it's amazing when you break through that stuff and create new habits and traditions. Today I'm very independent and those things never bother me" —*Nina*

We acquire a lot of habits when we're in a relationship, which provides familiarity and comfort from the routine and battle of daily life. Yes, old habits die hard, but by making a conscious choice to let go of them we are investing in our future.

Many women described to me the various adjustments they underwent from the rhythm of living as a couple to the acclimation of flying solo. It's hard to let go of that daily check-in, or that comforting feeling that someone has your back. Letting go of even mundane routines that at the time meant absolutely nothing can seem so weighty now. Creating a new life that is defined by you is indeed challenging, but it is also so empowering.

The decision to move in a new direction will open you up to new experiences and allow you to be the very best that you can be. If you test yourself every day in simple ways you'll be delighted to see how quickly old habits are replaced by new, endearing ones. I suggest you take some time to think about some of the old habits you are missing, and create new ones to replace them with. If you enjoyed watching a certain television show with your ex, you may consider discovering a new show, or inviting a friend to watch with you. Do the same with restaurants and other routines that you once shared. As you replace the old with the new, you'll be opening yourself up to new experiences and getting some great traction in your recovery.

The Last Hurrah

> "When I got the call from my lawyer that my divorce had gone through, I felt like a huge weight had been lifted off my shoulders. That was the day when I finally said to myself, 'I am so done!'"   —*Sage*

Several women I spoke with described a single incident that helped them see the light of day and finally allowed them to cut the ties. I call this moment "the last hurrah." This is a little gift from the universe that gives you a big hint that it's time to let go. Sometimes these incidents are gentle and subtle, and other times they bang you over the head. I heard some crazy stories that were upsetting and horrifying, and others that were downright comical. Whatever the case may be, this is good material for growth, and if you allow yourself to see the lessons contained within, it will help you get additional closure. Now you may be scratching your head and saying, "Hmm, nothing I can think of," but I promise you, if you allow yourself to be open to this concept, you will discover your personal hurrah.

Jennifer's last hurrah came with a crash. Her divorce was unexpected, and for a long time she held on to hope that her husband, Alan, would return to his senses and rejoin their marriage—until the night he smashed the planter. "Alan had his visitation with our daughter for the weekend. When he returned her to me on Sunday evening, she was in a foul mood. We argued, and she called him asking him to come back and get her. Well, instead of telling her to yield to me, as he should have, he came flying over to our home, banging on the door and calling me every name in the book. I told him to calm down and go away, but he refused. Truly, I was petrified. I said, 'Alan, you've done a lot of nasty things to me, but you can't call me a bitch in my own home. Now go away, and we'll talk another time.' Then I heard a loud crash—he smashed this huge and beautiful planter on my front porch that we had purchased together on our honeymoon. I heard so much hate in his voice, and that rage was frightening. This was the most disrespectful and mean thing anyone had ever done to me. At that very moment, a power came over me. A strength I didn't even know existed. I was finally finished."

Gabriella's hurrah: running into her ex with his new girlfriend. "I had such a hard time letting go. I hung on for a ridiculous amount of time—hoping, hoping, hoping—until the night I ran into him with a girl. I was at a bar with some friends and he waltzes in, stares me straight in the eye, and sits right down and proceeds to make out with her in front of me! He totally knew what he was doing. He left me, and he knew how hurt I was—what kind of a man behaves like that? What was he thinking? Wait a minute—forget what he was thinking. What was *I* thinking? That was the night I finally pulled out of the race. If it took that sick and disrespectful act for me to let go, I'm thankful now, and consider it a gift!"

Believe me, every woman experiencing a romantic ending has many hurrahs. But the last hurrah is that crystalline moment where you say to yourself, 'This just isn't right, and I need to move on.' Remember my story about the boyfriend who cavalierly announced he was leaving town with his other girlfriend? That was my last hurrah. If you take a few moments to honestly think this through, I promise you will discover several incidents where your ex did something really foolish that hurt or disappointed you. Sometimes these incidents happen in the course of the relationship, and other times during or after the breakup.

Please write a list of every single upsetting, spiteful, disrespectful, or inappropriate thing that your ex has ever done to you—and consider using this list to help you finally let go.

A Transitional Relationship

I do maintain a belief that our best shot at becoming part of a healthy union happens when two people come together after they have fully let go of past relationships and completely transitioned into their new lives. When we take the time to learn valuable lessons, rebuild

Letting Go of the Ring

Every married woman described to me the day she took off her ring as enormously notable. Some women took it off immediately, and others describe a lengthy process toward baring their naked fingers. In our society wearing a ring is especially significant. It's a symbol that we are "spoken for" and no longer available. For many, our rings are extensions of ourselves and they hold memories of the day we became engaged and married. Our rings are physical symbols of our relationships—and letting go of that is colossal. As I write this sentence, a friend is preparing to sell her ring and travel the world with its proceeds. "I was a different person when I wore that ring, and back then it was important to me to have a nice big diamond. But today in my new life, my passion is travel. If my divorce can fund that, hurray for me!"

ourselves, and become transformed, it sets us up to make great romantic choices and enables us to perform optimally once in a new romance. Nevertheless several women I spoke with described how a premature romantic or sexual connection with another helped them to let go.

Transitional relationships do have the potential to be rather messy and even dangerous. I know more than my fair share of stories of women getting profoundly hurt by a new man when they have not yet recovered from their original breakup. Alternatively, these romances can also be the catalysts that help some detach from unhappy or unhealthy relationships or advance to a new stage after a breakup.

Kristen recalls a brief transitional relationship following her breakup as a vehicle for her awakening. "I remember it was New Year's, exactly seven months after my breakup. I felt it was the right time to cleanse and heal. I started dating a cute younger guy. We had kind of a passionate affair. The relationship lasted only a few months, and it was mostly for fun and distraction, but it definitely showed me that there were other men out there who were attracted to me and liked me—and vice versa. It definitely helped me let go. I remember a friend telling me, 'The best way to get over someone is to get under someone!'"

My friend Erin, separated for nearly two years and in early transformation, blushed while telling me that she's been spending time with a few different men. "I realize I'm not ready for a full-blown relationship yet, but I have been casually dating a few guys. It's been fun, plus a confidence builder for me at fifty-five to be flirting and, well, more than flirting again! Also it's great to see that there are single men out there who are smart, interesting, and interested in having a real relationship with a mature divorced woman."

I can only imagine that some of you who have not had a transitional relationship now wish that you had! We all fantasize from time to time that there is someone out there who will take away our sorrow and rescue us. If you want to be in a new relationship in the future, you *will* be in one. We will discuss this in chapter 15, "Dating Again." But until then, keep working on your personal growth because that is the best medicine for recovery!

Forgiveness

"I didn't need to forgive him. He didn't abuse me or leave me. He was just a big jerk. I take full responsibility for staying with him—so I had to forgive myself." —*Iris*

"I read a story about a family whose daughter was murdered, and they advocated for the murderer not to receive the death penalty. It made me think, if these people forgave their child's murderer, why should I hang on to my hate? Once I forgave, I felt so much better about my life. Forgiveness is so powerful." —*Sharon*

To my surprise, the concept of forgiveness stirred up a lot of debate and controversy within our community. This made me weigh in on some of my own convictions. How, I pondered, does one go deep into one's soul and forgive someone who has caused a tremendous amount of pain? Should we absolve someone who has hurt us through words and deeds? And is forgiveness a necessary step in our quest toward letting go? I spent a great deal of time discussing these questions with a variety of women, and many were quite conflicted over this hot topic.

Most breakups are messy affairs that can cause a lot of pain and suffering. Many of you are still coming to terms with your feelings about your ex. There is a good chance that no matter how your relationship ended, you endured a lot of distress during the process. And if you share custody of children, there is a possibility that he is still causing you aggravation from time to time. Several women I spoke with told me flat out that forgiveness was not in their repertoire. Some explained that their ex's behaviors, in their opinions, were completely unpardonable—and they had no interest in further exploring the subject. Yet others firmly believed that forgiveness was their key to letting go and expressed disbelief when I told them that many of their "sisters" disagreed with them.

Forgiveness is a conscious decision to let go of unpleasant feelings about your ex. It's about releasing the anger, resentment, and the thoughts of revenge. Forgiveness is about reaching deep into your heart, and discovering some degree of empathy or, better yet, understanding for the person who caused you pain. This doesn't mean you have to exonerate or minimize what your ex has done to hurt you—but it is about being able to look past those transgressions and say, "Yes, I can forgive this person." Believe it or not, uttering those words can really help you get on with your life.

Intellectually I'm sure you can relate to what I'm saying, but of course it does take longer for this concept to sink in. Using both love maps (yours and his) for this exercise is a great tool. There are many factors that played into why your ex behaved as he did, and comprehending what motivated his actions—no matter how vile they were—will certainly help you in colossal ways. Once you truly reach understanding, it may enable you to feel some empathy, and empathy is a huge component of forgiveness.

My feeling is that forgiveness can be extremely useful to any woman's recovery. It can accelerate your healing and should be considered a gift to yourself. If you truly challenge yourself to look past the anger, the bitterness, the disappointment, and try to find compassion for the person who has hurt you, you may surprisingly find yourself in a much better state of mind. Being able to forgive another is an extremely powerful act. It's a huge investment of consciousness and the rewards can be so profound when we discover that we are capable of going beyond ourselves and doing something that feels pretty foreign, but is in fact quite virtuous. I have made a deliberate effort to forgive every person who has ever hurt me. We are all imperfect, and I don't desire to go through life carrying resentments on my back—it serves no meaningful purpose.

Liz, a divorced woman, felt that she didn't handle herself as well as she could have during the breakup of her marriage. She had a lot of anger toward herself, and realized it was holding her back until she reconciled those feelings through forgiveness. "I had to forgive myself. I told my kids too much—things they shouldn't have known. I talked very poorly about my ex. I was too self-centered during that period. I deeply apologized to them. I didn't know at the time how much I hurt them. I didn't handle it as well as I could have, and that weighed heavily on me for a long time."

I heard a sweet story today about forgiveness that I'd like to share with you. Claire's parents divorced when she was in college. It was a contentious divorce and a difficult time for everyone involved. Her parents spent many years without contact. Decades later, while in her seventies, Claire's mother telephoned her ex-husband. What she said was, "Bob, so much time has passed. We're not getting any younger, and we're not going to be around forever. I apologize for all that I did to hurt you, and in turn, I forgive you for how you treated me. I miss having you in my life, and was wondering if perhaps we can be friends." Well, Claire's father was absolutely delighted to receive this call. He accepted her apology, and apologized to her in return. Today, in their eighties, they have a wonderful friendship and spend quality time together, which includes vacationing on cruises. As you can imagine, Claire and her siblings are delighted with this turn of events.

When you reach the point in your journey when you can finally forgive, that's one definition of coming full circle. This is when the magic happens, and then you really can let go.

Exploring Rituals

When I have a client who for one reason or another is having a particularly difficult time letting go, I reach into my bag of tricks and offer some rituals. An avid newspaper reader, I always love when I discover a story about someone making the best of a difficult situation. Several years ago I read an article about a woman who, after a bad divorce, started an online company for women wanting to sell their engagement rings. The company had become very successful and helped her fully recover. It made me think. In our country we have rituals for everything, and there are so many rituals around love, engagement and marriage, and even death. But how about rituals that can help us through the difficulties we experience through the loss of love? It seemed to me that we were lacking in those! That's when I realized that rituals could be very useful for women recovering from break-up pain, and since then I've been offering various ideas. Several women I interviewed described how rituals helped them, and here are a few of their comments:

• "On the day my divorce became final, I threw myself a party. I'd been through so much, and I needed to make this a happy day for me. There were many people who supported me through my ordeal and I wanted to say thank-you to them. So I took about ten people out to dinner and showed them my gratitude. This was my way of celebrating the beginning of a new chapter in my life. No more crying, no more bitching, moaning, or complaining. This was the day my new life began."—Kim

• "Selling all the jewelry that my fiancé had given me was my ritual. I just couldn't stand looking at it, and I knew I'd never wear it. I sold it all, and there were some expensive pieces! My ex was better with money than with emotion. With the proceeds from the sale, I put it toward the down payment on a home. For me, that was a great move."—Kali

• "I gave his clothes to Goodwill. Frankly, I considered destroying them, but I decided a charitable act would be good for my soul. I giggle to think about my ex's reaction if he knew some homeless person is walking around in his Gucci loafers!"—Hayden

Discovering your own personal rituals can be a fun and creative project. You can research old rituals from your family, religion, or culture—or create one on your own. Here are a few additional suggestions that will help you let go:

• Go to a spiritual retreat to officially cleanse yourself of the grief and toxins experienced from your breakup.

• If you are married and have taken your husband's last name, consider changing it. You don't have to change it back to your maiden name; you can change it to any name you desire. I met a woman who changed her name postdivorce to her grandmother's maiden name. She adored her grandmother, and remembers hearing stories that her great-grandmother was a pioneer feminist. She felt she needed a completely fresh start, and was excited about adding a new name and identity to her life.

• Enroll in a marathon or walkathon for a good cause. Raise money and challenge your body as a way to say good-bye to old memories and hello to charity.

• Create a funeral-type ritual. Write a prayer to be read. You can do this solo or invite a few good friends. If friends are included, they can speak too. Then bury or burn a memento of the relationship.

Many of us are given messages that we shouldn't be so deeply affected by our loss, but truly, no one is exempt. Letting go is a process, and rest assured I'm not standing above you with a stopwatch measuring or judging your progress. I'm confident that you will use the suggestions I have offered to begin your voyage out of understanding and into transformation when you feel ready. Please use all that you have learned so far, plus your abundant wisdom, to find meaningful strategies that will enable you to walk through this next set of doors.

~~~~~~

Letting Go
Tips and Tools

1. Full recovery requires us to eventually let go of our ex and move with intention into transformation.
2. If you carry the scars of old wounds, you must first heal those in order to fully let go of your ex. These wounds, which complicate our mourning, could be from your parents, other family members, or people or situations that have previously injured you or caused you pain.
3. The best way to heal old wounds is to look at the personal love map of the people who inflicted harm upon you, and try to comprehend what transpired in *their* lives that made them treat you as they did. Acknowledge how it affected you and prepare to work through the pain using all the tools I have given you. Then make a conscious decision to let it go.
4. The best way to heal the wounds inflicted upon you by your ex is to look at *his* personal love map and try to understand what transpired in his life that made him behave as he did. Acknowledge how it affected you and prepare to work through the pain using all the tools I have given you. Then make a conscious decision to let it go.
5. We tend to hang on to many things that interfere with our ability to let go. Please acknowledge what you are holding on to and prepare to start letting go of those various thoughts, feelings, and habits.
6. Although some women report that transitional relationships helped them let go, please be careful of getting involved with someone before you have finished your healing, understanding, and transformation. Relationships have a

much better chance of succeeding when they're conducted between two healthy individuals and there are no lingering ghosts.

7. When feeling stuck, try to remember a few last hurrah moments. Return to your hurrah list and study it whenever you need to.

8. Please consider how forgiveness may be useful to you in your journey of healing both old and new wounds.

9. Craft some interesting rituals to help you let go and move on.

PART III

Transformation

It's the fire in my eyes,
And the flash of my teeth,
The swing in my waist,
And the joy in my feet.
I'm a woman
Phenomenally.
Phenomenal woman,
That's me.

—MAYA ANGELOU

13

Creating the Best Life Ever

"When I think back on my breakup and what I've been through, and where I am today, it's unbelievable. I swear, I'm happier today than I've been in the past ten years. No, I take that back. Happier than I've ever been in my entire life!"   —*Lisa*

"Open all the windows in yourself and everything comes in. You invite in all the possibilities. You can't wait for things to come to you—you have to put yourself out there, even when it's scary. That's how you start to feel good about yourself."   —*Tova*

I had a dream last night. We were all together on a long hike in the woods. I was leading the way with a determined clip and a destination in mind. Finally I saw the marker I was on the lookout for, a sign that read "Transformation Up Ahead." "Perfect timing," I thought. We had passed healing hours ago, and the ground was slippery, but we soldiered on without a hitch. Understanding, which was more challenging, was filled with rocky terrain, yet we stuck together and prevailed. Moving along we encountered a wide stream with rushing water, and on the opposite bank was a vast, neon Las Vegas–style sign screaming out WELCOME TO TRANSFORMATION: THE FIRST DAY OF THE REST OF YOUR LIFE. "Figures." I sighed. "No rest for the weary. But we're an unwavering crew, we've beaten many odds. We'll just slowly wade across, supporting each other, as we always have."

I hitched up my pants and started to cross the stream when I noticed that absolutely no one was with me. Everyone was standing on the shore refusing to budge. I was baffled. Things had been going so well—why this mutiny now? Each of you had reported that you had completed your prep work, and were ready and committed for transformation. We hadn't taken any shortcuts that I was aware of, but maybe I missed something. I started a roll call.

"Jenna, did you build your support system and rely on family and friends?" She nodded yes.

"Margo, have you been eating well and exercising?" A resounding yes.

"Isabelle, have you been going to yoga, meditating, and building a spiritual practice?" "Yes, ma'am!" she cried out.

This was not making any sense. You had all been so cooperative until now. I scratched my head.

"Siena, are you still involved in a negative engagement dance?" "No, I'm not—I have had no contact with my ex at all," she said.

"Janet, did you fill out your story and history break-up reasons and take accountability?" "Definitely," she shot back.

"Georgia, are you keeping hope alive?" "Positively!" she shouted out.

"Jessica, did you create your personal love map and study it hard?" "Of course," she answered. "Well, did you do it for your ex?" I said. "Certainly," she replied. "And, did you contemplate forgiving him?" I asked. "Not only did I forgive him, I forgave my father for his ambivalent attachment style too."

Finally, it hit me. I surveyed the faces in the crowd and this is what I saw: fatigue, frustration, and fear. Of course! The three F's will always slow you down. But I realized there was more. You have all been through so much and worked so hard, naturally letting go and preparing for the passage into transformation is going to take a leap of faith. Several of you were contemplating turning back, so I had to think quickly because defeat was absolutely not an option. I've always believed in you and promised to coach you through your complete journey. It was my responsibility get you over the river and through the woods before sundown. We had navigated tricky waters before, and I knew, together, we would prevail. I took a moment to calmly survey the situation and weigh my options. I took a deep breath and gathered the troops. "Ladies, I get it. You're all exhausted and have temporarily lost your drive. It's scary to let go of the comfort and even the *discomfort* of your old lives, especially when you don't know what's up ahead. But please, don't give up now—we're almost there. You can do this, and I promise it's well worth the endeavor. Transformation is right there, waiting to welcome you with a tender hug and a big celebration."

Although clearly not of inaugural quality, my little speech did the trick. Everyone was back on her feet with smiles and fresh optimism. And that was because you actually did want to cross to transformation—you just had a little hesitation, that's all. While we rested and gathered our strength, the water had slowed and the stream was now shallow and ready for an easy crossing. What a miracle! Truthfully, I just used everything we've learned together to solve the dilemma. I pushed past my own fears, stayed positive, and didn't lose sight of the mission. True recovery is about being resourceful. It's also about putting yourself first, and knowing when you need to take a break to rejuvenate yourself. When the going gets tough, and occasionally it will, believe in yourself and trust that good days are around the bend. And that's the real definition of a miracle.

Embracing Transformation

Transformation is a very potent word. Scientifically speaking, transformation is a central concept that results in the actual alteration of a cell. Wow. On further research I discovered that transformation also describes formulas and concepts in the areas of math, natural science, computing, law, English grammar, economics, design, and more. Pretty astonishing stuff. Transformation is also the title of several books spanning various topics, a dozen films, and quite a few songs. Clearly transformation is such a powerful and evocative word that it has been adapted by wide-ranging industries, professions, and walks of life. I'd say it is quite apropos that we are calling this last phase in your recovery "Transformation!"

Now, you may ask, what is so special about transformation, and what's in it for you? Excellent question! See how you're inquiring, looking out for yourself, and using your new radar to determine if something is useful for you or not? That, my friend, is transformation. It's the phase where you are pushing yourself forward, stepping out, taking more chances, practicing what you've learned, and preparing to launch a new you. It's about challenging yourself to go beyond and explore. It's about fully letting go of the past and carving out a new life. It's getting to know yourself better and even becoming your own best friend. But it's also about expanding your social circle, making new friends, and contemplating romance. It's opening your mind and absorbing new knowledge. It's defining yourself, creating a legacy, and finally claiming the happiness that you most definitely deserve. By embracing transformation you are making a huge effort to get your groove on and experience life's abundant bounty.

As I have mentioned throughout this book, full recovery takes *time* and *toil*. If you have meticulously worked through healing and understanding, used most of the exercises, and are *continuing* to use the ones that are most beneficial to you, there is an excellent chance that you are feeling better, healthier, more balanced, and back in control (hurray!). If this is the case, you are ready to enter transformation. However, if you have not completed these steps yet, I urge you to please go back and spend some more time in the previous chapters. I completely understand that burning desire to get your breakup behind you, but please believe that you will achieve recovery when you take the time to follow my method fully. Transformation generally begins between approximately six and eighteen months after your breakup. If you try to transform before you are emotionally and physically ready, before you have built a solid foundation through the work of healing and understanding, I'm afraid that you just won't have the strength or confidence to accomplish the new set of tasks I'm about to lay out for you.

Transformation will be so much more meaningful to you when you have *completed, incorporated,* and *sustained* the vital work of healing and understanding. I regularly hear frustrated women moan,

"It's been a full year—why aren't I feeling any better?" And, upon investigation it always turns out that these women have put in the time and the suffering, but regrettably, not the endeavor. So please don't allow yourself to fall into this common trap. If you do the work and *maintain* everything you have learned, you will not only recover in totality, but you will have a blueprint for happiness and success that you can work from for the rest of your life.

However, when we go through a breakup, especially when it's unexpected, we lose so much control, and that can be such a terrifying feeling. So, if you are someone who likes to know what's coming your way, or likes to have some "control" over your destiny, be my guest and please go ahead and skim through the transformation section. It will let you know what's on the road ahead, and you may take comfort in that. Then go back with some markers and notebooks and dig right back in to healing and understanding with renewed dedication.

Here's a small example of this concept of sustaining growth. Several months ago I enjoyed a fantastic vacation. I readily admit that I had become careless in the months leading up to my travels—I had not been tending to myself in ways that had proven to be effective in the past. I was working too hard and regrettably being led by my stress. In other words, I had allowed myself to slip back into some bad habits. I wasn't getting enough sleep or taking time for

Gathering Strength from Your Ancestors

When you feel that life is too overwhelming and you can't get over that next hurdle, consider gathering strength and wisdom from your lineage. Contemplate the immense struggles that your ancestors endured. Whether it was poverty, religious persecution, immigration, famine, prejudice, sexism, or extreme weather—our great-great-great-grandmothers faced excessive difficulties and prevailed. Dedicate that challenge to their hardships, and remember to feel blessed about the abundant gifts you have in your world today.

myself, and the result was that I was tired, grumpy, and had temporarily misplaced my gratitude list. I used my holiday to relax and enjoy, explore and learn, and most important, to reconnect with myself. I spent at least one hour every day alone, getting reacquainted with my soul and thinking about what was working in my life and what needed to be adjusted. I reminded myself that in order to be a good therapist, mother, wife, and daughter I needed to be sure that my happiness quotient was being met. I made many important realizations through my daily date with myself, and I made a commitment to sustain this activity upon my return. I'm pleased to report that when I got home I completely fulfilled my commitment, and I've sustained it since because (1) I know it's good for me, (2) it gives me immense pleasure, and (3) it provides a much-needed release.

Now that you know what is meaningful to me, let's discuss what you've learned from healing and understanding that is meaningful to you. The goal is for you to be able to sustain the spiritual, emotional, and psychological growth that you have been accumulating for many years to come. It's all there for the taking, so do be greedy and grab all that you can. Let's take a moment to review the most important concepts and exercises that we have covered thus far and see what is working best for you. Please ask yourself the following questions while reviewing this list:

- Have I practiced this exercise or considered this concept?
- Has working through this issue made me feel better?
- If I haven't tried it, why not? Is something obstructing me? If so, how do I get around the obstruction?

Healing

1. Have you been validating your feelings and comforting yourself?
2. Did you create an actual or metaphorical "room for yourself," and are you using your alone time in a meaningful way?
3. Have you taken enough time to properly mourn your loss?
4. Have you accepted that true recovery takes time?

5. Have you been journaling with regularity?

6. Have you used grounding exercises to alleviate anxiety?

7. Have you created a support system that consists of family, friends, and colleagues? And are you continuing to rely on these folks as needed?

8. Have you used the friendship formula to expand your support system?

9. Did you consider adding individual or group therapy to your system?

10. Have you thought about using faith and/or animals to provide comfort?

11. Have you been eating healthfully, exercising, and getting enough sleep?

12. Have you been avoiding overusing alcohol and other addictives?

13. Have you been taking time to nourish your soul?

14. Have you navigated the entire emotional roller coaster and spent time contemplating every stage?

15. Have you been using the exercises from chapter 4, "Navigating the Emotional Roller Coaster," that are most helpful to you, such as:

    a. Recognizing when you are slipping into the denial or bargaining stage and giving yourself a gentle reality check.

    b. Eliminating hero worship by writing a list of everything that was wrong with your ex and your relationship.

    c. Using the exercises for decreasing depression and anxiety.

    d. Writing a gratitude list.

    e. Talking back to negative, depressing, or anxious thoughts.

    f. Doing some volunteer work to combat loneliness.

    g. Delaying obsessions and ruminations.

    h. Identifying feelings of abandonment and rejection and working toward eradicating them.

  i. Being very mindful of your dance with anger.

  j. Being careful of getting overly involved with guilt, regret, failure, and self-blame.

  k. Remembering that you have nothing to feel embarrassed or ashamed about.

  l. Fighting to keep hope alive.

16. Have you accepted that there is a slim chance that you will ever receive validation or closure from your ex?

17. Have you stopped or cut way back on inquiring and spying?

18. Are you aware of your negative engagement dance, and have you committed to using the art of positive dialoguing when speaking with your ex?

19. Have you created your own set of rules of engagement and disengagement and are you sticking with them?

20. If you have children, are you doing all you can to help them adjust? Are you being sensitive to their needs and feelings when discussing your split or your ex with them?

Understanding

1. Have you uncovered and explored the story and history behind your breakup?

2. Have you taken full accountability for your part in the ending of your relationship? What have you learned from this exercise, and how is that knowledge benefiting you today?

3. After reading chapter 9, "The Most Common Causes of Breakups or Divorces," did you learn some additional particulars about where your relationship went off track? And did you get some new perspective about what a healthier style of relationship might look like?

4. Did you create your personal love map in entirety?

5. Did you identify aspects from biology, psychology (attachment theory), and social/cultural factors that combined to form your personality?

6. Did you do the same for your ex?

7. What have you learned about yourself *and* about your ex from this exercise?

8. Do you suffer from repetition compulsion or abandonment depression?

9. If so, have you been working toward your psychological repair through the study of your love map? And have you been using the exercises put forth in healing and understanding to help you mend?

10. Did you write your personal autobiography? How did this exercise benefit you? Might it be something you may revisit and update yearly?

11. Have you worked toward healing old wounds from your family or others in your past who have hurt you or caused you harm?

12. Have you worked toward healing the new wounds inflicted by your ex?

13. Have you finally let go of both old and new wounds?

14. Have you considered working toward forgiveness?

15. Have you used rituals to help you let go?

Wow, that is some long list! Now that you've read it through, please think about your voyage over the last few months. If you have enacted most of this list and have witnessed substantial growth, you are ready to enter transformation. Alternatively, if you have reviewed this list and realized that there is much more you can put into your recovery, I urge you to please go back and "do your time." If this is the case, please remember that this does not mean you have failed in any way at all—you are fabulous and have worked really hard. It just means that you may need to put some additional focus into the earlier phases. There is never any need to rush and there is absolutely nothing at all to be frustrated about or ashamed of. I know I may have mentioned this before, but let me say it once again:

True recovery takes significant time and a lot of hard work. The more you put into your recovery, the greater the benefits will be.

Transformation is the culminating phase of our work and it's where all the excitement begins. It was not difficult at all for me to find women to interview for this section of the book. Honestly, I heard so many mind-blowing transformation stories that I drove myself mad trying to decide which ones to share with you. I met many remarkable women who had completely re-created themselves in fascinating ways. Some were even near bankruptcy during their split and transformed their lives by returning to the workforce after a long absence, changing careers, and even starting their own businesses. Every one of these women had difficult separations and today they are living lives that are wondrous and very full. And if they can do it, so can you!

Now I understand that even if you are ready for transformation, your old worries may still surface from time to time—but by now you know what to do. Just keep pushing forward and believing in yourself. The best is yet to come!

Discovering Your True Nature

After a traumatic event like a breakup or divorce we lose our foundation. A normal response to our personal upheaval is to question everything in our lives. Suddenly, things we often took for granted as the norm become disputable. One of my friends during her healing phase took an intensive workshop on the history of religion. When I asked her why, she responded, "Nothing in life seems to make sense any longer. I'm searching for answers and hoping that by studying the origins of religion I'll discover something—anything—that seems tangible." I'm sure you've felt that way too.

As you may recall, I had previously suggested that you put any major life decisions on hold (if possible) until you complete your healing and understanding phases. So now that you're finally in transformation, it's time for some deep contemplation about what you genuinely desire from your life today.

Transformation is all about the discovery, development, and launch of your brand-new, powerful self. I will make many suggestions that will afford you abundant opportunities to question and challenge yourself in interesting and exciting ways. Through the process of deep contemplation *plus* action you are going to get to know your new self and figure out exactly where you need adjustments, improvements, or changes. Also, through challenging yourself and then succeeding in these endeavors, I assure you that you'll be really proud of yourself, which will be a massive confidence booster. Just wait and see how your confidence will rebound, or better yet, come to life.

Reevaluation

It's very important that you fully devote yourself to this section of the book. Although I wrote it for women transforming after a breakup, these concepts and remedies can be used throughout your entire life whenever you go through hardships, or feel stagnated and want to shake things up. However, before we jump into the next chapter about rebuilding, let's spend some time assessing your life today in preparation for the deeper work ahead.

Early transformation begins with a reevaluation of our lives, and what you're going to need to do now is ask yourself some very important questions. Change can be so intimidating, but the time has come to start doing some serious thinking about what is working in your life and what needs to be altered. There's a pretty decent chance that you've felt too depleted in the earlier phases of recovery to tackle this task. I know you are now finally ready to roll up your sleeves and do this thought-provoking work.

Let's do some more journal work. Please create an introductory "transformation list" that will continue to develop and expand. First, write down everything you *love* about your life and what is working for you right now. Not only is this your updated gratitude list, it is proof that there are many worthy things in your life today that you have created and do not need to be touched. Please take comfort in this fact, and keep adding to your gratitude list, as I do daily.

Now, start the initial process of reevaluating what needs to be modified and where real change needs to occur. Are you content with your current relationships and your career? Do you have enough passions and hobbies that give you pleasure? Might there be new places you want to travel to, or do you have a yearning to learn new things? We will be visiting all of these topics in chapter 14, "Rebuilding," but for now, write down whatever comes to mind. Challenge yourself and please have the courage to think big. The more time you spend mindfully contemplating your list and your life, the more ideas will flow. And the more ideas that you allow to come forth, the more excited you will become about creating a new life. So much that we think is not possible in actuality really is. When you are done, this will be your initial "transformation list." You will continue to add to it after you've completed reading this book, and hopefully, for an eternity. With time and attention, I promise, your transformation list will really bloom.

The next chapter, "Rebuilding," is so exciting and thought provoking—I just know you're going to love it. I'm going to propose a bunch of really great transformation ideas, and you can freely pick and choose from the delicious menu until you have a plan tailor-made just for you. You're going to meet some fabulous relaunched ladies, and that's just the beginning. By the end of this book, you can join their ranks and write your very own chapter about the fully transformed you.

Creating the Best Life Ever
Tips and Tools

1. Be mindful of the three F's: fatigue, frustration, and fear. When you find them creeping into your life, and they occasionally will, take some deserved time to relax, rejuvenate, and refocus.
2. Full recovery takes time and toil. Please remember this.
3. The more you focus on maintaining what you have learned and found useful in healing and understanding, the grander your recovery will be.
4. Commit to choosing a few exercises from both healing and

understanding and make a pledge to embed them into your life.

5. Keep up your gratitude list. Ask yourself each day, "Are there three new things I can be grateful for today?"

6. Create your initial transformation list before reading the next chapter. This is your first attempt at creating a wish list for the future. Ask yourself, what areas of your life need rebuilding, or simply adding on?

14

Rebuilding

"I knew that there was a lot in my life that needed to be revisited, and I understood that I was the only one who could make that happen. It's your life and it's 100 percent up to you what you're going to make of it. When you own that and commit to the changes—well, that's the most amazing gift you can give yourself!" —*Rene*

"It's not that I had a 'bad' life, but it wasn't fully the life that I envisioned. Then one day it hit me: In order to accomplish what I deeply wanted, I needed to turn my world upside down. You can't be afraid to shake it up. Once I took action—well, I created exactly the life I had dreamt of!" —*Nicole*

I'm so excited that you are ready to begin rebuilding your life in healthy ways! You have been through so much and worked so hard to reach this turning point, and truly, the best is yet to come. As with everything in this book, and in life, really good things come to those who put in the most effort, and I know by now that you really want to succeed in reaching full recovery. I understand that you may still occasionally fear that you live under a black cloud, and that others have it easier, or are luckier. It is completely normal to have periodic trepidations, but the good news is that transformation, and especially this chapter on the topic of rebuilding, is going to turn those doubts on their head.

I encourage you to take as much time as you need to heal from your ordeal—even in transformation. I want you to relax and breathe every day. I want you to soak up the pleasure of simply having a good day, which could be the pure relief that you have finally gotten over the daily drama of your breakup, or that you can now go an entire day or even a week without having your ex take up space in your head. Once you've established that—when you're feeling good and ready, when you have the desire to add some new layers to your life, when you're prepared to challenge yourself and try something new—we'll begin. I'm going to describe to you in full detail how to begin the spectacular process of rebuilding your life. I'm going to present quite a few suggestions and then back them up with proven exercises *plus* voices from the recovered community. We're going to have a lot of fun together while we try out new ideas. It's all part of the process, and I'll be with you every step of the way.

Rebuilding Self-Esteem

> "When I opened my eyes and looked around, I saw I was not alone. There were many women in my position and they didn't seem pathetic to me at all. They actually seemed to be in better places than they were when they were in relationships. They were changing their lives in really big ways. That gave me comfort, courage, and the confidence to get my act together." —*Chelsea*

Whatever the circumstances behind your split, there is a good chance that it took a great big hit on your esteem. We women are so hard on ourselves to begin with, and most women I interviewed described a period of doubting their belief in themselves after their relationships ended. If you are someone whose self-worth was not stellar to begin with, you are going to have to do some rigorous work in rebuilding to break out of that mind-set.

I'm going to tell you a secret now, and I'd really appreciate it if you'd sit quietly and seriously contemplate this concept. Here it is:

In order to change your external world, you've got to build yourself up from the inside out.

The rebuilding of confidence is one of our top goals in transformation, and most of my text and exercises are designed with this objective in mind. When your confidence is robust, when you really believe in yourself, everything you strive for becomes a possibility. Alternatively, a lack of esteem will always trip you up and leave you lagging behind.

Confidence boosting, an integral part of our work, is a bit of a catch-22. Here's why:

1. I'm going to ask you to accomplish a variety of tasks that are more easily accomplished when you have good self-esteem. Yet in order to develop better self-confidence you're going to have to accomplish these tasks.
2. Thus, you're going to need to take a leap of faith and really push yourself in a variety of ways to accomplish the duties that I'm going to assign in these next chapters.
3. Many of the things I'm going to ask of you will be initially intimidating and uncomfortable, and your first reaction may be "No way, Jose." Perfectly normal!
4. But here's the rub: The entire definition of building confidence is pushing your limits and then basking in the glory when you succeed.
5. Trust me, trust yourself, and push forward. Even when you're afraid, the rewards are well worth the risk.

Embracing this concept and making the commitment to thrust through your fears, doubts, negativity, and anxiety produces a snowball effect. Remember those snowballs many of us played with when we were kids? The more you packed into them, the bigger they got. And if you rolled them down a hill, they became huge. And when they got really gigantic—that's when the real fun began. Better snowball fights and the ability to build great big snow-women and makeshift igloos. Pushing past your limits creates more and more possibilities and opportunities. Each tiny accomplishment builds esteem, and that fresh esteem gives you the muscle to try something new again, and again, and again. Every triumph builds upon the next, and so on.

Here's a great story I'd like to share with you that fully nails this concept. Grace was seriously involved for a long time with an emotionally abusive man and stayed in the relationship longer than she should have because of her low esteem and abundant fears. When her relationship ended she immediately went to work with healing and understanding in preparation for her final act, transformation. In her own words:

> "When my relationship ended I was a shadow of my former self. I was a meek person with no confidence. But I couldn't wallow—I knew I had a limited amount of time to get my life together. The initial work I did to heal myself and make sense out of my relationship behavior slowly brought me back to life. Then I had to do all I could to hold on to my new soft-boiled self. I knew I needed to keep pushing and growing in order to get fully cooked. I evoked my new self to start doing things that I imagined would make me feel great. I spent time with my friends, exercised, went to museums—I did all the things that I love to do. Then, once I was feeling better, I really started focusing on my career and pushed myself even further. Suddenly, my career, which had been stagnant for years, started to take form. I noticed that all of my hard work was being actualized. Acknowledging this gave me gratification and satisfaction, and this perpetrated even more good feelings, further propelling me to go out there and take even bigger risks and make even more changes. It was all materializing before my eyes—and I was so proud, confident, and happy!"

When you make the conscious *decision* to turn self-loathing into self-loving, when you commit to facing your fears, when you make the *choice* to expand your life, you are opening yourself up to all the little miracles.

Here are a few esteem-building tidbits that you can freely rely on if that old friend "fear" stops by for tea. And by the way, by the end of transformation, that old friend will have completely disappeared, and I promise, it will not leave a forwarding address.

• Energize yourself. Do not underestimate the transformative powers of eating healthy foods, getting enough sleep, and exercising.

• Create optimism. Use positive affirmations on a daily (or hourly) basis. Tell yourself, "I am beautiful and amazing. I can accomplish every single thing that I set out to do."

• Set a few small achievable goals every day. Pat yourself on the back when you complete them.

• Be very aware of negative thoughts. When you catch yourself going to a dark place, please use the techniques I taught you in healing to talk back to them.

• When you are nervous about a challenging situation, do not retreat. Instead, "act as if." Visualize your most powerful self completing the act at hand (even if you are terrified) with ease. Now take that fantasy of your confident self and act on it. And once you arrive where you need to be, you'll never need to act at anything again!

• Celebrate progress and all small victories. Learn to be an excellent cheerleader.

Rebuilding Yourself as an Individual

> "It's about changing your identity. For so many years you're defined by being a wife or a mother. You have to take time to find out who you are. Once you dive in and start doing it, it gets easier. Then it actually gets fun. That's the journey!" —*Nikki*

We all suffer from a bit of selective memory after a breakup. Many of us led a full life before our relationship, which included individual pursuits and independence. Yet we tend to forget this important factor when we've temporarily lost our grounding and feel unsure about ourselves. In the early stages of a breakup, accomplishing simple acts on your own can feel so daunting, and, at times, completely unattainable. Breaking through this mind-set is central to the theme of this section and to your personal growth.

Many women complain to me, even when feeling notably better, that their life has narrowed and they have difficulty filling up their time. Upon further discussion most readily admit that they do have things that they'd like to accomplish, but are too intimidated to tackle them solo. Let me tell you that one of the many benefits of being single is taking time to discover what turns *you* on, and who *you* are at your core. Your new status affords you the tremendous opportunity to become reacquainted with yourself, and in the process, to rediscover old passions and interests, while creating some fabulous new ones as well. Transformation is about defining *and* defying yourself. This is the perfect time to try things you've always wanted to do but never have. You will have many discoveries about yourself—things that you didn't know existed or never thought were possible.

Here's a nice example of this concept. Liz was married for many years to a man who insisted on calling the shots. She gave up her career to devote herself to managing his needs and caring for their children. During their marriage they collected art, and over the years amassed a substantial collection. Liz always thought that she liked this arrangement, until after her divorce when she was working toward redefining herself.

> "I love art, and I thought I liked the type of art we collected, but after the dust of my divorce settled I came to realize that my ex had to have all the control. We always bought the type of art that he liked, and I really didn't have a say. As a single woman I came to discover that I loved drawings. He would never have let me buy drawings. The further I got away from him the more things that were 'me' came out. These were things that were suppressed. I had not acknowledged them before. They were buried. My new home is filled with the art that I have discovered and purchased on my very own. I can't even express how much satisfaction this gives me."

No matter where you live there are so many wonderful activities that you can carry out on your own, and this is how the snowballing begins. There are abundant positive consequences of stepping out unaccompanied, such as planning your own schedule without checking with others, combating loneliness, doing things that interest you, and enabling you to meet others who will enrich your life. Another benefit: the more comfortable you are venturing on your own, the easier it will be to attend holidays, functions, parties, and weddings by yourself. That's important because I don't want you turning down invitations because you feel awkward attending events without a partner.

A great exercise to get the snowball rolling is challenging yourself to dine out alone. Learning how to eat at a restaurant on your own can accomplish a lot. It teaches you to enjoy your own company, helps you get familiar doing an activity by yourself, and it gets you out of your house to where you may have the potential to meet others. You can certainly start with lunch, but I challenge you to work yourself up to a dinner out with your new best friend—you. I suggest you choose a restaurant that you feel comfortable in to begin this assignment, and then, over time, work your way up to establishments you've never visited before. Initially you can bring a book, magazine, iPod, computer, etc. You can write in your journal about how this new experience makes you feel. Please observe how over time this activity gets easier and easier. Try not to stress about what *you think* people are thinking—tons of people dine alone and it does not mean they are lonely or something is odd about them. When I'm eating dinner out by myself I generally pick a restaurant that serves food at its bar. This gives me an opportunity to talk to others and make some new friends. I've met many fascinating people (some appearing on these pages!) in this way. Don't limit yourself, and try to talk to strangers—everyone has something to offer.

Once you tackle this activity, try doing the same with movies, plays, concerts, sporting events, lectures—anything. The more gambles you take on your own, the easier it will become, and you'll have so much pride. Please do all that you can to make your world inflate, and when you feel unnerved, use the confidence-building exercises to give you an added boost.

Rebuilding Through Your Career: Reenergizing Your Current Profession

"I supported two kids one hundred percent with my own job. If that's not empowerment, what is?" —*Karen*

You've all heard the saying "Do what you love and the money will follow." Hands down, one of the best ways to rebuild your life and create self-esteem is through an honest day's work. Doing something you are passionate about and making a living from it is a true form of bliss. Having a meaningful career affords you a wide range of opportunities. Many positive things happen when we commit ourselves to our jobs. Here are just a few of the numerous benefits:

- Expanding your social circle
- Using your brain power
- Feeling connected and important
- Being creative
- Enjoying the satisfaction of accomplishment
- Making a difference
- Financial independence
- Combating loneliness
- And for some, changing the world

When times are tough, having the routine of a job to go to is just the sort of consistency we crave, plus it's something you can sink your teeth into every day. Work enables you to feel competent, and that is empowering.

The majority of women I conversed with described how refocusing on or escalating their existing career helped them transform after their relationships ended. I also heard some amazing stories of women returning to the workforce or changing careers either out of financial necessity or as a consequence of their self-evaluation process. Since this was such a central theme for many women, I have decided to spend several pages in this chapter discussing the world of work and the abundant opportunities that having a meaningful career can afford you. Transformation is all about getting the most out of your life through challenging yourself to go beyond, and a great way to start the snowball rolling is through the assessment of your current employment situation.

To further demonstrate this concept, here is a story from a woman who began her transformation process through examining her career.

Rita, an artist, described to me how focusing on her career completely altered her existence.

> "My ex-husband called me 'a housewife dabbling in art,' and partially because of this I didn't concentrate on my craft as much as I should have. But after my divorce I was determined to turn my life around, and I did it through my art. I rented a studio and started painting every day. Then, when my confidence started to build back up, I became an insane marketer—something completely foreign to me. With the Internet today there are so many resources to help anyone promote their careers. A lot of positive changes came from this—and with each step I took, the next one became easier and easier. Today I'm fully making a living from my fine art, commissioned portraits, and I'm teaching. I have a solo show coming up in Philadelphia, and I've been featured in magazines, in a major advertising campaign, and on the radio. I feel very proud of my accomplishments and I'm ecstatic to be making a living from something that I love!"

If focusing on your existing career is something that interests you, I encourage you to pursue this path. Here are a few questions you can mull over during your career evaluation process. Ask yourself:

Connecting with a Mentor

One suggestion I consistently make to clients wanting to advance their career is to consider finding a mentor. I've regularly used mentors and without a doubt their guidance and encouragement has been a big factor in my career success.

Mentors are useful to everyone—it doesn't matter whether you're starting out in your career or advancing through the ranks. A mentor can be a senior person in your company, in your industry, or someone in your life that has a lot of useful knowledge and is generous with sharing their time and insights. Don't be afraid to ask someone you respect to be your mentor—the mentoring relationship is a two-way street. I often mentor and receive a tremendous amount for satisfaction from it.

- How might I get more satisfaction from my current job?
- Am I doing all that I can to be a stellar performer?
- Are there growth opportunities available in my firm? And if so, how might I chase after them?
- If there are not, should I consider applying to work at a different company in my field?
- Do I need any further education to advance my career? Are there workshops or classes available to strengthen my skills?

During this process you may discover that you want or need to change firms or even contemplate a new career. This is all part of the journey, and you are acquiring the power to make it all happen.

Going Back to Work

Some of the most profound stories I heard in my travels for this book involved women returning to the workforce after years of raising children, caring for husbands, and running households. Some turned to work because they wanted to expand their lives, and others because they were left nearly destitute by their divorces. Many I spoke with hadn't worked outside the home for decades. A common denominator with all of these women was that they had to push through intense doubt, fear, and at times paralysis to reinvent themselves. Here is a story I'm proud to share with you—it's a perfect representative of my philosophy, which is that any woman can accomplish exactly what she sets out to do.

Ashley, a former model and actress, hadn't worked in a decade because she made a decision to say home and raise her daughter. She was married to a lawyer and living in a small town, and a contentious divorce left her nearly penniless. "One way a man can kill his wife is with finances—and my ex really tried to kill me. His last words to me were, 'You'll be back—you'll never make it on your own.'" He obviously didn't know who he was dealing with because he was completely wrong. This is how Ashley turned her life around:

> "I was forty-two at the time my marriage ended. I needed a job immediately, and of course I had no idea what I was going to do. I was afraid—I didn't go to college, I feared I had no skills. I went to the nearest mall and got a job at Banana Republic making seven dollars an hour. I was so grateful to have a job and be working. I worked very hard. I'd do anything they would ask of me. I'm a people person and discovered I really liked sales. In eight months I was the top-selling person in my entire state. After a while when my confidence starting coming back, I knew I needed a different job making more money. I realized now that I could sell, so I de-

cided to look for a job in sales with any product I felt I could relate to. I took the first job I was offered. I remember being interviewed by the owner of this successful company. He was a wealthy man and drove around in the most beautiful shiny black Jaguar—and I said to myself, 'One day.' I worked my butt off, went full-speed ahead. I refused to let anyone or anything deter me. In less than two years I was the top producer at that firm. Years later, when I really succeeded and had money in my pocket, I bought a black Jaguar of my very own. The day I got it I went to pick up my daughter at my ex's home. Well, he ran out in his underwear screaming and yelling like a maniac when he saw me pull up in that car! Watching him that day was worth all my struggles!"

I fully understand how scary it can feel to pick yourself up and start over after years out of the workforce. In fact, the fear of supporting oneself keeps too many women in unhappy or unsafe relationships for too long. Please use these inspiring stories, plus your personal resources, to help you make haste and get back to work. You will be so proud of yourself when you see that you have a tremendous capacity to both reinvent yourself *and* make a living.

There are several routes you can take when faced with the prospect of going back to work. If you are someone who once had a career in an industry that you enjoyed, you may consider starting your new journey where you left off. If that is the case:

A few days ago I heard a great story about a young unemployed woman who desperately needed to make money after her breakup. She owned a Prius and decided to advertise to drive people to the airport—providing an eco-friendly alternative for travelers wishing to reduce their carbon footprint. Today she supports herself from that one innovative idea.

• Spend time researching your former industry. How has it changed and how has it remained the same since you departed?

• Are your skills intact, or might you need to read some books or take some classes to refresh them?

• Do you keep in touch with former colleagues? If so, this may be an opportune time to reach out to someone and begin a dialogue about returning to work.

• Review your industry on job-posting websites. What sorts of jobs are advertised and what do they pay?

• Consider contacting a headhunter covering your industry. A good headhunter knows the market and understands what employers are looking for.

• Be prepared for interviews, especially if you've been out of the workforce for a length of time.

If you are an executive or a senior person in your firm, you may wish to have a few sessions with an executive coach. These coaches can help you define your goals, map out a professional strategy, and teach you how to negotiate your contract or compensation package.

Even if you are in dire straits and need to make money fast, please try to give yourself time to create a solid strategy that will work best for you. If returning to your old career is not an option, or if you have decided that you'd like to embark on an entirely new journey, read on.

Dare to Dream: Changing Your Career

As I've described, a key component of transformation is the process of looking deep into your soul to discover what you truly desire from a new life. It's all part of the journey and it's important that you allow yourself this exceptional experience. If you were working out of your home when your relationship ended, at some point during your recovery you may question your current profession. If you are not getting enough satisfaction from your job, your new circumstances may be a major catalyst to rethink your career path. We spend so much time and energy in the workplace, and the effects of doing a job that you don't love takes a huge toll. Alternatively, working in a field that you are passionate about is one of life's greatest joys. Transformation is all about getting the most out of life, so this may be an opportune time to explore a change in your vocation.

Culturally we are living in times where it is completely normal and acceptable to be in a career transition, and people regularly change careers—and do so at any age. You just have to have the desire to do it and the motivation to see it through. Clients often talk to me about wanting to change careers, but they don't always initially know what they want to do, or how to begin the process. These unknowns can certainly be unsettling, and due to this too many folks understandably retreat back into the comfort, security, and routine of their weekly paycheck. However, I met quite a few women who had done career 180s after their breakups, and every one of them described the elation they felt once they busted through their fears and literally got down to work. They uniformly depicted how much richer their lives became and how amazing they felt about themselves in the aftermath.

I'm going to give you a tutorial on career change using my personal circumstances as a model. And as I've repeatedly said, I'm no different than you, and if I can do something and succeed, so can you.

I had been unhappy in my former profession (sales and marketing) for several years, but I felt stuck and was deathly afraid to leave. I had no idea what I wanted to do or how I would support myself in the process. The very thought of redoing my résumé made me extremely nauseous. My first step was to *do some deep contemplation about why I was unsatisfied*. This was my version of a "pro-and-con" list and this is what I determined:

1. The rationale I used to choose my previous career was no longer applicable in my current life.
2. I felt that the work I was doing was not benefiting hu-

manity. I wanted an emotional satisfaction from my job
that I was not receiving.

3. I wanted more of an intellectual challenge from my
career.

4. My industry was mostly male, and I longed to have a
female collegial experience that wasn't being afforded
to me.

5. I have an entrepreneurial streak (which doesn't always
make me the best employee!) and I have always wanted
to own my own business.

Once I made that list I saw with my own eyes that my rationale was
sound, and that gave me the boost to carry on ahead. Then I made
a second list, which consisted of *what aspects of my career I actually
did like*. It is very important to ask yourself this question, because in
reality very few of us fully despise our jobs. There is always something—even if it's minuscule—that we fancy, and determining that
brings forth more data. What I discovered was:

1. I enjoyed all aspects of my job that had to do with human
relationships. I had a close connection with many of my
customers—some had become good friends over the
years—and I eagerly anticipated forging new relationships with new customers.

2. I also realized that I enjoyed both managing and mentoring junior employees. Several people on my staff
were going through difficulties in their lives and I had
a great deal of empathy for them and always offered assistance.

What I took away from this exercise was that I wanted to be in
a career where I would have the opportunity to become involved
with people's lives and provide support in meaningful ways. That
became my "mission statement," and I used it as a basis to begin my
vast exploration process. My particular investigation took several
months and included a combination of research, volunteer work,

taking classes, visiting a conference, and informational interviewing, until I came to the conclusion to become a therapist.

Once you determine what your new career is going to be, a second-tier procedure begins. This process consists of creating an action plan that lays out everything you need to accomplish to move from your current line of work into a brand-new one.

If a career change seems appealing to you, here are several ideas to get the juices flowing and the ball rolling:

- Make your own "pro-and-con" list, as I did, and see what pops up.
- Is there something you've always wanted to do but haven't been able to for one reason or another?
- What is that something, and how can you overcome your obstacles?
- If you woke up tomorrow and had your dream job, what would it be?
- What are your passions, interests, and values? How can you turn one of those into a profession?
- What are your best "skill sets"? What is unique about you, and what do you have to offer the world?
- Have there been messages from various people in your life directing you toward a certain profession?

There is a chance that after doing the above exercises you still have no plan that you wish to pursue. If that is the case, don't get frustrated or give up. Try some of these suggestions:

- Consider seeking vocational counseling.
- Spend some time with a person who has a job that seems interesting to you and ask him or her everything you can think of about the job.
- Add a part-time job to your schedule in a field that interests you.
- Do volunteer work in fields that attract you.

Once you figure out what you want to do, then head straight for rebuilding. Create an action plan and carry it forth. Here are some questions to ask yourself during this final stage:

• What type of research might I need to do to learn more about this type of career?

• Is my current skill set transferable to my new career? If not, how do I prepare to relaunch myself?

• If I need to reeducate myself, can I do so during my evenings or weekends? Or do I have to quit my current job and take this on full time?

• Who can I contact who could help me learn about and transition into this career?

• If I need to leave my current job, how will I support myself? Will I use savings, take out a loan, or work part time? What about health insurance?

• Some companies are actually helpful to employees wanting to transition out. If you think your company may be career-change friendly, perhaps you can discuss a plan with them where you will have the flexibility to interview or to cut back on your hours.

Please use setbacks to retrieve important facts, and never, ever give up! I know so many people who have changed careers—it is entirely possible. If you take your time to do accurate research and make a fail-safe plan, you will succeed. As a side note, people had been telling me my entire life that I should be doing the work that I am doing today. So be sure to pay close attention to the messages that the universe is sending you!

I fully understand that some of you are either uninterested in having or unable to have a career. You may have small children at home, be retired, or have received a divorce settlement that afforded you financial security. If that is the case, I still strongly suggest that you consider adding a few new valuable activities into your life. In the "healing" phase we discussed the importance of building a support system, and I gave you ample guidelines on how to achieve that. And because transformation is about adding on, there is so much to gain by accruing new folks and activities in your wonderful expanding life.

I really want you to do all that you can to continue building your confidence and experiencing emotional growth. That comes from repeatedly accumulating more areas of interest that provide you with stimulation, fun, accomplishment, and satiation. Plenty of fresh ideas are waiting for you on the next few pages.

Rebuilding Through Charity

> "I joined an organization rescuing and placing aban-
> doned animals and gave at least one full weekend day
> to them. This decision produced great results—I met
> wonderful people and felt good about myself that I was
> helping these innocent creatures. It was good for my
> soul, and for the community." —*Kristen*

The allotment of time or resources to a charitable program is unquestionably an extremely satisfying experience. Consider this saying: "Esteemable acts build esteem." A mentor once told me this, and it really is true. Accomplishing activities that you feel are meaningful—such as giving yourself an important cause or to a friend in need—will make you feel good about yourself, and in turn will help to build up your self-worth. But that's only one of the abundant benefits of bringing volunteerism into your life. I wasn't surprised at all to discover the central role that philanthropy played in the lives of so many women's recovery. Loads of you told me stories about putting yourselves out there for the greater good, which created fulfillment *and* opportunities. A lot of snowballing resulted from simple acts that came straight from the heart.

Committing yourself to charity can be quite rewarding, and here are just a few of the numerous benefits:

- Volunteering creates personal growth.
- You will feel a sense of accomplishment and it will make you feel really good about yourself.
- You will become more compassionate and develop more empathy.
- Working with an underserved population puts your life in perspective.
- It's a great way to meet people.
- It's an opportunity to learn new skills and pad your résumé.
- If you sign on for a project outside of your state or country, it gives you a chance to see the world and experience different cultures.
- If you have children, you are setting an excellent example for them.
- With your own two hands, you will be changing the world.

Katherine was in her fifties when her complicated marriage ended. A stay-at-home mother of three, she hadn't worked in thirty years. Her transformation included relocating from France to an American city where she had few friends. Katherine knew she had to rebuild her life from the bottom up and eventually secure a job, but she was frozen in fear. After much reflection she decided she wanted to work in the arts, as it had been both a passion and a hobby for many years. Her decision to begin with volunteerism completely transformed her life.

> "I immediately got involved with a nonprofit organization benefiting the arts. They really appreciated me and after several months they offered me a paying job! This opened up a whole new world to me. Slowly I started feeling better about myself. I made new friends. I had perspective. I realized that I was valued. I was OK. People were giving me opportunities and I was jumping on them. The job gave me more and more responsibilities, and my self-confidence really evolved."

I have been an enthusiastic volunteer for much of my life, and I can speak firsthand of the joy and opportunities it has created for me. If doing service is something that appeals to you, use some of these guidelines to help you get involved today:

- Commit to volunteering and create a strategy that works best for you.
- Think about a population or cause that is important to you.
- Look for an organization to partner with. Most religious organizations or local community centers have charity projects that you can join. Large organizations have useful websites with instructions on how to sign up.
- Consider signing on for a onetime event like a fund-raiser or a walkathon; or perhaps you are interested in a more regular commitment.
- Consider inviting a friend or a group of friends to join you.

As an aside, after a bad breakup my sister met her current partner through volunteer work, and they've been happily together ever since!

Enrichment Through an Expedition

When I was in my midtwenties I suddenly found myself out of a job. Now you know how I feel about work—I had been employed since I was fifteen and this experience was very unsettling for me. The old fear-based part of my personality took over and I frantically prepared to begin a job search. Suddenly my newly emerging self piped in suggesting that perhaps this would be an ideal time for me to shake it up and try something completely different. I was aware that a friend of a friend was about to embark solo on a trip to Europe— it made me think. I had started working full time literally the day after I graduated from college, so the ubiquitous "take some time off to travel" had never been in my overachieving vernacular. Suddenly I realized I had a major opportunity to turn my misfortune into something extraordinary. I pushed past my fears, called this woman I had met just once, and invited myself on her trip. With barely an itinerary and a few bucks in our pockets, we headed overseas and spent two amazing months traveling through Europe. We tested our mettle every single day, met fascinating people, and had a blast. We even ended up at the Princes Ball one evening in Monte Carlo. It was an extraordinary experience that made me feel so powerful and filled with pride. I have not stopped traveling since.

For me, traveling is like tuning my brain into an entirely new frequency. When exploring a new destination, colors become more vibrant, smells more pungent, and my thoughts become clearer. There is something about opening yourself up to a new land, culture, and language that is intoxicating, stimulating, captivating, and liberating. It also makes you feel accomplished, confident, and allows you to get some real perspective. This is why I always recommend an interesting travel experience to every woman in her transformation phase.

Several women I met echoed what I already knew, that traveling after their breakup or divorce helped transform their lives. In fact some of the best stories I heard involved travel. The common thread was that they were all nervous before their voyages, second-guessed themselves (some even missed airplanes or spent the first few days holed up in hotels), yet described unbelievable elation as they pushed past their hesitation and proved to themselves that they could be resourceful and independent. Some called their travel experience the most important component in their recovery.

Sheryl described to me how a visit to the desert in New Mexico helped her rebuild. "It's important to go somewhere new after experiencing a breakup. I went away with a male and female friend to an isolated cabin in the desert. The sky and the colors of New Mexico were so breathtaking. It was so quiet that my ears hurt—it was a silence like I never experienced before. There weren't even any birds because there were no trees! It was very intense but really good because it forced me to think. It was amazing being in the middle of nowhere with good friends."

Reaching beyond our comfort zone to create something unique is attainable to any woman. Anyone can have a vision *and* turn it into a reality. Please consider adding travel to your transformation repertoire. Even if you are employed or have children at home, anything is possible, so don't let that stop you from having an adventure. Be creative. We all get time off from work, and friends and relatives (and ex-husbands) make excellent sitters. If you aren't comfortable traveling alone and can't find a companion to tag along, sign on to a

Expanding Your Mind

An important aspect of rebuilding is keeping your mind razor-sharp. These activities will expand your brain, an important component of healthy aging. As an added benefit, staying informed will give you plenty to talk about when you're out there socializing.

• Consider taking a class or a workshop. Pick a topic that you are drawn to, and then find a locale. Most colleges offer classes for nonmatriculating students. You can also try your local community center or Learning Annex. If you are not sure what you'd like to learn, look through a class catalog and see what turns you on.

• You can also expand your mind by taking an online class or a Web seminar, or purchasing a book, video, or podcast on any topic that you'd like to learn more about.

• Exercise your right brain by trying something creative. Consider taking a class in cooking, the arts, learning how to play an instrument, or taking up a language.

• Book clubs are great vehicles to both learn and socialize. You can explore new authors and subject matter this way, plus you get the immediate gratification of reading a book and discussing its meaning in a community setting.

Taking on a Hobby

When you do something that you enjoy, like a hobby, it stimulates your brain's "feel-good" zone and actually makes you happy! That's because research from the State University of New York shows that new experiences activate the brain's reward system, flooding it with dopamine and norepinephrine. Making time for enjoyable activities can also enhance your creativity, help you to think more clearly, improve your focus, increase your self-confidence, *and* give you additional energy. Those are things worth striving for!

tour. If cost is a factor, contemplate doing a home exchange (which I've done several times), or joining a charity mission. Stay in hostels instead of hotels. Does a language immersion trip where you live abroad with a family appeal to you? Try an art history tour or an archaeological dig. Look for off-season deals. You'll be surprised what you can come up with and how it can change your life.

Challenging Your Body

Regardless of your age, body type, strength, or coordination level, starting a fitness program is a wonderful way to build confidence, feel your power, see results, and experience real joy. In the healing section we discussed the plentiful benefits of exercise and I gave you quite a few suggestions for designing a routine tailor-made to your interests and lifestyle. If you completed that assignment, and have sustained it, great job! If you haven't, I suggest that you revisit chapter 3, "Nourishing Your Body and Soul," and do your best to add some form of enjoyable exercise into your life right now.

I'm going to take this project one step further by discussing the advantages of raising the bar on your existing program, or adding to it by signing up for a team sport or a new physical challenge.

If you join a team or decide to train for a particular sport with others, it will:

- Be a great way to meet new people (both men and women) and form lasting friendships
- Provide support and structure
- Enable you to improve your skills through being coached by a team leader or more experienced members
- Work on relationship- and communication-building skills
- Tap into your hidden potential
- Be more fun and interesting than going to a gym and running on a treadmill

Forty years old, five feet tall, and barely a hundred pounds wet, Meryl decided to join a football league during her rebuilding stage, and much snowballing came from this novel idea.

> "Football is my passion. I dated a quarterback in high school and played in college. I needed to add more to my life, and I wanted to do something outdoors that would get me out of my house and allow me to meet people. I contacted my alumni association and discovered that they had a football league in my city! I was so excited about this, so I joined up. It turned out to be such a great decision for me. I made many new friends and it made me feel alive, and it was so much fun. The team had mostly younger people, but they really responded to me and wanted to be my friend—no one treated me any differently. This gave me something to look forward to every weekend, and surprisingly, it expanded from there. Now we play, watch games together, and socialize. As an aside, I had my first post-break-up sexual experience with a cute young guy, and it gave me some added assurance to begin dating."

I just love that story because it's so representative of the variety of ways that women can rebuild their lives, even in arenas that are mostly male-dominated. Here's another story that I'd like to share with you because it's so impressive and fully displays how psychological growth can actually stem from muscular growth. One afternoon, on a cross-Atlantic flight, Katherine, newly divorced, sat next to a woman who was a flight attendant. The two women struck up an easy rapport, and the attendant mentioned that she was a triathlete. At that moment the flight attendant turned to Katherine and said, "When was the last time you did something in your life you have never done before?" It made her think.

"Well, she really inspired me and got me thinking. I decided that I needed to challenge myself in an entirely new way. When I returned home, I found myself a trainer and began to train for a triathlon. Now mind you, I'm not a biker, a swimmer, or a runner. And I'm in my midfifties! I told everyone I knew so I'd be too embarrassed to quit. A friend of mine who had done triathlons before was going to do the event with me, and a week before the race she injured herself and dropped out. I called my flight attendant friend and told her my friend had dropped out—and she flew from Seattle, where she lived, across the country to my home city and entered the race with me! My trainer joined up with me too. I didn't really have a time goal, I just wanted to complete the race alive. But I did it under two hours, which was actually an amazing time. I swear I was high for two months afterward. It was so empowering. Everyone was so proud of me. It made me feel so great about myself, so accomplished. I challenged myself in a way I had never been challenged before. I knew right there, on that day, that I had come full circle. I had arrived."

If that's not challenging your everything . . . what is?

Rebuilding from the Outside In: Getting a Makeover

I have continually proselytized on the importance of taking care of your body and soul, especially in times of transition. I am confident by now that the majority of you agree and are continually using my suggestions to maximize your welfare. When you make a commitment to take excellent care of yourself, to be healthy from the inside out, you are also making a commitment toward full recovery.

Now that we are in the last section of "Rebuilding," I believe it's time for some girl talk. You have worked so hard to heal, understand, and learn valuable lessons from your breakup, so isn't this a perfect time for some personal rewards? When was the last time that you truly pampered yourself from head to toe? Are you keeping up with your haircut and color, treating yourself to an occasional manicure or pedicure, and updating your look? Have you had an honest moment with your closet?

Do not undervalue the importance of feeling great about your appearance. When I leave home each morning—if my hair is nicely styled, if my makeup is applied, if I've used a touch of perfume, if my outfit is fashionable—I feel like a million bucks. And if I feel like a million bucks, my confidence soars, and my day is going to go so much smoother. Looking and feeling stunning is a big part of transformation, and as more than one of my transformed women humorously put it, "Looking fabulous is the very best revenge!"

Many women in the community described to me how upgrading or updating their appearance was yet another ingredient of self-improvement, which paved the way to self-fulfillment. One of my clients in mid-transformation—a stunning young woman with jet-black hair—appeared for a session one day with lighter hair. When I inquired about this change, her response was, "My black hair represented a time in my life that was dark and gloomy, and I decided that I wanted an updated look that better fit my new light and airy personality!" With a little help from Clairol, Sasha added to her already-blooming confidence, plus noticed a few stares from the

opposite sex. There is a good chance that men were always appreci-
ating her looks, but this time she was recognizing and embracing it,
and she finally had the gumption to flirt right back.

No matter where you live, fresh style is either right around the
corner or achievable via your computer. So don't be shy, hesitant, or
fret that it's superficial. You deserve to feel and look your best because it's all part of becoming a phenomenal woman. Here are a few
tips to ensure that you are putting your best possible self on display
for the world to admire:

- Sometimes even our tried-and-true style needs to be turned
on its head. Experiment with a new haircut or color, or a trendy nail
shade. Even a little change, like growing out those high school bangs,
goes a long way toward a renewed sophistication.

- This year gray hair is all the rage, so maybe it's worth a shot to
put the hair color away. Two of my most stylish friends have never
colored their hair, and they look marvelous. Think of the time and
money you'll save—and you may love the real you.

- Have you considered a cosmetic update? Every few years I go
to the makeup counter and have a skilled professional give me a current look. Don't be afraid to experiment with color at any age.

- Are you getting too comfy in your "mommy" jeans? There
is nothing like a trendy new pair to turn staid into hip in seconds.
There are tons of stores that sell stylish jeans for a fraction of the
price of designer ones. You are never too old to wear a cool pair.

- Whitening strips are a cost-effective way to brighten your
smile. And I want you to be comfortable grinning as you walk down
the street each and every day.

- If your wardrobe needs an update and money is tight, consider adding accessories for a more modern look. A scarf, new belt,
and some chunky costume jewelry can go a long way. Also consider
visiting a tailor to lengthen or shorten hems as current style dic-
tates. You can also make your flared pants straighter through this
cost-effective method.

- Are you in touch with your sensuality? Do you have a couple
of outfits that make you feel sexy? There's no day like today to get

comfortable with all aspects of your body. If you don't already own some items that will allow you to show off your fabulous new self, and this includes revealing your curves and displaying a little flash of skin, pick up a few.

• If you are someone who hates shopping, bring in reinforcements. Call a friend and ask her (or him) to be a cohort in creating the new, special you.

A Makeover Story

Here's a cute story to conclude this chapter and prepare you for the next. My friend Marla, a beautiful woman both inside and out, is two years past the termination of her marriage. Marla epitomizes the spirit of *The Breakup Bible*, and her recovery has been very inspirational to me. She fully used and continues to use her healing and understanding tips and tools, and she is presently making great strides in transformation. She travels, has built a great network of single and married male and female friends, regularly takes classes, and is currently in the process of changing careers. We met for coffee recently and she told me she is ready to explore the world of dating. After some banter she told me this funny story about how a recent conversation with a friend produced some added personal growth, which included a trip to the mall.

"I was chatting with my friend Denise and I told her I was ready to date. Excitedly she started rattling off names of all the single men we mutually knew. Then I said to her, 'I've been thinking that this time around, I'm finally ready for a real man. I want someone to adore me—someone who can't keep their hands off me. That's what I really want.'

"Denise sat back and became silent. Finally she blurted out, 'Well if you want a man to be all over you you've got to stop dressing like a piece of modern architecture!' After I picked myself up off the floor, I realized she was not entirely wrong. I love fashion and style, but my taste can be simple and austere. After further contemplation I came to the conclusion that in the past I have not been comfortable displaying my body. I haven't always been at ease with my shape, and because of that I realized that I don't put off a sexual vibe. It hit me that if I wanted to date and attract men, this was something I needed to work on. So Denise dragged me out shopping and 'sexied' me up! We bought a few really cute things that were more revealing, but still very much me.

"The first time I headed out in my new attire was a complete bust. I was invited to an event and everyone there was gay. But I didn't give up and wore the same outfit to a dinner party the following weekend. There were several single men there and I was really feeling good about myself and finally at ease in my own skin. At one point a very attractive man sauntered up to me and whispered in my ear, 'That's not fair. You look too damn good.' I said to myself, 'Another mission accomplished.' I can really get used to this!"

Rebuilding Tips and Tools

1. Internalize the concept of snowballing, one achievement building upon another, and remember that pushing through your fears will always create marvels.

2. Use your confidence-building exercises as often as necessary.

3. It's vital to embrace your individuality. Create some small challenges for yourself so you can get the hang of stepping out solo.

4. Get serious about your career. What aspects are working for you and what needs alteration?

5. Become involved with charitable activities.

6. Venture out to see your state, the nation, and the world.

7. Challenge your mind and body.

8. Make new friends and keep the old ones too.

9. Do all that you can to feel and look fabulous.

10. Create your final transformation list and keep adding to it regularly.

11. The revolution is here. Put your list into action today!

15

Dating Again

"If you don't open yourself to love, if you don't open yourself to pain—what's the point of life?" —*Julie*

"After much soul-searching I finally figured out what type of relationship I wanted, and guess what? It didn't look anything like my old one!" —*Christie*

Stop! Wait! I know what you're thinking, but please, please, don't put the book down! Before discussing this new theme, allow me to digress for a moment. It is so exciting that we are here together, approaching the finale of *The Breakup Bible*! You all deserve such a huge round of applause and my hat goes off to each and every one of you. You have given so much of yourself and put in abundant time and effort. Congratulations, you are now an official member of an enormous recovered community. I hope you feel great about your accomplishments, because you certainly deserve to. So now that I've disarmed you (a good trick, by the way—charm first, then hit between the eyes), sit back, relax, and let's have a serious talk on the topic of dating, the last leg of our amazing journey.

By now you recognize that I'm not one to brush things under the rug or hide from an uncomfortable subject. But there is always a method to my madness, and I would not steer you here today if I didn't feel you were ready to ponder some new data or tackle yet another snowball challenge. This book would not be complete without an honest discussion about the contemplation of a new relationship at some future point in your life. In fact, I would be doing you a grave disservice if I omitted it.

Now that we've established that, this chapter is not intended to pressure you back into the world of romance. It is simply here to provide an open forum for discussion among good friends. Reentering the dating scene is a decision that should not be taken lightly, and for many of you the mere thought of this will stop you cold in your tracks. I'm sure some will read this chapter with a bit of skepticism, and that is perfectly understandable. On the other hand, several of you have been chomping at the bit to arrive here. Others feel that the healing road you have traveled has taken you to this point, and you are finally ready to venture out. Whichever account describes you, it is never my intention to pass judgment, push you out, or rein you in. I just want to present the facts, and with all the growth you have acquired, you will intrinsically know when the moment is right. And when that time comes, as always, I'm merely here to offer support, guidance, and coaching.

After a painful breakup or divorce it is natural to think that you lost the true love of your life, that you will never have another soul mate, and that it's too late for happiness. And if you've left an unhappy or complicated union, you may feel that you are done with men and content to be alone. I'm sure quite a few of you feel that you can never trust again, or that you could not handle another rejection or broken heart. If this resonates with you, I implore you to keep an open mind while you read this chapter. Please don't allow your previous relationship to map out the rest of your life. Try to remember that there is an excellent chance that with all you've learned, you are in a better position to make a much better match. And there is an excellent chance that this new match will have a great outcome. But mostly, I want you to be open to all that life has to offer and not limit yourself in any way.

As we conclude this "transformation" section my wish is for you to be at a place of true contentment—and that definition is yours, not mine. I do however maintain a belief that we women are happiest in loving, connected relationships, but those relationships can and should come from a variety of sources. I am here to tell you that if you have completed your three phases of recovery, if you are over your breakup and your ex, and if you have created a great life for yourself—if you want to fall in love again, you can.

In this chapter I will help you determine if you are ready to date, or need to take more time. If you are ready, I will provide you with thought-provoking info to mull over, arm you with tips and tools to make you a really great dater, and I'll give you suggestions to help you pick the right man. I'll also offer directives on how to have a healthier relationship this time around.

Alternatively, if you don't feel it's time to begin dating, no worries at all. There is absolutely no rush here, and in fact, dating before you are emotionally ready or enthusiastic about it is a really bad idea. However, I will challenge you to make sure that you are postponing romance for sensible reasons. Together we will discuss regaining trust and I will dispel some of the dangerous dating myths that are floating around out there that make many shy away from taking any chances with love.

The art of skillful dating is a topic that I simply love to discuss, and I have so many insights and so much information that this chapter could be an actual book in itself. But I understand we are rapidly approaching the time for me to exit stage left and for you to take over my role. So I will try to spare you too much detail and instead leave you a bunch of ideas to mull over at your own pace. Finally, I will conclude with a variety of voices from the community who will pass on their wise dating anecdotes to you.

I think it's great to be here today, talking about *you* and planning *your* future and the prospect of a new and more satisfying love affair. I'm just thrilled for you and so excited about the possibilities. So please never, ever forget how far you've come, and always remember that the more you focus on your personal awakening, the faster your memories of the past continue to fade into oblivion. How cool is that!

When to Date? The Right Reasons
vs. the Wrong Reasons

Timing is everything with life and romance. Dating is a skillful process and one that should not be rushed. I don't want you "out there" until you're good and ready, and that means until you're wholly recovered and primed to be a great dater. By wholly recovered I mean that you have thoroughly worked through all three phases of recovery and can fully profess that you are a changed woman. As I've often said, if you begin to date before you are ready, your recovery will be greatly endangered, and unfortunately this can set you back several giant steps.

Dating works best in late transformation. If you feel that it's time to dip your toes into the waters of the dating pool, that is definitely another milestone in your recovery. Still, it's important that we take a moment to review your rationale for dating. Even if you have fully completed your healing and understanding and are well under way in transformation, it is my job to continually poke and prod. I want you to be an extremely mindful dater, and that means being fully aware and accountable for all of your decisions and actions. It also means thinking things through (benefits vs. risks), and understanding your motivation before setting out to try anything new. And, most important, it means always protecting your new life and doing what's best for your emotional health.

Now that we've established that, let's discuss what makes someone a great dater. You are ready to begin dating if these statements describe you:

The "Right" Reasons to Date

• You are a fully transformed woman and want to continue expanding your already-expansive life.

• Your state of mind is optimistic and enthusiastic, and you feel confident and empowered.

• You completely understand all the reasons why you picked

your ex, why the relationship derailed, and what part you played in the relationship and the breakup.

- You have a new or renewed positive association with men and romance and see many benefits in participating in a new relationship.
- You have an open mind about dating and are up for the process, even if it means some occasional bad dates, rejection, frustration, and disillusionment.
- You refuse to allow sporadic rejection or disappointment to put you back into a break-up tailspin.
- You understand that it will take time to meet someone and you will not try to rush it.
- You fully understand what a healthy relationship consists of and have made a deal with yourself that anything less than a great one is a colossal waste of your precious time.
- You feel that you have so much to offer to the right person and have the confidence and motivation to put yourself out there until you find a match that meets the majority of your realistic criteria.
- If you previously suffered from repetition compulsion or abandonment depression, you have put ample time and resources into your healing, and feel strongly that you are firmly in recovery.
- You have a great support system in place to cheer you along.

If you agree with all of these statements, you have a strong foundation and are ready to move ahead. Alternatively, if any of these statements do not resonate with you, you would greatly benefit from putting some additional time and commitment into your recovery before uploading your Match.com profile. Please don't be upset with yourself at all, just put some more emphasis on what needs to improve. Remember that the more seasoned you are, the better your outcomes will be.

Now please review this next set of criteria.

The "Wrong" Reasons to Date

- All of your friends have boyfriends or husbands and you are sick of feeling like the odd woman out.

• You are lonely and/or bored.

• You still miss your ex and hope that a new relationship will help you forget him.

• You want to take revenge on your ex by letting him see you are dating or have acquired a new boyfriend.

• You are competitive with your ex and want to be in a relationship before he is in one, or because he is already in one.

• Your family and friends are pressuring you to get back out there.

• You are desperate to have children or to be in a relationship.

• Fear of never meeting anyone and always being single is your main motivator to date.

• You still have many days where you feel negative, angry, anxious, or depressed.

• You have lingering trust issues and don't predict a happy outcome once you start dating.

• You think that all of your friends are in awful relationships, and therefore you are not convinced that there is such a thing as a "healthy" relationship.

• You have a laundry list of traits your new man needs to have— and it is seven pages long.

You Can Tell a Lot About a Guy by the Type of Date He Crafts

Although dining atop the Eiffel Tower may be every woman's fantasy, in fact it's probably not realistic unless you happen to live in Paris. I do, however, give points to the man who puts some thought into planning an appealing date. It shows that he is motivated, interested, and creative (or not!). My friend met a nice guy for coffee the other day, but crossed him off her list when he took her to a food court in a local mall for their second (and last) date.

If any of these statements describe you, you are not quite primed to date; this does not mean you didn't pass the test. It just means that it would be sensible to put some more effort into your program. When you have eliminated all the checks from the "wrong" list, and feel illuminated about the reasons on the "right" list, then by all means, move ahead!

Learning to Trust Again

> "Yes, I had trust issues, and yes, I dated before I was fully recovered, and yes, I got hurt—again. My first reaction was, 'Solution found—I'm done with men!', but then, thank God, I reconsidered after putting a lot of work into myself. You've got to learn to trust again, you've got to let yourself love again. It's all part of the magic of life." —*Melissa*

When women profess their concerns to me about starting over, the ability to trust again is one of the top issues we chat about. If your breakup came out of left field, if infidelity or deceit was involved, learning how to regain trust can certainly be a challenge. And if you had issues with trust before your split, you will probably think, "I will never date again!" When I meet someone whose relationship ended ages ago, and she won't even consider dating, rest assured she had trust issues going back way before her ex. And sadly for these women, their inability to trust often becomes a self-fulfilling prophecy.

Trust is a cornerstone of any healthy relationship, and once trust is broken by someone we deeply love, it is certainly a harrowing experience that takes a long time to recover from. Alternatively, you cannot have a healthy relationship with anyone if you have lingering issues with trust. So how do we solve this tricky paradox?

Dealing with the loss of trust is vitally important to your full recovery, and before you can move forward or consider dating, being able to trust again is paramount. Trust is such an important component of being close to a partner, and the absence thereof makes for complicated unions. It is fully possible to trust again, and I don't want you going through life being suspicious or untrusting of romance or men in general. You will limit yourself in so many ways if you hang on to that sort of baggage.

If you still find yourself grappling with the profound question "How can I ever trust again?", try to take some time and ask yourself why you are still feeling this way. Is there anything in your love map that may help you trace the genesis of this feeling? If so, please work diligently toward repairing the initial problem. Or, if it's just a normal by-product of your breakup, what can you do to expedite its departure? It may be very helpful to put some additional time into the rebuilding stage of transformation and practice forming trusting relationships with some of the new people who cross your path. Please regularly remind yourself that there are plenty of people out there who are trustworthy—and look among your circle of friends so you can prove this fact to yourself firsthand.

A better question to ask yourself before you date is "How can I try to protect myself this time around?" That is a great query and we will discuss it throughout this chapter.

Once you are completely recovered, one of the best ways to fully regain trust is to allow yourself to fall in love with a wonderful person this time around. Someone who will be true to you, and who will never destroy your trust. And yes, they do exist.

What's the Rush?

Making a great match and falling in love is a very slow, thoughtful, and somewhat organic process. When we take our time and make good decisions, magic can happen. Alternatively, when we barrel ahead like a Mack truck with extreme anxiety as our fuel, accidents repeatedly occur. I regularly implore my clients to take it slow and steady, yet surprisingly I don't always get resounding cooperation. We live in an instantaneous results–oriented world, and unfortunately too many people feel that they want what they want when they want it. And while that philosophy may be useful for some in their career or other aspects of life, it doesn't necessarily work for human relationships and romance in particular.

Rest assured, for every one of you who is grappling with trust or the decision to date again or not, there is one of you who is overly impatient for the games to begin. If this sounds like you, eager beaver, it is not going to get you where you want to go. Desperation and dating make very poor bedfellows. After the question I regularly hear about regaining trust, the second is always, "Will I ever meet someone again?" And it is the fear that lies underneath that completely normal question that makes many rush a process that simply cannot and should not be rushed. So before we move any further, let's address that ubiquitous question.

Yes, you will meet lots of potential suitors *when you are ready to date,* and that means fully transformed, dating for the right reasons, taking your time, making good decisions, and both respecting and enjoying the process. Maybe you're thinking that the phrase "enjoying the process" is an oxymoron. Most of you confess to me that the prospect of dating again is very intimidating, especially if it's been years since you were single and "out there." Some women I spoke with explained that they were never single and had zero dating exposure—they went straight from home into a committed relationship, or they were serial monogamists. And many feel that dating is an unpleasant means to an end—kind of like interviewing for a job. What I say to those folks is of course, no one loves to be out of work, but remember that the better you are at networking, the job hunt process, and the actual interview, the higher the chances that you will get offered the very best job! This same philosophy pertains to dating.

I want to address two important points, and they are (1) that the "process" of dating needs to be respected, and (2) dating can be really fun. If you rush out there with your panic leading the way, it will severely impede your chances of success. Alternatively, if you take your time and stay relaxed and learn to embrace it, dating will be a profound growth experience.

There is much to be gained by taking it slow. You will have the opportunity to meet a variety of people from different walks of life, and the more you date the closer you'll get to knowing what you truly desire from a new relationship this time around. Over time and with practice you can learn to be a really great dater, and the better you are at dating the sharper your antennae will become. So slow down and please enjoy a smooth ride.

I know you all have heard a story like this, but even so, I'm going to tell you one of my favorites because we all need a reminder from time to time. Several years ago, a lovely thirty-five-year-old woman purchased an apartment next door to mine and became my neighbor. I was impressed that such a young woman was buying a home for herself. Tara was friendly and kind and we fell into easy banter in our common hallway. Smart and competent, she had a job she was passionate about and a very full life. One day the subject of dating came up and Tara joked to me that she was in "recovery" from being on a frantic dating track. She explained that for many years she felt extremely pressured to be in a serious relationship leading toward marriage, and that pressure caused her to make some poor choices that resulted in a few broken hearts. Eventually she saw the light and realized she was on a bad path leading nowhere. That's when she decided that it was perfectly OK to be single, and that's when she

Look Terrific on That First Date, But Always Look Like You

It's important when dating to be yourself. That doesn't mean showing up without a shower or some nice attire. But it does mean dressing in a way that reflects whom you really are. If you're a sporty gal who rarely takes off her Converses, don't show up in seven-inch heels just to impress. If your hair is supercurly and you only get it blown out once a year, maybe tonight is not the night for a blowout. And if you rarely wear makeup and don't plan on changing, why cover yourself in Maybelline for a date? Love yourself and let your true essence shine through. That's better than any accoutrement.

decided to slow down, breathe, and transform. Tara felt so relieved once she made this important discovery, and she finally started to really enjoy herself and her life. Purchasing her own home was a declaration to herself that being single, even if it meant forever, was perfectly fine. Shortly after we had that chat a cute consultant was sent to her company to work with her on a project. Interestingly, he also happened to be from her hometown of Toledo. A year after our conversation, I had a brand-new neighbor, Mike, an affable guy who was crazy about Tara. This summer they wed and now Tara's apartment is up for sale as they prepare to move back to Toledo together. Once Tara took herself out of the race, no matter what the outcome, she won it in spades.

Dispelling Myths

In our culture we have many myths about dating and love. Both of my grandmothers regularly spewed folklore about man trolling; perhaps yours did too. Grandma Estelle begged me always to wear makeup and heels when I left my home—even when using a public Laundromat—because "you never know who you'll meet." Grandma Syd implored me to wear perfume in order to attract a man. And those were the more playful tales floating around back then!

Many years ago a popular magazine ran a cover story stating that single women past their late twenties faced dismal odds in tying the knot, and if you were over forty, you had a higher probability of getting killed by a terrorist than finding a husband. I can only imagine the horror that any single gal experienced when she learned of that unverified and misleading stat. Unfortunately myths such as that awful one regularly abound, and I hear the same silly ones today as when I was dating. And with all we know about the powers of subliminal advertising, I can only imagine the anxiety (both unconscious and on the surface) that most single women carry within themselves due to these disturbing messages.

I encounter the manifestation of mythology every day with my clients, both male and female, who are working with me on dating. And regrettably it is the acceptance of these untruths that keeps too many stuck in unhappy unions, and makes singles deathly afraid of dating. I feel strongly that part of my job as a therapist and writer is to be an educator, and part of the education I offer my clients and readers (and, frankly, anyone who will listen to me) is to completely dispel these harmful tales. And I'm in a great position to take on the title of "senior myth buster," because in my line of work I regularly see that they are simply obtuse fables and nothing more. Every fully transformed woman I have ever encountered will agree with me.

I know you've all heard the scary myths floating around out there, but I'm not so sure you actually understand the toll they take on everyone's psyche, including yours. So let's take some time and dispel the most damaging ones.

The Top-Ten Most Deplorable Dating Myths

Your job now is to acknowledge the ways in which these myths affect you, and to make a deal with yourself that you too will prove that they are wrong. I'm going to present a myth and then next to it you'll see my response. After you read mine, please add several myth busters of your own.

    1. **All men are cheaters.** Sure, some men cheat, but many do not. And by the way, the most recent study I read noted that men and women cheat in equal numbers. The best way to guarantee a monogamous union is to have great dating radar, pick the right man, and do your part to keep the relationship strong and "affair proof." By that I mean jointly committing to ensuring that the maintenance and sustenance of your relationship is always on the front burner.

    2. **All men want younger women.** Our culture prizes youth, so naturally some men and women dream of dating a little arm candy. Sure, a certain type of man will only date women a decade (or many decades) younger, and it's good for you to understand and identify this because it says a lot about his personality structure (and is a red flag). These men care more about the flash than about the substance and consider their young babe an extension of their tiny ego (and maybe some other smallish body part). So unless you adore sugar yourself, stay clear of this type and date men who seek an

age-appropriate match. And by the way, there are many men out there who have no interest in dating women young enough to be their daughters.

3. **There are no good men out there.** There are plenty of good men out there—never, ever forget that. If you are convinced that this is true, please ask yourself where this dangerous falsehood originated. The roots of this myth may go way back to your childhood, especially if you had issues with your father or another male authority figure. If that is the case, please work to repair the original wound if you desire to be in a healthy relationship. Maybe your last man was a "no-goodnik," but there are so many kind, generous, and honest single men available who are looking for wonderful women to make a life with.

4. **There are no single guys; all the good ones are taken.** See, there are "good ones" as this saying goes, and guess what, they are not all taken! Do I need to remind you about the breakup or divorce statistics? That means for every one of you divorced women, there is a divorced man. And, for those of you living together, the break-up rate is even higher. New singles regularly cycle in and out of the dating pool. Stay optimistic and practice all that you will learn in this chapter and you'll meet plenty of good ones.

5. **Men love bitches.** Yes, some men love bitches, and there is a name for them: masochists. Stay away from those guys and find someone who will love you for who you are!

6. **All men are players so I have to play games to be successful at dating.** You don't have to be a "player" to be lucky at love—but it's always good to have some skills and a strategy. And that's why I wrote this chapter! Yes, some men are "players" and they generally like women who play back. But rest assured, those types always end up in my office with a boatload of problems because they get lost in the game and that causes all sorts of dysfunction. Meanwhile, there are plenty of men out there who love sports but do not view love as a game. Look for one of those.

7. **No men want to commit.** Believe it or not, just as many men as women really want to be in happy, healthy, and committed relationships with wonderful women. So if you meet someone who is a

commitmentphobe, pass him by and look for someone who wants exactly what you want.

8.   **Men only want sex.** Good sex is a great part of any healthy relationship, and I know just as many women as men who love sex and enjoy being coupled so they can have lots of it. Men want many things in a relationship (as do we!), and sex is undeniably *one* of them. But that doesn't mean they "only want sex." Figure out what's important to you in a relationship and in a partner, and look for someone who will meet your criteria and then some!

9.   **Men don't want to date women with kids.** There are thousands of single dads out there who are looking for single moms to get cozy with. If you have children and date men with kids, you'll have more in common with them and lots of hysterical (and not so hysterical) stories to bond over. Alternatively, there are also plenty of childless men out there who are very open to dating women with children. I know many successful blended families, and you'll hear some of their stories up ahead.

10. **You have to kiss some frogs before you meet your prince.** Sorry, this is true. But remember, the more frogs you kiss the closer you'll get to knowing what you really want in a relationship.

It's so important to be aware whenever these negative myths crop up, and please do your very best to talk back to them. They are very pesky and will stick around and cause havoc if you allow them to. Use your skills to exterminate them and don't let them take up one more second in your head.

One final point—I know this is not a myth per se, but some do tell me that they are not eager to date because they are so happy in their transformed lives. And because of this, they are afraid of any setbacks and are not willing to settle for just any partner. Believe me, I want you to love your life, and choosing whether to date or not is completely up to you. I would never tell you to date before you are ready, and I would never allow you to settle for someone who didn't add to your already plentiful life. So just keep an open mind while reading this chapter and see how you feel over time.

What Are *You* Looking for
This Time Around?

Now that we've busted those troublesome myths, we're getting closer to the first round of dates. But before you apply your final coat of mascara and slip into your heels (or flip-flops) let me ask you an important question. Have you taken some time to contemplate what you're really looking for in a partner or in a relationship at this stage of your life? Identifying this is essential, and it is our next step.

Let's face it, we all have our "fantasy" list, which contains words such as tall, sexy, rich, and buff. We'd like him to resemble Ashton Kutcher or sing like Bono. But the operative word here is "fantasy," and right now I want to help you create a list that is honest, original, authentic, and representative of the newly transformed you. If you are exiting a lengthy relationship there is a very good chance that you are looking for something completely different this time around. If you have identified repetition compulsion in your DNA you are definitely going to look for someone who has absolutely nothing in common with your ex! In actuality, some of the most delightful transformation romance stories I heard involved women falling in love with men who were not their usual type, or in fact, who were completely different from others they'd dated. And the wider the net they cast, the more fish they easily procured. I know great tales of women opening their minds and hearts and going "off type" only to discover mind-blowing love in places (and packages) they never would have dreamed of finding it.

With all the incredible insight you've acquired, plus the firm understanding of who you are today, whom might that special someone be who is deserving of your love?

Keeping an Open Mind

When people come to me for dating advice, the first question I ask them is what they are looking for. Answers generally range from "I don't know" (a biggie), to the delivery of a ten-page list (it really happened). Of course the correct answer lies somewhere in between. I nearly scream when I meet someone who emphatically exclaims that she will never settle, and her dream candidate has a résumé longer than a roll of paper towels! The best daters, and the most interesting people, keep an open mind when it comes to romance. Some of my forty- and fifty-something friends and clients joke with me, "You'd be surprised what I'd settle for today!" What they are really saying is if you want to be in a relationship, you have to have a very open mind. Other women confess to me that as they age, brains are so much more important than brawn, and that character far outweighs money . . . and hair. My friend Amanda recently joked, "At our age, Rachel, you have to be attracted to a feature like a bright smile or blue eyes, instead of the whole package!" And I'm always thrilled when twenty- or thirty-year-olds proclaim to me that "nice guy" status has replaced other qualities they were previously attracted to that were more superficial.

A great sense of humor would be on top of my list of traits I want in a man, but what about yours? Think about some traits that are meaningful to you and write them down. Here are some of the top contenders from me and the community, and I'd like to see a few of these or similar ones on your list. Why don't you review this list with a pencil in hand and then circle the ten traits that are the most important to you. That will give you something tangible to review when evaluating a potential contender:

Important Traits in a Man

Kind	A prolific reader
Respectful	Friendly to the earth
Intelligent	Fun
Honorable	Interested in others
Honest	A joker
Funny	An optimist
Loving	Down to earth
Devoted	In the know

Active	Worldly
Interesting	Good to his parents
Open-minded	Giving
Creative	Has integrity
Charitable	Mindful
Caring	Thoughtful
Athletic	Energetic
A good father	Considerate
A good dancer	Stable
A good person	Solid
Adventurous	Grounded
Committed	Masculine
An animal lover	Metrosexual
A nature lover	Is in touch with his feminine side
A food lover	Has good boundaries
Loves travel	Passionate about life
Independent	Healthy
Confident	Secure
Patient	Sensitive
Empathetic	Emotionally intelligent
An adult	

Furthermore, I also urge you to challenge some of your own myths and mind-sets. How about considering these possibilities?

• If you are childless, would you consider dating someone with kids? My sister's boyfriend has two young daughters and she is a devoted step-girlfriend.

• How about a long-distance relationship? Don't rule it out—I know of some great ones.

• Have you considered dating someone from a different ethnicity, race, culture, or religion? As we mature it frees us up to make decisions that benefit us, and are not made because of pressure from our parents or communities.

- How about age range? Would you date someone older or younger?
- What about profession? If you've only dated businessmen or lawyers, try a professor, a geologist, or an artist.
- What about income? Too many women discard perfectly nice guys because they aren't "rich enough." If money is important to you, please ask yourself what *you* can do to bring more wealth into your life without having to rely on a partner. And if you are financially secure, perhaps you'd consider dating someone who is less financially successful than you. Remember that there is not always a correlation between dedication, ambition, hard work, and wealth.

As a reminder, there is a huge difference between keeping an open mind and settling for someone who is too dissimilar, or whom you have no interest in or attraction to. And never allow yourself to become involved with someone who is of poor character, mistreats you, or doesn't always have your best interest at heart.

Modern Love

Whether it's Match.com, Facebook, Chemistry.com, eHarmony, JDate.com, or ChristianSingles.com, with the advent and advancement of the Internet, there have never been more opportunities to both fine-tune your dating skills *and* meet potential quality men. And if you haven't dated in decades and are out of practice, the Internet is a superb way for you to ease back in. Still, even with the capacity of making a match right in your living room, too many women tell me that they either don't like or won't try Internet dating sites, because, "The guys on those sites are all total losers." Oh my, another myth to bust!

There are numerous social networking, singles, and dating sites on the Web today, and rest assured, perfectly normal people are successfully using them. I know of many great stories that consist of meeting and matching in cyberspace and eventually becoming a

Is It Safe to Date a Man Who Is Separated But Not Divorced?

I get asked this question often. Some marriages take years to unravel, so it is indeed possible for someone who is separated to be fully recovered and ensconced in a brand-new lifestyle without much unfinished business. Alternatively, some men with unresolved issues are bitter or negatively engaged with their ex for years post-divorce. What really matters is that you date someone who has fully healed, understood, *and* transformed. Use all the tools in this book and this chapter, and then look for one of those!

committed couple. More than a few of my good friends and clients have met terrific partners online. My friend Corrine was matched up with her boyfriend of seven years by her best friend—online. Corrine's friend had gone on one Match.com date with a nice man and said, "I met this sweet guy, but I think he's more your type than mine."

Remember my "Keep an open mind" concept? Please don't limit yourself in any way when it comes to dating. The best daters I know use what I call a "360-degree approach," and that means they are completely open to meeting all sorts of prospective suitors in a variety of different ways. The Internet is a great tool that works best when it's part of an entire dating program as opposed to the only method you are using. And if you are using it, take it slow and please don't get obsessive with it or too frustrated when you have the inevitable disappearing act or bad date.

The Art of Skillful Dating: Rachel's Top Tips

We're halfway through this chapter and I can see that you're finally becoming curious about this dating thing. We've covered a lot and you're sticking with me—a very good sign! I'd now like you to contemplate what else you can do to become a really great dater. Great daters are not born, they are made, and with practice you too can be part of this group. I know we all have accomplishments that we're proud of, and I regularly hear women refer to themselves as great moms, daughters, friends, partners, tennis players, or cooks. But when was the last time you heard someone refer to herself as the world's best dater? Well, it's a new category that I have invented, and I am looking to invite tens of thousands of single women into this elite club. Read my next set of tips over and over again, and definitely keep adding to it from your own experience. And when you become the "top chef of love," please write to me so I can learn a few new tricks from you!

• **Do whatever you need to stay optimistic and enthusiastic, but also be very realistic.** It's a challenge to balance optimism and realism, but it can be done. I want you to try to put your best face forward and have fun without being too invested in the results. Keep your expectations in check. Try not to obsess "Is he the one for me?" or "Did he like me?" Instead just relax and enjoy meeting someone new and having a different experience. A much better question to ask yourself is "Did I like this person enough to spend another second with him?" That puts you right back into the driver's seat, where you belong.

• **Be sure to laugh after a bad date.** Believe me when I tell you that laughter is powerful medicine when it comes to dating, so hang on to your sense of humor! I've spent many hilarious moments with friends and clients giggling over their dating antics. Yes, some dates are going to be really really bad, and some men are going to be superboring or highly arrogant. It's all part of the experience. My friend Ellen gives every guy she dates a humorous fake name. According to her, "I've dated Boring Rich Guy, Maniac Party Man, Short Man, Cheap Man, and Plant Man. It gave me comic relief. Sometimes after a bad date I'd say, 'Is it me, or am I just having some bad inventory?' But then I would look at my list and know it wasn't me at all and I'd have a good laugh!"

• **Learn how to flirt.** It you're exiting a lengthy relationship it may have been quite some time since you've had a good flirt. Perhaps you forgot how, or maybe you were never comfortable with it. Flirting is actually a wonderful way to display your confidence, emit pheromones, and communicate in a nonverbal way. Eye contact, a bright smile, and a swing of your hair or your hips can definitely be a gateway to romance. So if you're feeling a little rusty, please start practicing today, because it's fun and empowering.

• **Develop a really strong radar and always listen to your instincts.** After all you've learned about yourself in "Understanding," you are in an improved position to identify potentially problematic men and steer clear. I think that most men fully reveal themselves by the fourth date—you just have to know what to listen and look for. But that being the case, I don't want you too skeptical either. Just be yourself, and see what you notice about the personality of your date.

Developing Your Dating Radar

Here are my top red flags to be aware of, and write down some of your own warnings as well. If any of these crop up, is it really worth a second or third date?

Potential Red Flags
Talks too much about his breakup or divorce
Talks too much about his ex or his kids
Asks you too much about your breakup or divorce
Bad-mouths his ex
Talks too much about himself
Too much flash; throws around money, brags, and name drops
Makes too many jokes
Seems negative, caustic, or pessimistic
Asks inappropriate questions or makes inappropriate or insensitive remarks
Doesn't ask enough questions about you, or seems disinterested in what you have to say

Repeatedly checks his electronic devices

Talks about past sexual experiences or conquests

Attempts to get too physical too soon

Is too complimentary

Seems controlling or jealous

Drinks too much

Appears too eager to plan a second date, or calls or texts too
  much between dates

Is thirty or older and has never had a serious relationship

Talks too much about his mother—or his dog

Here are a couple of examples where a finely tuned radar proved
to be very useful:

Jaci liked John on their first date and agreed to the next one by
the end of the evening. On the second and third dates she noticed a
pattern. "John was very rude to the waitstaff wherever we went. He
also made a statement about ex-girlfriends, and said when his relationships end, he never speaks to the woman again. Those two clues
made me see that he had a mean streak, and I decided that a fourth
date was not in order."

Here's an astute story from Emily. "I had my first date with Todd,
and it went very well. He was attractive, interesting, and seemed very
bright. He did say one thing that gave me a hint that perhaps he
wasn't a flexible person, but I let it go. On the second date I saw he
was a total control freak. He had to have the entire night go his way
and was not interested in my feedback or suggestions. He cut me off,
talked only about himself, and when I did try to break in or give an
opinion, he negated it. A few times I actually broke out laughing. I
knew halfway through dinner that he was not for me. The next night
I went to a dinner party and sat beside a very nice man who was
kind, thoughtful, and respectful. He really valued what I had to say
and listened to me intently. I felt the universe gave me this experience to prove it wasn't me—it was him!"

Please make your own list of red-flag issues and stay very tuned
in during the first few dates. You'd be surprised how much aggrava-

tion you will save yourself when you eliminate men who aren't right for you early on in the process.

Here are a few additional tips to coach you along:

• **Make sure you have great supports in place.** You've put so much into creating your new life, and your number-one goal is to keep your transformation going strong. Don't cancel plans with friends to have a date, and do make sure you have plenty of friends to call when you have a bad one, or a wicked crush.

• **Try planning something fun the night after a date so you have an activity to look forward to.** It also serves as a good reality check that you have a great life and are going to be fine with or without romance in your life.

• **Do not let dating rule your mood.** If you find yourself getting obsessive, anxious, or depressed, that is a sign that something is amiss. Take a few steps back and reassess your situation. Your recovery and happiness are paramount—don't ever let anything or anyone interfere with them.

• **Leave the past where it belongs.** In the past.

• **Don't drag it on.** If he's not right for you, break it off. Don't keep it going because you are afraid to say no, or you don't like confrontation, or you don't want to hurt someone's feelings, or you are afraid to be alone again.

• **Be honest.** Be gracious and simply tell someone if you don't want to see him again. People really appreciate honesty and you'll feel better about yourself when you act with integrity.

• **There is not strength in numbers.** If you date too many guys at once it will be confusing and your radar will crash.

• **Date someone at the same recovery phase that you are in.** Since I know you won't date until late transformation, I suggest you not date anyone unless he is in the same place as well. If you meet someone who has recently ended a relationship and hasn't gone through his three phases of recovery, he will not be at a place where he is able to sustain a healthy relationship.

• **Use every date as a learning experience.** From time to time you are going to have dates or mini-relationships that hurt or disappoint you. This is completely normal and happens to everyone. Please use these experiences to both gather and dissect data. There is a lot of good information here, so please be wise and commit to learning valuable lessons instead of throwing up your hands. I recently heard a good story that verifies this point. Darlene was just beginning to contemplate dating when an acquaintance set her up with Dan. According to Darlene, "I didn't know much about Dan, except he was a doctor. I was proud of myself because I was taking a chance—I didn't even ask to see a photo. Over the e-mails I really liked him. He was smart and seemed interesting. The night we finally agreed to meet up I had a bad cold and considered canceling, but I realized we both had insane schedules. When I got to the restaurant and met him, I'll admit I was disappointed by his looks. He was very short, heavy, and dressed extremely messy. Not my physical type at all. My immediate reaction was, 'So this is what dating is about—I'll never meet anyone, I'll be alone forever.' But I had a quick pep talk with myself and pulled it together. He was actually a very sweet guy. He was very attentive to my cold and gave me some great advice. He was kind and empathic. It made me think, 'My ex-boyfriend *never* would have been so sweet to me if I was sick!' Ultimately Dan wasn't for me, but it was a great experience and helped me think about what I actually wanted in a man this time around!"

• **Be careful with alcohol.** If you drink too much your radar will get waterlogged and it will malfunction.

• **Manage dating anxiety and don't let it spill over.** We are all nervous during first dates and the early stages of a relationship—that is perfectly natural. Be sure to use your anxiety-reduction tips and tools to help you glide through. Try exercise, yoga, meditation, and deep breathing to calm and sooth you. Remember to talk back to negativity, delay obsessions, and use your confidence-building exercises. Don't sit and wait for the phone to ring—use your supports and stay busy doing wonderful things.

• **Take breaks as needed.** There will inevitably be moments when dating will be challenging. If you find yourself becoming frustrated or pessimistic, take some time to get your bearings back. However, one of the biggest mistakes I see women making is to completely stop dating when they've had a new breakup, a stream of bad dates, or a dry spell. When this happens, please spend some time taking care of yourself and get back to doing things you love. But also use this time to analyze data. Think about why things have not been going well for you and what you can do to change course. Then get back on the saddle and try try again.

Please never forget to continually add to the rebuilding of your new life, especially when dating. The more interesting activities you have going on, the more fulfilled you'll be. And the more fulfilled you are, the better dater you'll be!

Let's Talk About Sex

No book gets published these days without some sex talk! All kidding aside, I couldn't send you into the trenches without a little love strategy. Face it, as much as the thought of fooling around with someone new may unnerve you, you'd be pissed at me if I left this topic out—and I'd be doing you a disservice. So don't be shy or repressed, and let's have a chat about some sex.

When it comes to hooking up, not much has changed. Women are as conflicted today as they were decades ago about when is the right time to become intimate with someone. I regularly have the same conversation with women in their twenties, forties, and sixties—and they all want to know when they should sleep with someone they like. And if they have already taken the plunge, they completely doubt themselves and wonder if they should have waited longer. I'm certainly not here to tell you that I have the answer to this universal quandary, but nevertheless, as you may imagine, I do have some thoughts to share.

Sex is exciting, fabulous, and fun, and it's also extremely intimidating and scary. Opening yourself up to someone new—emotionally and physically—is not without some risk. If you have been with one partner for years, the thought of getting naked with someone brand-new will be met with equal parts of intrigue and panic. Alternatively, if it's been ages since you've had a regular lover, you may be so obsessed with having sex that your radar will most definitely collapse. My friend Alicia, married twenty-three years and divorced for two, called me giggling one night to shyly announce that she had "lost her virginity" to her new boyfriend. I was very pleased for her, especially since the fear of being intimate with someone new was originally overwhelming to her.

So back to that question of when to have sex with someone. Many feel that sex has always been a game since the beginning of time. If that is the case, I want to tell you that the rules are yours and only yours to make. Just keep a level head and do your best to make decisions that are beneficial to you. Here are a few concepts you may wish to think through before dimming the lights:

• Remember my fourth-date theory? Perhaps it would be wise to wait until you feel trusting and comfortable with your new paramour before heading for home base.

• What's the rush? Men love a little mystery and intrigue.

• Before agreeing to sex, it's important that you ask yourself how you will feel if you never hear from this person again after you have slept with him. Unfortunately it can happen and I want you to do your best to protect yourself.

• When women make love to a partner they release the hormone oxytocin, known as the "snuggle chemical." This may make you feel more attached to your new partner, so please be mindful of this.

• Do not confuse sex with love. They are two entirely different things.

• Do not sleep with someone unless you feel somewhat in control. If you have doubts that he likes you, or feel uncertain about his character, using sex to win him over is never a wise choice.

Here are two stories I'd love to share with you because they both have sex as a theme, yet they are quite different in nature.

Amy had been single for a few years when she met Tom and described him to me as the first guy she'd been attracted to for a very long time. She was definitely in transformation and felt ready to date, but she was also fiercely independent and very protective of her recovery. After a few months of dating, Tom told Amy that he thought she was holding back emotionally and sexually, and it was affecting the way he was feeling about her. After some thought, Amy came to the conclusion that Tom was right. She had built up a solid wall to keep herself safe, and it was affecting her ability to let go and become fully intimate with him. Although the relationship didn't last, Amy didn't fret, because she felt it was a great learning experience. It taught her that if she wanted to be in a full-fledged relationship she had some work to do around issues of trust so she could be more accessible to both sex and romance.

Donna was in early transformation when she ran into Larry, a high school boyfriend, at a restaurant. "Larry was a player back then, and apparently still was, because he was laying it on thick with me! He was very cute and he was the first guy I was attracted to since my divorce. We exchanged numbers, but I knew right away I wasn't going to date him because he was just like my ex, and I was really trying to go for a very different caliber man this time around. But he was awfully sexy and I knew I needed to get back out there. I was about to turn thirty, and I didn't want to ring in my new decade with my ex being the last man I had sex with. So I made a move and I called Larry. I invited him over to my place and we had amazing hot sex. I knew this was just for sex and nothing else and because of this I was able to have a great time and a fabulous orgasm. Then I kicked him out. It was very empowering and liberating—I just felt it was something I needed to do!"

The House That Love Built

Before turning it over to the community for a concluding round of stories, I want to take one last opportunity to leave you with my final words on love. There is an excellent chance that in the future, if you want to be in a new relationship, you will. And if that is the case, it is my deepest wish that it be a wonderful and rewarding experience. I would be overjoyed if you told me that you were in a healthy and equal partnership with someone special. And I would hope that he or she would embody many of the positive traits that I listed earlier in this chapter. If you fall in love again, let it be the icing on your perfectly baked cake—and nothing less. You deserve everything from life, and never settle for anyone who doesn't deserve you. With all you have learned from the ending of your relationship and this chapter, you are now in a superior position to make excellent decisions about romance. Moreover, you are also in a great place to keep this new relationship on the right track for as long as you wish to be in it.

So I leave you with my closing list, called "The House That Love Built." My analogy is that a strong relationship is like the foundation of a beautiful home—if you give it the maintenance it needs, it will always stay robust and retain its value for years to come. Alternatively, if you let it hang out there through stormy weather, it will slowly crack and bring the walls down with it. If you find yourself falling in love, good for you—it's yet another milestone in your journey. But remember you have a huge responsibility now to both care for yourself and tend to your partnership. I suggest you return to the "understanding" section occasionally for a refresher course on the most common causes of breakups, just to familiarize yourself with the traps that we all fall into from time to time. So here's my last list on love. Read it, and then, by all means, write yours. The healthiest relationships are built on (put the word "mutual" in front of each description):

Deep love
Strong intimate bond
Sexual connection *and* compatibility
Respect
Trust
Honesty
Friendship
Kindness
Understanding
Support

Tolerance

Gratitude

Interdependence (not codependence or too much independence)

Ability to negotiate and compromise

Life philosophies

Interests

Ability to take responsibility for your actions and apologize
  when wrong

Dating at Any Age

Dating in Your Twenties

Rena. "I met my ex in college. He was my first serious relationship, so being single at twenty-four is a new experience for me, and
it definitely took some adjusting.

"I'm not big about thinking I'll meet someone at a bar. It's loud,
and you can only have a brief conversation that's superficial. So
don't go out with your friends to a bar thinking you're going to meet
someone. Just go out to see your friends and have a fun night. And
if you do meet someone and give him your number, don't get your
hopes up that he will call. Many girls get excited too quickly when
they meet someone new, so don't get too ahead of yourself. You have
to temper your expectations. There is never any reason to settle for
someone who isn't right for you. Have a clear idea of what you like
and what makes you happy. Relationships should only be adding
value to your life. If it's adding stress or negativity, that's something
to worry about."

Hailey. "I was moving to a new city three years after my divorce
and I signed up on a dating website before I even arrived at my new
destination. I actually did meet someone nice online and we started
chatting regularly. He seemed like a really sweet guy and we made
plans to go on a date as soon as I relocated. It definitely took me
time to let down my guard—I had boundaries and barriers up. After

about eight months, Michael sat me down and said, 'It's been awhile now and I'm not feeling the love. I know you have it in you because I see how affectionate you are with your dog. What's going on?' After that conversation I realized that he was right and I wasn't allowing myself to fully let go. I understood that if I wanted things to progress, I had to let myself be vulnerable again. I had to trust him and trust that I'd be OK if we didn't work out. Then when I finally let go, it was so much better between us. We've been together for over a year now and it's a really great relationship.

"The best advice I can give to other twentysomethings is take your time. The first time around I was in such a hurry to get married that I missed some obvious signs. But having said that, do be very open to the process of dating. You have to go on a lot of first dates. It's important to get out and see what's out there."

Dating in Your Thirties

Elena. "I was thirty-four when I started dating after my marriage ended. I really wanted to be married again and to have children, so it was important to me to get back out there as soon as I was healed. I was determined, but I was definitely not desperate— and there is a huge difference. A lot of people are very negative and warned me that the statistics were not good. But I was not going to let this deter me.

"When I went to file for divorce, I mustered up the courage to make the first appointment with a lawyer. I prepared myself well that day—I wanted to look like I had it together. I walked into his office, and the lawyer who came out to greet me was a handsome man I had met at a party the year prior when I was unhappily married. His name was Eric and it turned out that we knew a bunch of the same people. There was clearly chemistry between us at that first meeting, which ended up lasting hours! I wasn't sure what his status was, but I found out from friends he was divorced and had a teenage son. Eric was a gentleman and wanted to be professional, so he didn't actually ask me out until after all my paperwork was filed, which was several months later.

"We started dating and got serious quickly. He was a real

grown-up. Finally, I was dating a man instead of a boy. Eighteen months after our first date, we were married. Today we have two daughters of our own and a wonderful life. No one's life is perfect, and sometimes we have issues, but we work them out like two responsible adults. I was thirty-six when I married, thirty-eight when I had my first daughter, and forty-three when I had my second. Anything is possible—never, ever give up hope!"

Belle. "I was thirty-two when I separated and had a four-year-old daughter. I had met my ex-husband in college, and I had long-term boyfriends in high school, so I'd never really dated. But I was optimistic and felt that even with a child I would meet someone one day.

"I knew I had to learn how to date, and that felt a bit daunting to me. I discovered that men *were* interested in dating someone who had a child. For the right man who is in the mind-set of looking for a woman who will be a wife and potential mother—well, I was that 'ready-made' person. I was presenting the whole package to them. I was young, attractive, I had a full life, a job that I loved, and was able to raise a child on my own.

"I met the man I'm currently married to at a singles event after three years of dating. I liked Ross from the get-go. He is five years younger than me—and I didn't let that deter me at all. You've got to keep an open mind. We took it very slow—I had no idea if he was the right person for me or not. I was in no hurry and wanted to see how it all played out. We married after dating for two years.

"Ross always wanted to have children, but he also saw he had a role in my daughter's life. I was thirty-eight when we married, so we didn't have that much time. Eventually we decided that having children together was something we both wanted, and I became pregnant at thirty-nine. Having a blended family is not without challenges, but marriage and parenting are not without challenges either! I get along very well with my ex, and there are occasions where we are all together as a large blended family. That makes my eldest daughter feel very happy and secure. We all try hard, and that's so important when kids are involved. I'm extremely content in my life today. Truly, it couldn't have turned out better."

Dating in Your Forties

Kristen. "I was doing a ton of animal volunteer work after my breakup, and Jack, who became my partner, came in with his two small daughters to adopt a kitten. I remember thinking he was kind and a good father. We chatted and I gave him my card. One day he called saying that his daughters wanted me to visit them and see the kitten. That night he formally asked me out. I had never dated anyone with children before, so that was very new to me.

"The most important thing I want to say is that I never would have been able to get involved in this healthy relationship if I wallowed in my situation. I either would have continued making poor choices or I would have stayed a victim—stuck and depressed. I really did my work, and that's the reason I was able to not only heal but create a much better life for myself. I will not make the same mistakes today that I made in the past.

"I think women in their forties must be open to dating someone with children. You don't want to limit the choices of people you'll meet. Men with kids are generally more mature and have worked on their relationship skills. Plus you can learn a lot about them by the way they treat their children. Also, it opens you up to the world of step-parenting, and for me, having a nice relationship with his daughters has been such a pleasant surprise!"

Hillary. "I had just turned forty when I started dating my current boyfriend. I had been divorced twice and I had no interest at all in getting involved with someone new. Plus I was applying to law school, and nothing was going to distract me from that. I live in Alabama now, but I'm originally from Memphis. I was visiting home one weekend and I was out with friends when I met Pete. He had recently divorced and relocated to Memphis, and he was friends with some of my friends. He pursued me for over a year, and I kept saying 'no . . . no,' but he didn't give up. I was not up for a long-distance relationship—plus I was extremely busy working full time and studying for my law boards.

"My previous experience with relationships told me that no man would put up with my independence and my being in law school. But Pete showed me that he was completely open to folding into my life wherever there was room for him. It took me a while to trust him, but we really got to know each other before I agreed to date him. After a while I let my guard down and realized he was the real deal.

"I'm so happy with him today, and we have an unbelievable relationship. We're still long distance, but we see each other whenever we can, and it's so fresh and amazing when we do. He's super supportive of my life and does whatever he can to help me out. It's a true partnership, and I'm very pleased that I eventually let go of my preconceived notions about men and long-distance relationships, and opened myself up to this special kind of love."

Dating in Your Fifties

Anastasia. "My boyfriend, who was a friend of a friend, is a composer. I was at a party one evening and I heard his music and I liked it. I asked my friend to set us up, and she gave me his e-mail and said, 'You should contact him. He's a foodie—invite him to your store.' I own a mail-order food company, a business I started on my own when my marriage was ending. I didn't think I had it in me, to send an e-mail to someone I didn't know and just introduce myself—but I did. One day, unannounced, he walked into my store. At first, I'll admit, I was disappointed—I didn't feel there was chemistry. He's eighteen years older than me and I thought he looked younger in the photos I'd seen of him. In actuality, he's in great shape and looks younger than he is, but my fantasy was different. As in my past relationships, I felt I needed instant chemistry—but we talked and got to know each other first. He was so nice to be with. When we eventually kissed, we had chemistry. Now I think he's the most handsome man in the world!

"One mistake I did make was trying too hard to blend him into my family—and in actuality, you don't have to do this. I was putting too much pressure on all of us. My kids are in high school and they are my priority. His kids are out of the house. I think my daughters felt competitive with him and didn't want to hang out with him. I keep it all separate now and it's so much better that way. We both have busy lives but try to see each other as much as we can. I see him when my girls go to my ex's. I'm a calendar-oriented person, which is very important when you're trying to have a relationship with kids at home. I block out two to three nights a week for him. He grounds me and he's so interesting and exciting. We travel on each other's business trips or take vacations together when we can. We cook, have sex, connect. We're enjoying an adult relationship—it's about quality time. I'm even a better mother now because I'm so happy. I get along great with my daughters and we talk about anything and everything—and then when I'm with him I'm no longer a mom, I'm a woman."

Dating in Your Sixties

Liz. "I had some boyfriends when I was newly divorced before I had fully built out my new life. I realized I was making some mistakes and I was still looking for men to complete me. When I eventually created a wonderful life for myself, dating seemed less important. I'm not going to compromise for anyone at this stage. I'd rather be alone than compromise. I have so many friends and I'm not lonesome at all. Sure I'd have a relationship with someone if I could have a deep soul connection, if he was politically very liberal, and if he was brilliant—otherwise it's just not worth my time."

Monica. "I met my current husband five years after my marriage ended. We both divorced around the same time and started communicating as friends, and then we became involved. He pursued me—and it hit me out of the blue—I didn't expect it.

"I had dated others before him—and you know the first person you date or have a relationship with may not be the one you will become serious with, but it will help you break your fall, and that's really important. My fall had been broken by the time I met him—we were both at places in our lives where we were ready to be in a committed relationship. I was in a place of strength, not neediness—and that is key. But falling in love again did bring my spirit back to life.

"After several years of dating we decided to get married. People say, 'Why marry at your age?' I suppose I felt if I was going to go through life's ups and downs plus aging with this man, I wanted the public validation and the religious validation and the legal validation of a marriage.

"This time around I married for healthy reasons, not for neurotic reasons! I married to be a companion, to be a lover, and to be a friend to someone in this stage of my life's journey. It's very important to recognize when you remarry that what you see is what you get. He is who he is, he's not changing, and neither am I!"

Dating in Your Seventies and Beyond

Anita. "I've been dating since my midfifties, when my marriage ended, and I just turned seventy. Yes, it can be a jungle out there, and some men definitely do want women in their twenties—and there are a lot of young women who will do anything for a Barneys credit card. But many women my age want younger men too. When I see a cute guy he's always younger, and I'll think, 'What a hunk!' But even with all of the craziness, I have been very successful at dating, and I've had at least six boyfriends over the years. I love to go out, to date, and to have sex—and yes, I'm still sexually active! There is always someone who I'm seeing, but I've never wanted to take it to the next level. I'm very independent and like waking up alone—I'm like a man in that way! Some of my boyfriends have wanted more, but I shy away from that. I know many women want more permanent relationships, but I was married for a very long time and I really don't need that or want that again. Being alone doesn't scare me at all. I like myself. I'm an avid reader and music lover. I have a great group of friends, which is so important, and I'm very close to my children."

Margie. "My marriage ended when I was thirty-five, and I was single from then until fifty-seven, when I met someone special and we married. During the years I was single, I had three boys to raise and I worked sometimes two or three jobs. I did occasionally date, and I had a few boyfriends, but my kids were totally my priority.

"I had a wonderful second marriage to a man who was kind and very generous, and we had many happy years together. Unfortunately he died a few years ago when I turned seventy. When I was seventy-two, I met Charles, the man I live with today. Charles and I were set up by mutual friends, and that's the same way I met my husband who passed away. Really, that's how I've met every man I've dated. I think it's the best way to meet someone. My friends' husbands have always had my back too, and that's because they see me as a woman who has a lot to offer. I'm smart, career-minded, I volunteer. The more you have in your life, the easier it is to meet people—and you are a more interesting person that way too.

"Dating is a process and you have to be open to it and stick with it. Yes, I met some crummy men, but I also met some crummy women! Never think of yourself as old—I'm turning seventy-five this year and I feel like thirty-five!"

~~~~~~

Dating Again
Tips and Tools

1. Dating works best in late transformation. It's best to delay dating until you have worked through all three phases of your recovery, are completely recovered, loving your new rebuilt life, and primed to be a great dater.
2. Only date for the right reasons.
3. The ending of a love relationship may cause you to have some issues with trust, which is perfectly understand-able. Healthy relationships, however, are built on trust, so please continue to work on becoming a trusting person before you venture out into the dating pool.
4. Dating is a process and should not be rushed. Take your time, be mindful, and always weigh the benefits vs. the risks.
5. Think of dating as an enjoyable prospect that will lead to many rewards. Be optimistic, enthusiastic, and open-minded, and view it as a learning experience.
6. Don't let any harmful myths stop you from feeling positive about dating, men, and relationships. Do all you can to dispel negative or anxiety-provoking myths.

7. Before dating, take time to think about what you are look-ing for in a partner and in a relationship this time around.

8. Keep an open mind and cast a very wide net for the great-est chances of success.

9. Study my rules on how to be a very skilled dater—and cre-ate a few new ones of your own.

10. Develop a finely tuned dating radar, and be very aware of "red flags."

11. Think about where sex fits into your dating life, and make your own set of rules.

12. Memorize "The House That Love Built," and don't settle for anything less. And when you are involved with someone fabulous who adores you, commit to doing your part to keep your new healthy relationship going strong.

Conclusion

Today is such a spectacular day! It's the inauguration of the "First Annual Breakup Bible Phenomenal Woman Marathon." Here in New York City, two million women are about to cross the finish line, which is representative of their triumphant completion of all three phases of recovery: healing, understanding, and transformation. Most of these athletes have trained for at least a year, and some even longer. Like you, they've challenged their minds and bodies in amazing ways, and even when the going got really tough, they never gave up. I'm here at the finish line ready to greet them with a grand hero's welcome. And next year at this time, you will be successfully completing this race too. Picture yourself on that day—strong, powerful, confident, unstoppable. And I will be there to personally give each of you a congratulatory hug and a massive trophy.

Bravo! Hurray! You did it! You finished this book and are fully committed to your total recovery. Truly, it has been such an honor to be your guide on this unbelievable journey. You impressed me every single day. You worked so hard, you were indefatigable, you rarely complained, and you never, ever surrendered. I am so incredibly proud of you, and more important, I know that you are so proud of yourself.

As you know by now, full recovery takes time and toil. And just like a marathon, slow and steady always gets you through. No shortcuts, just honest hard work. I have learned so much and grown in many ways through hearing your inspirational stories. Please allow me to thank every one of you— your bravery always takes my breath away. I hope our friendship will continue to flourish, and I encourage you to keep in touch through visiting my website at RachelASussman.com. I am committed to building our community and would be honored to hear your rousing tales. Let's pledge to support and inspire each other from this day forward.

As a final farewell, please indulge me by reading one concluding list. It's my parting gift to ensure your sustained recovery. And as you know by now, I love a good list. And admit it, so do you!

Rachel's Final List: Recovery Tips and Tools

1. Full recovery takes time and work. There are no shortcuts. Take plenty of time to mourn and heal. You are on a long marathon, yet there is a finish line ahead.

2. Validate yourself every day. You are part of a huge community and you are never alone.

3. Build up an incredible support system and learn to lean on it now and forever.

4. Love yourself and take excellent care of yourself.

5. Do not be afraid to explore, experience, and express your emotions. This is part of what makes you a curious, fascinating, and exceptional woman.

6. Understanding is the linchpin of your recovery. Be inquisitive while you honestly explore your psyche to discover what makes you tick.

7. Full recovery entails a complete understanding and ownership of your personal love map and that of your ex.

8. Please be willing to take accountability in all areas of your life, and always strive toward expanding your personal growth.

9. When the time comes, let go.

10. Take your rebuilding seriously and regularly add new snowball challenges to your emerging life.

11. Consider delaying dating until you are fully recovered and then only date for the right reasons.
12. Commit to being a great dater and never settle for a relationship that is not in your best interest.
13. Always strive to be hopeful, even when times are tough.
14. You are a phenomenal woman. Never forget it!

Acknowledgments

*N*umerous people pitched in, offered guidance, and supported me along my journey, and I am eternally grateful to you all. I am enormously indebted to every woman who agreed to be interviewed for *The Breakup Bible*. Your honesty, bravery, insights, and anecdotes continually moved and inspired me. This book would not have been possible without all of your generous contributions.

Applause to my wonderful husband, Gary, who was present, proud, and served as a first-rate amateur editor. Today he knows more about female breakups than he ever bargained for. Thanks to my daughter, Izzy; you always brighten my day and make me laugh, and that is such a gift. To Lisa Gallagher, my literary agent, a million thanks for your expertise, encouragement, and dedication. Thank you for taking a chance on a first-time author. Truly, I couldn't have accomplished this without you. Colossal thanks to my talented editor, Hallie Falquet, and to her team at Three Rivers Press. Hallie, your abundant enthusiasm, patience, and guidance kept my nose to the grindstone even during challenging moments. Christina Lindstrom, my dear friend and mentor, thank you for your endless teaching, coaching, devotion, and your unflappable belief in me. Your sage wisdom pours forth on every page. There is a slim chance I would have fulfilled this or numerous other dreams had our paths not crossed once upon a time. Bravo to the brilliant Nancy Newhauser, who insisted on reading every chapter, even when you were not feeling your best. So much of my energy comes from your strength. Deepest thanks to my father; sister, Nina; and brother, David—for your encouragement and love. Nina, your courageous story helped inspire me to write this book. I am tremendously grateful to all of my friends who lent a hand and cheered me along. Many of you shared your own personal accounts or introduced me to others who became important aspects of this project. A very special thanks to Joan Overlock, whose spirit epitomizes this book. I am grateful for all of the assistance, knowledge, and sound bites you generously provided. *Merci* to all my pals at CGPS for your friendship and enthusiasm. Every one of you helped me out in a meaningful way. I'm especially grateful to Ellie Levin and Beth Stern, who fielded a lot of annoying phone calls over a prolonged period. I am indebted to the many colleagues and professionals who were generous with their time and expertise. I would like to express my appreciation to Kim Allouche, Joy Bauer, Dr. Robert Grossman, Ellen Oler, Sylvia Rosenfeld, and Dr. Maria Sullivan. The spirit of my grandparents guides me every day. I love and miss you, Mom. You are, and will always be, a huge part of my essence. I know you would have been so proud.

About the Author

Rachel A. Sussman, LCSW, is a licensed psychotherapist, writer, and lecturer. As the founder of Sussman Counseling, a psychotherapy practice devoted to treating couples and individuals with relationship dilemmas, Sussman had counseled patients in all phases of dating, marriage, and breakups for more than a decade. Ms. Sussman lives in New York City with her husband and daughter. Visit her online at www.RachelASussman.com.